Animal Architecture

BEASTS, BUILDINGS AND US

Paul Dobraszczyk

T0408644

REAKTION BOOKS

To Patrick

Published by
Reaktion Books Ltd
Unit 32, Waterside
44–48 Wharf Road
London N1 7UX, UK
www.reaktionbooks.co.uk

First published 2023
Copyright © Paul Dobraszczyk 2023

Printed and bound in Great Britain by TJ Books Ltd, Padstow, Cornwall

A catalogue record for this book is available from the British Library

ISBN 978 1 78914 692 9

CONTENTS

Jeanne Gang's Aqua skyscraper, Chicago, 2010.

Introduction:
Going to Ground

When the Aqua skyscraper was completed in Chicago in 2010, by architect Jeanne Gang, it was lauded as a shining example of a building constructed for human occupation that also took into account the lives of other animals. Its wave-like facade and fritted glass were designed to stop birds flying into the building's windows, injuring or killing themselves. A low bar to set, perhaps, for an architecture that accommodates animals, but that is hardly surprising given our long history of seeing animals as outside of, even beneath, the human. More usually, animals are designed for only when they are deemed of use to humans, whether as livestock, domestic pets, spectacles to consume in zoos, menageries and aquaria, or objects of scientific manipulation in laboratories. If animals cannot be instrumentalized, they are usually ignored; if those animals take it upon themselves to inhabit buildings, they are invariably regarded as pests and removed or annihilated. When the global construction industry is one of the principal drivers of climate change and species extinction, there is an urgent need to transform our relationship with animals, to build with animals not just in mind, but also as cohabitants that seeks some measure of recompense for the long, sad history of human exceptionalism.

We need, in short, an animal architecture, the subject of this book. It will consider thirty different animals in order to open up new ways of thinking about the relationship between architecture and the more-than-human. It moves from some of the smallest visible organisms (insects) to the largest (elephants); from the domesticated (cats and dogs) to the despised (wasps and rats). What if architecture were to simply become more deeply attuned to the other life forms that already use it? Examples in this book include spiders spinning their webs in the dark corners of rooms; swallows finding ideal purchase on brick walls for their saliva-mud-based nest cups; rats making their homes in the subterranean spaces of the city; beavers working alongside humans as landscape engineers; cats and dogs appropriating our furniture and fittings as their own places of rest. There is hardly any part of the human-built environment that cannot be inhabited or changed by non-humans, yet people are usually very selective as to which animals they allow in and which they diligently keep out or eliminate.

To open up space for animals in architecture is to first become aware of how non-human life is already enmeshed in both our buildings and our imaginations. By paying close attention to how animals produce and/or occupy both space and structures for themselves, this book asks what might be required to design with animals. By focusing on imaginative engagements with animals, it stretches the possibilities of solidarity with more-than-humans. At the same time, though, it provides an unflinching account of what non-human life gets sacrificed for human inhabitation: an opening up to more discomfort in the face of this; a moving towards rather than away from the mess and pain of entanglements that cannot be controlled. In short, *Animal Architecture* is about building in a world where humans and other animals are already entangled, whether we or they like it or not.

In this introduction I will sketch out some of the broader arguments that inform how this book explores the relationship between animals and architecture. These are, first, questions about origins in architecture and the latter's relationship with nature; second, arguments about why it's crucial that architects and planners move beyond a solely anthropocentric approach to building; third, why animals are important to consider in human constructions; and finally, why it is critical to start to care more about building for and with animals. The overarching aim of the book is to challenge prevailing understandings of the value of animals (and more generally nature) within architectural practice, namely as 'others' that are only ever construed in terms of their usefulness to humans. Undermining this holds open the possibility of a richer but uneasy approach to animals that lets go of instrumental thinking in favour of much more open understandings.

Architecture: destroyer of worlds

In what is the oldest surviving treatise on human construction – the multi-volume *De architectura*, compiled in the first century BCE and usually translated into English as *Ten Books of Architecture* – the Roman architect Vitruvius speculated on the origins of architecture. He set the scene by imagining a gathering of early hominids (always male) around a fire that they have recently created for the first time. Here, the men 'first began to make shelters of foliage, others to dig caves at the foot of mountains and yet others to build refuges of mud and branches in which to shelter in imitation of the nests of swallows and their way of building'.[1] When Vitruvius' writings were 'rediscovered' in Renaissance Italy, they precipitated a renewed obsession with the origins of architecture that lasted until the twentieth century. In the eyes of many different writers, the 'primitive hut' first suggested by Vitruvius was variously inspired by the boughs of trees, the older art of weaving branches and reeds, mud-built termite mounds, the excavations of ants and burrowing animals and the nests of birds.[2] According to architectural historian Joseph Rykwert, this preoccupation with the origins of architecture was rooted in attempts to renew the discipline, with the repeated stress on the examples in nature as inspiration for human building a way of affirming universal – even divine – sanction for a particular way of conceiving architecture.[3]

As Rykwert has pointed out, speculation on origins can also reinvigorate thinking by calling into question some of our basic assumptions. And who can argue that this is not an urgent task for the construction industry, which, even by the reductive standards of bald statistics, is a leading participant in the orgy of destruction that now characterizes human relations with the planet that are based on capitalist consumption? In 2021 the global construction industry accounted for 38 per cent of anthropogenic emissions of carbon dioxide, the highest percentage for any single economic sector, and a share that is expected to grow to 42 per cent by 2030. Every week, across the planet, a city the size of Paris is built, and only 1 per cent of the resultant buildings are assessed for their carbon footprints.[4]

Sometimes it takes an outsider to draw attention to the true scale and horror of the destructive impact of the construction industry. In his 2016 book *Vertical*, geographer Stephen Graham considered the ways in which the human-built world has increasingly dominated the vertical axis of the planet, from satellites to bunkers. In the final chapter on mining, he brought to light how today's supertall skyscrapers are only made possible through an almost unimaginable level of destruction. Here, Dubai's 830-metre-high Burj Khalifa (until the completion of the Jeddah Tower in 2025, the tallest building in the world) is revealed as a monstrously destructive edifice – the Burj's 55,000 tonnes of steel, 250,000 tonnes of concrete, 700 tonnes of aluminium and 85,000 square metres of glass (not to mention tonnes of Egyptian marble and Indian granite for the interior fittings) all requiring the mining, extraction and processing of countless tonnes of other materials from all over the world, particularly iron ore and sand.[5] And these material statistics tell us nothing about the organic life annihilated as a result of these technologies of extraction and fabrication; that level of destruction is rarely, if ever, accounted for in the realization of a building. Viewed in this way, the spectacular shiny surfaces of the Burj (and almost every other skyscraper, however 'green' their credentials) are really just a very effective cover for the gigantic level of destructiveness required for their realization. These buildings are quite literally destroyers of worlds.

Given this intensely depressing reality, it is easy to understand the desire of some architects to revert to small-scale building in order to model something different. Thus the thousands of eco-villages that now exist around the world are predicated on creating 'restorative' environments where building grows out of immediate needs and renewable materials. For example, Tao and Hoppi Wimbush, two of the residents at the Lammas eco-village in Wales, founded in 2009, used locally sourced timber (where possible fallen trees from carefully managed woodland) as the principal construction material for their self-built house. The argument here, and in many other eco-villages, is that by returning human builders to a direct engagement with materials, methods of construction and also infrastructure, a new kind of relationship is struck with nature, that of respect and, moreover, mutual enhancement. However, even as the Lammas community have genuinely enhanced local biodiversity in their careful management of the land they occupy, it is impossible to circumvent architecture as a fundamentally destructive art.

Felling a tree for use as a building material means destroying a life-world (regardless of whether this act is offset by planting another tree in its place). Even if we do not consider a plant to be a living being (and most

Interior of Tao and Hoppi Wimbush's self-built house at Lammas in 2019.

plant scientists would now dispute this), a single tree nevertheless supports a huge array of animal life, from insects burrowing into its bark to birds nesting in its canopy. Using deadwood is arguably *more* destructive, given that fallen trees generally support more life than growing ones, as decaying wood provides sustenance to all manner of other animals, fungi and protozoa. Even the most primitive act of dwelling described by Vitruvius – excavating a hole in the ground or retreating to a cave – results in some level of destruction: other lives are always displaced and sacrificed for the sake of our own. Indeed, the very act of being alive, whether of a plant or animal, means an ongoing and unrecoverable expenditure of energy that will eventually result in the death of any organism. In this more realistic mode of understanding, speculating about the origins of architecture is not a way of imagining human building returning to nature (unless this refers to a thoroughly human understanding of nature), but rather the opposite, namely, retreating to a world inside by disconnecting from nature that is seen as threatening (the same applying to other animal architectures such as termite mounds and birds' nests). To build a shelter means to purposefully exclude what is outside: the very act of construction encloses and partitions the world, even as it also creates something new. The outside of the 'primitive hut' is precisely the 'nature' that, millennia later, would become so revered by those seeking to justify architecture's supposed 'natural' basis. Perhaps the more truthful question to ask about architecture's destructiveness is not whether the latter can somehow be 'solved' (namely, reduced to zero), but rather how it can be both accepted and mitigated – a far more troublesome question than that of finding sustainable or resilient architectural solutions.

Thinking of architecture's relationship with nature as a difficult negotiation as to what will inevitably be destroyed results in a different way of thinking about concepts such as sustainability. Anthropologist Tim Ingold has put forward the idea of 'correspondence' to describe how humans can relate more respectfully to the world they inhabit. Acknowledging that all living beings – human and more-than-human – are always enmeshed, correspondence 'goes along' with the world rather than seeing it as a series of problems to be solved. In this mode of understanding, 'lives, in their perpetual unfolding or becoming, simultaneously join together and differentiate themselves, one from another'.[6] A useful way of thinking about architectural correspondences is to consider the nature of the ground; and Ingold does this himself in an essay responding to the makeshift dwellings created by artist Tim Knowles in the Scottish Highlands from 2015 to 2019. Here, Ingold recasts the origins of architecture as 'going to ground', that is, constructing a hide that aspires to invisibility because concealment offers the best form of protection against nature. Contrasting the characteristic way in which the built environment tries to make the ground impermeable – think of asphalt road surfaces or concrete floors – the hide is 'an intricately folded or crumpled volume of heterogeneous materials', where the human inhabitant 'nestles into a fold much as you would into a cradle, co-opting its existing features with only the barest of additions'.[7]

Architecture that is a folding into the world does not try to make an impermeable ground between humans and nature, but instead engages in creating correspondences. When I visited the Lammas eco-village in spring 2019, I was struck by the way those in the community are more open than is usually the case to accommodating animals in their buildings. For example, in the guesthouse where I stayed, a newly emerged queen wasp was beginning to construct a new nest on the ceiling. Most noticeable was the buzzing sound of her wings, vibrations that liquefied the wood pulp she had collected with which to build. Next door, in Tao and Hoppi Wimbush's timber-built house, a robin repeatedly flew through the open

One of artist Tim Knowles's shelters, created in the Scottish Highlands as part of his Howff Project from 2015 to 2019.

front door to take tidbits from the kitchen, while a succession of birds, including barn owls, made their nests inside the roof-space, accessing it through a circular hole intentionally cut into the wall. It was the porosity of both buildings that allowed animals to come inside, whether deliberately designed or a consequence of makeshift approaches to building that left gaps between doors, windows and walls. In more conventional buildings, it is precisely this kind of porosity that is so assiduously avoided, with all kinds of specialist materials designed to seal up any gaps. What the unconventional openness of the buildings at Lammas revealed was the multiple animal lives that desire to become enmeshed with our own, if they are facilitated to do so. My distinct discomfort in the face of a nest-building wasp demonstrated to me that perhaps the biggest obstacle to a genuinely ecological architecture is the human sense of revulsion at nature, unbidden, trying to get back in. But gaps in buildings are, ironically, ecological anathema to many, namely because they wastefully leak precious energy. It is even the clarion call of the protest group Insulate Britain: poorly sealed buildings account for a large percentage of not only the UK's carbon footprint, but those of many other countries with sizeable historic housing stocks.[8] But perhaps the point is that instrumental 'solutions' to perceived architectural problems tend to focus on the gains and ignore the inevitable losses that come with any kind of building.

Human constructions are, at every moment, assailed by a nature that is always trying to get back in; only ceaseless maintenance prevents buildings from being overtaken by the world outside. At the smallest level, impermeable matter is always being broken down by either its own internal entropy or the friction of other things on it, whether we regard those things as inert (weather) or alive (plants, animals, fungi and protozoa). In architectural terms, it is perhaps ruins that are the most potent expressions of the attritional relationship between nature and culture: ruins stand testament to the inevitable folly of the human idea of permanence – the impermeability of architecture to decay an illusion that ruins forcefully shatter. If architecture is to ever open up to what is outside of itself, it must relinquish the pretence of permanence.

We can now return to challenge the idea of the primitive human shelter imagined by Vitruvius. Instead of a technologically empowered man becoming the measure of all things, including his first house, we instead encounter humans that are only all too aware of their vulnerability, namely their entwinement in a world of other lives that ceaselessly spill into theirs, however much they would like it to be otherwise. With acceptance of this vulnerability, these humans already know that any shelter they construct will inevitably be folded back into the ground from which they and it were both born. Thus the origins of architecture inevitably lead to the *ends* of architecture, to a greater sense of awareness of what happens when buildings die.[9]

A new realism

Opening up to animals means de-centring ourselves. Challenging the long-standing anthropocentrism of human thought and ways of being in the world has become the principal driver of what has been broadly termed the 'post-humanist' turn in philosophy and other disciplines in the last two decades or so.[10] Many of these attempts to de-centre humans from the world stem from the current realization that human dominance of the planet has already been catastrophic for other life forms, particularly animals, which have seen, in some cases, a decline of 60 per cent or more in their numbers in the past half-century alone. For architects wishing to confront the legacy of such destructive anthropocentrism, one particular recent philosophical strand – Object-Oriented Ontology (sometimes termed 'Triple O' or OOO) – has proved significant in opening up other ways of conceiving of architecture that take into account more than humans alone.[11]

Since the beginning of the Enlightenment, mainstream philosophical and scientific thought in the West has assumed that reality only exists in a meaningful way as and when it relates to human thought, a foundational assumption known as correlationism. On the face of it, such anthropocentrism may seem absurd – after all, it seems so obvious that things such as animals and plants and rocks really do exist despite us. Yet to acknowledge that things other than the human really do exist (or rather that they exist *equally* and *independently* to humans) creates a deep philosophical problem, for it directly challenges our supposed ability to gain exhaustive knowledge about the world – a claim that is often made by science. For those associated with Object-Oriented Ontology, the solution to this philosophical problem is to simply accept that all things exist equally and that human knowledge of other things can only ever be partial rather than exhaustive. Prominent theorists Graham Harman and Timothy Morton have gone further, arguing that this partial knowledge is much more akin to aesthetic experience than to empirical observation, and that aesthetic perception actually precedes scientific method. In their estimation, the way things in the world relate to each other is always indirect, or 'at a distance', because equal existence implies that one thing can never know another exhaustively.[12]

If we accept such a proposition – indeed, some scientists, particularly in the fields of quantum mechanics and cosmology, now do so – there are profound implications for the ways in which architects think about their work. In his many books Morton, in particular, has repeatedly returned to architectural analogies to illustrate his arguments. For example, in *Humankind* (2019), he argues that we need to cultivate kindness towards non-humans in our approaches to design, imagining an ecologically minded architect who decides to build a house that is 'affected by how frogs and lizards and dust see it'. He then turns this thought on its head by drawing attention to the types of infrastructure in buildings that already acknowledge, albeit negatively, the presence of non-humans, namely the 'filters and air conditioners and mildew-resistant paint [that attempt to] eliminate non-humans'.[13] We might add sealants, glues and mortar to this list of ubiquitously present defensive materials in architecture. Turning this negativity around would clearly result in a very different kind of house, from top to bottom, inside and out. The point here is not to force architects and occupants to welcome mildew or dangerous or destructive insects into their homes, but rather to foster a renewed sense of fascination with the non-human things that humans all too readily dismiss; this is precisely what is required first and foremost to foster human solidarity with other beings. In Morton's estimation, this is about allowing other beings to 'have pleasure' alongside us; he cites the example of sparrows, which, along with other building-loving birds, favour constructing their nests in cavities in roof spaces.[14]

Another way of opening up to animals is to acknowledge their agency as builders. Even though the sophistication and complexity of animal-built structures, such as termite mounds or the bowers of bowerbirds, has been affirmed by animal scientists such as Mike Hansell, there is still a widespread assumption that only human architects are able to imagine

Moss growing on the rubber gasket of a metal rivet on the Urbis building, Manchester.

what they want to build; other animals build because they are merely obeying preprogrammed instincts that are hard-wired into their genes.[15] As will be explored more fully in the first chapter of this book, most recent scientific studies of animal behaviour now assert quite the opposite: that even animals without brains, for example ants and termites, exert some measure of individual agency when they build collectively.[16] Moreover, studying animal architecture reveals that what humans like to call the 'environment' – meaning a separate domain outside of the human-built world – is actually fully entwined with architecture. Notable examples are the dams and lodges constructed by beavers. These do not merely 'sit' in an environment, enclosing and cordoning it off; rather beaver-built structures actively constitute the environment over time. The fact that beavers are now being co-opted by humans in the search for 'natural' solutions to the increased incidence and severity of climate-change-induced flooding shows that some are becoming more attuned to the intermeshing of buildings and environment and their co-constitution. Yet what many are still slow to realize is that this coexistence of buildings and environment applies to every single living organism, whether they build anything or not. For the environment is never something that is outside of any given life-form that inhabits it; rather it amounts to a single gigantic organism made up of innumerable parts that actively constitute and change it.

That such a concept should sit so uneasily with us is a powerful reminder of the continuing strength that anthropocentrism holds over understanding of the human-built environment. But this is hardly surprising. On a recent walk in my home city of Manchester with an architect friend, we stopped to admire the technical prowess of local architect Ian Simpson's Urbis building in the city centre, a striking curvilinear structure built from steel and glass in the 2000s. As we were talking, my friend observed a clump of moss growing at the edges of one of the building's metal supports and carefully removed it. His justification for this action was that the moss was a sign of the building's imminent decay: the moss would, over time, break down the rubber gaskets that held the rivet in place and thus require expensive, and energy- and time-consuming, repairs. I was struck by the way in which my friend argued that this was a more ecological approach than sanctioning the moss to remain, with its teeming ecology of microfauna; surely allowing a building to go to rack and ruin would result in more expenditure of resources in the long run? For my friend, careful preservation of the structural and material integrity of the building was precisely what constituted 'sustainability' in architecture.

To argue for the opposite means perversely inviting disorder and ruin into architecture, an idea that is understandably anathema not only to architects but to those who occupy buildings. But can a truly ecological architecture arise from any other place? Those who promote design as a solution to the ecological crisis are perhaps missing an obvious contradiction. For example, purchasing a bespoke birdhouse to mount on a wall may seem like an ethical action to mitigate the precipitous decline of many bird species in cities, but a large part of this problem stems from an increasing human intolerance of what the birds would probably prefer, namely crevices and cracks in the material fabric of buildings themselves – what would generally be pejoratively termed 'disrepair'. Opening up to animals undoubtedly means changing attitudes towards what is perceived as threatening. Perhaps, contrary to my architect friend, what is needed is greater tolerance of the mess and ruin that other lives bring in their wake.

Moving beyond anthropocentrism in architecture is, in some ways, counter-intuitive. Allowing all animals to exist equally is certainly possible, but when it comes to our own homes, George Orwell's famous assertion seems always to apply, namely that 'all animals are equal but some are more equal than others.'[17] In buildings there is almost always a hierarchical system of values when it comes to animals: pets (dogs and cats especially) at the top; pests (insects, spiders and rodents) at the bottom. Yet such a value system is always open to modification – it can be challenged in ways that promote a richer engagement between humans and animals, although this will undoubtedly result in discomfort for the former. And modest gains are possible, even in the wake of the all-too-obvious colossal destructiveness of human construction. There is a cumulative effect that comes from a willingness to experience the discomfort that comes from allowing other beings to share our spaces. At present, my own small contribution is to let spiders remain in their webs in the dark corners of my house.

Becoming animal

If humans were to become more attuned to the lives of animals in architecture, can they ever really know what those animals actually want? Is it really possible to think like another animal, even another human being? In 1974 the philosopher Thomas Nagel asked, in a famous article, 'What is it like to be a bat?', a work often quoted in studies of consciousness, human or otherwise.[18] Nagel chose bats as his subject because of their ability to perceive using sonar receptors, a quality humans simply do not possess. In Nagel's estimation, attempts to understand bat sonar through scientific analysis can only lead further away from the desired human empathy with bats: such objectivity is always about creating distance between the observer and her/his subject. But Nagel also rejected imaginative modes of engagement – these are merely superficial human projections of what it is like to be a bat – very far indeed from actually *being* a bat. Nagel's conclusion was that there is no way of understanding what he termed the 'alien' perception of bats (or, indeed, any other life form, including other humans). For individual humans are intractably locked into their own subjectivity when it comes to perception and, indeed, imagination. They cannot help but anthropomorphize everything they try to understand.

Nagel's disparagement of the human imagination has been forcefully challenged by Object-Oriented Ontology. For example, Ian Bogost, in his book *Alien Phenomenology* (2012), asserted the value of imagination as an invaluable faculty because it allows humans to empathize with things that are inescapably alien. We can, as Bogost himself did, imagine bat sonar as being like that of a submarine, or of an aircraft control system: we readily create images of what is, to us, an invisible form of perception (as you are no doubt doing at this very moment).[19] These are of course, wholly anthropomorphic metaphors, but that is to be expected; Bogost contests Nagel's pessimism in his assertion that anthropomorphic analogies take us outside of ourselves because they are attempts to create empathy with things that are genuinely alien to us. Unlike scientific objectivity, imagination never claims that knowledge of the more-than-human can ever be exhaustive; rather, as already stated, it is knowledge 'askance' or at a distance. Political theorist Jane Bennett has argued that the risks associated with such anthropomorphism (superstition, romanticism, animism and so on) 'work against anthropocentrism' because 'a chord is struck between person and thing, as I am no longer above or outside a nonhuman environment'.[20] In Bennett's estimation, the dangers of anthropomorphism are hardly comparable to those of anthropocentrism which, in its current form, is rapidly stripping the planet of its remaining biological life.

Nagel's pessimism has also been challenged by novelist J. M. Coetzee in *The Lives of Animals* (1999). Here, a fictional writer, Elizabeth Costello, delivers two lectures at an academic institution where she defends the human capacity for imaginative identification with animals. In a direct challenge to Nagel, she asserts that 'there is no limit to the extent to which we can think ourselves into the being of another' and that it is through the 'sympathetic imagination' that we can experience the way in which a 'living bat is . . . full of being' in just the same way as 'being fully human' is to be 'full of being'. In a damning and controversial indictment of the supposed 'neutrality' of scientific objectivity, Coetzee, through his invented character, argues that the horror of the Nazi death camps was a direct result of an inability of the killers to 'think themselves into the place of their victims': the holocaust rendered as a failure of imagination as much as the consequence of an inherently evil regime and its machinery of annihilation.[21] This may seem an extreme point of comparison to make in terms of how we think about animals, but it is meant to shock us into a realization of the true scale and horror of the almost ceaseless mass-murder of animals that humans have orchestrated (the tens of billions of animals that are now slaughtered for human consumption every year).[22]

The centrality of imagination in thinking ourselves into the lives of animals has significant implications for architecture. First, it can expand how we conceive of the relationship between buildings constructed by humans and those made by animals. For example, we might return to speculating about the origins of architecture through a deepened awareness of the evolution of animal-built structures, not as a means of reasserting the superiority of human faculties over and above those of animals, but rather of finding correspondences between the two. At a more prosaic level, we might pay more attention to animal builders, beginning with more sustained curiosity and tolerance of our discomfort in the face of animal agency. Many architects are already doing this, particularly in the field of biomimicry, a term that first appeared in 1962 and has more recently come to mean a conscious imitation of natural processes in design.[23] Yet, despite the fact that biomimetic design encompasses a huge range of practices too large to enumerate here, it is almost always predicated on a utilitarian understanding of nature. Here, nature variously reveals to us more efficient solutions to human problems, demonstrates 'closed-loop' energy transfers, or makes apparent structural forms we have not yet discovered. While it undoubtedly produces many striking buildings, such as two pavilions that were created by silkworms and the Mediated Matter research group at the Massachusetts Institute of Technology from 2012 to 2020, it does not alter, at a fundamental level, the long-standing assertion that nature lies outside of the human and is primarily there for us as an instrument to use.[24]

Opening up to non-instrumental ways of thinking about the relationship between architecture and animals requires precisely the kind of imaginative engagement prioritized by Object-Oriented Ontology. As I have argued in *Future Cities*, an emphasis on imagination can expand understanding of nature,[25] often with the result that the idea of nature 'out there' tends to dissolve into what is generally termed a 'nature-culture continuum'; or a 'mesh' in Timothy Morton's more succinct definition.[26] Imagination multiplies the correspondences that can be found between the lives of humans and other animals. In this book these correspondences are gleaned from animals in fiction, film and art alongside those in buildings, which include both executed and speculative designs. Architecture is not just buildings (let alone those that are actually designed by architects), but rather a whole series of connections – coexistences between makers and users; between spaces and forms; between materials and mind; and between flows of all kinds – people, non-human things, facilities, information, time and so on. In connecting animals and architecture, this book argues for an expanded field of architecture itself, one in which it connects with the 'nature' in which it is always enmeshed. In this mode of understanding, it is the correspondences between things that are actually the subject and focus, rather than any one thing in itself, whether that is a building, an architectural visualization or an immaterial idea. It is precisely the chains of connections between things that actually constitute what is real in the world.

This kind of imaginative openness might seem inimical to the creation of architecture, if we accept that design fundamentally rests in the transformation of an imaginative project into a material one (as, for example, architect Peter Zumthor does in his collection of essays *Thinking Architecture*, first published in 1998). But, clearly there is no harm in being more open to *not* building. After all, when the construction industry contributes so much to global warming and species extinction, taking the foot off the pedal of architectural production would surely be of benefit to the lifeworlds it so casually destroys, mostly unawares. Perhaps, as is often the case in architectural education, designers might stay within the realm of the imaginary for much longer than they currently do. Here, architects would come to understand, with Ingold, that to correspond with the world means not describing it from a distance, but rather living in it with others – humans and non-humans alike – and *answering* to it.[27] Animals themselves, engaged through the architect's imagination, would then be granted some form of agency.

Architectures of care

Focusing on imagination in relation to architecture and animals is fundamentally about instilling *care* as a principal motivating factor in human construction. It is easy enough to understand how this works in relation to animals that are classed as pets; as will be seen in Chapter Five, domesticated animals such as dogs and cats are increasingly being thought of as co-inhabitants in relation to design. It is generally taken for granted that pet owners know how to care for their animals, even if they often read the feelings of their pets anthropomorphically. It is much harder to care for animals that are generally regarded as unwelcome intruders into buildings – creatures that humans generally describe as 'pests' or 'vermin'. The Expanded Environment, a non-profit organization, has provided a helpful online resource in promoting awareness and care for a much wider range of animals in relation to architecture, most notably in their collaborative design proposals and annual competitions for novel types of animal design. The material on their website deliberately expands ideas about what might be considered appropriate animals for designers to work with as 'clients': thus insects appear alongside dogs and cats, birds with lizards, bats with oysters and so on.[28]

The very notion of an 'expanded environment' is dependent on a recognition of the diverse range of human responses to animals and the fostering of more care for those creatures that generally fall outside of human favour. In this book, that also means an expansion of what is generally classed as animal architecture. In the pages that follow, you will encounter, variously, structures built by animals (nests, mounds, burrows and shells); human buildings that are inspired by animal architecture, whether animal-shaped structures or buildings drawing on the engineering principles of animal architecture; structures and spaces designed for inhabitation by animals (for instance zoological and agricultural buildings); spaces and places which, without intentional design, accommodate animals (rats in urban sewers, for example); and metaphorical images of all of the above in fiction, film and art.

A powerful example of the potential breadth of such interspecies awareness, and one that I return to in the first chapter of this book, is artist Fritz Haeg's *Animal Estates* project, which ran from 2008 until 2013.[29] In nine different cities, Haeg organized events to encourage participation in creating structures and habitats that would be attractive to a variety of native species of non-human animals, including bats, birds and insects. These were the artist's 'wildlife clients'; each iteration of *Animal Estates* worked with animals that lived in the nine different European and North American cities in which the project was held. As well as building structures for animals to inhabit, the project also hosted events designed to stimulate interest in and knowledge about native animals (and, in many cases, to encourage urban inhabitants to make structures themselves). This holistic approach to ecological design aimed to foster more care for animals in cities – animals that would probably otherwise go unnoticed. It was also underlined by a subversive question: why should design be limited to just human clients? Back in 1998, geographer Jennifer Wolch described such attentive care towards urban animals as creating a 'zoöpolis', namely a re-naturalized city in which humans invite animals back in so that 'an ethic, practice and politics of caring for animals' can emerge. Wolch argued that the human division between wild and domestic animals must be understood as a 'permeable social construct'.[30] As *Animal Estates* demonstrated, all animals have differing subjectivities that must be taken into account if we are serious about caring and designing for them.

This may seem like a daunting and overly conceptual task, yet it can be rooted in everyday practices that involve not just architects, planners and academics, but everyone. The specific examples that I draw attention to in the rest of this book are many and varied. Thus we might learn how to build a 'bug hotel' in our gardens or schools, but equally we might become more curious and tolerant of insects that try to get into our houses. Leading on from the latter, we might simply pay attention to what animals are doing in our homes, for example watching a spider spinning a web between two walls. If we are fearful of arachnids, we might consider how to manage the revulsion that stands in the way of such an engagement. We might look up at tall buildings in the hope of seeing the increasingly common sight of an urban peregrine falcon, but equally we might see these birds at close quarters through a webcam. We might expand our knowledge of animals through education, but equally we might grow our sympathy through imaginative engagements in novels and films. We might consider installing nest boxes for birds on the walls of our house, but we might also become more tolerant of the 'defects' in our buildings that already provide birds with the spaces they need. Finally, we might develop more awareness of what animal life inevitably gets sacrificed for the sake of the human-built environment; and perhaps form or join activist groups that seek to redress this.

And there are many more examples in the pages that follow. The thirty animals chosen for consideration are but a tiny part of the vast network of sentient life generally termed 'the environment'. I have organized the selected animals according to typologies that provide loose unifying themes. The first chapter considers the miniature worlds of arthropods; it explores how insects and spiders build for themselves and also how they occupy human buildings and imaginations. The second chapter focuses on birds – consummate builders in their own right but also thoroughly alien to humans in their mastery of the air. Moving between what might be termed 'charismatic' species (peregrine falcons) and those that are either over-looked or despised (pigeons), this chapter negotiates human engagement with this most opportune class of animals when it comes to appropriating buildings. Chapter Three interrogates the way in which humans tend to favour certain 'wild' animals over others; by focusing on some animals that have become accustomed to living in cities (rats, bats and foxes), it challenges the distinction often made between domesticity and wildness. It also considers how certain animals (elephants, lizards and apes) challenge conventional ideas about what it means to be a human, especially when these animals are encountered in zoos. The fourth chapter moves to the medium that is arguably most hostile to humans – water – exploring how relations with aquatic animals are driven by both utility (the animals humans eat, such as oysters and salmon) and also estrangement (the extra-ordinary intelligence of octopuses and dolphins, for example). The final chapter returns to more familiar territory, considering how the domesti-cation of animals has profoundly affected how a select group of creatures share human-built spaces and structures. These considerations range from human intimacy with pets (dogs and cats) to animals that some might choose to eat (cows, pigs and chickens).

It is worth ending this introduction by reinstating a basic truth: that all life forms create their environments and that all environments are in reality the sum of these creations. Why then does anthropocentrism persist so strongly, namely the idea that humans live outside of 'the environment'? Perhaps, as any therapist will likely tell you, losing a fantasy is always much harder than losing a reality. Yet, as is all too obvious, the persistence of the fantasy of human exceptionalism is now endangering all life on the planet. It is humans, and humans alone, that, in Jane Bennett's words, have 'crawled or secreted themselves into every corner of the environment', while at the same time asserting that they are actually removed from that environment. Bennett urges us to give up 'the futile attempt to disentangle the human from the nonhuman' and instead 'engage more civilly, strategically, and subtly with the nonhumans in the assemblages in which [we], too, participate'.[31] If this book has one core aim, it is to promote just such a giving up of human exceptionalism in the way we imagine, design and live in our buildings and cities.

1
Miniature

A spider carries on operations resembling those of the weaver, and many a human architect is put to shame by the skill with which a bee constructs her cell. But what from the very first distinguishes the most incompetent architect from the best of bees, is that the architect has built a cell in his head before he constructs it in wax.[1]

Karl Marx, *Capital* (1867)

Karl Marx's well-known analogy of architects and bees promoted human exceptionalism because it assumed that only humans possess imagination. Spiders and bees may build admirable structures, but they lack the ability to construct, in their mind's eye, a fully formed image of what they intend to build before they realize it. Forty years ago, Tim Ingold argued, *contra* Marx, that 'it would be quite wrong to conclude from our inability to penetrate the experience of other species that we are uniquely endowed with subjective will.'[2] Today, research on the building habits of termites, ants, wasps and bees has comprehensively demonstrated the fallacy of Marx's assumption. Social insects' way of perceiving the world is clearly radically different from our own, but no less significant. It is perception without what humans would call a 'mind', meaning a complex brain or neurological network; rather, the lives of social insects are best described as ceaseless flows of communication between bodies, buildings and environments that nevertheless sometimes produce extraordinary works of architecture.[3]

As well as constructing their own homes, arthropods – here I consider beetles, spiders, ants, wasps, bees and termites – are also highly adept at exploiting human buildings. Entomologist Richard Jones has provided an eye-opening and skin-crawling encyclopedia of the dozens of bugs that find sustenance and safety in the hidden spaces of our homes, even as we mostly wish for their extermination. This is a veritable cornucopia of beetles, wasps, flies, bees, cockroaches, termites, ants, fleas, mosquitoes, gnats, moths, bedbugs, lice, mites, spiders, snails and slugs.[4] Despite their closeness to us – it is said that we are never more than two metres away from a spider – arthropods remain intractably alien, about as far as possible from domesticated animals and the human-like qualities we attribute to them. As horrifically demonstrated in David Cronenberg's 1986 film *The Fly*, bugs make us squirm. As its fly-man hybrid protagonist Seth Brundle says: 'I'm an insect who dreamt he was a man, and loved it. But now the dream is over, and the insect is awake.'

A powerful way of imagining the alien lives of arthropods is through the simple technique of miniaturization. Interest in the microcosmic world of arthropods first gained prominence in the nineteenth century, when the structures and social lives of insects and spiders were readily compared with human equivalents (for example, termite mounds as the insect version of the pyramids of Egypt).[5] That mode of identification has persisted, yet

Still from the opening sequence of *Antz* (1998).

it remains thoroughly anthropocentric in character, one example being the opening sequence of the animated film *Antz* (1998). Here, what we initially take to be the skyline of New York is in fact an ant's-eye view of blades of grass – a trick of scale being all that separates lowly insect from sophisticated urbanite. It might be argued that this kind of imagination merely reasserts the human exceptionalism argued by Marx even more strongly, with every aspect of the social lives of insects made to mirror our own. Yet ecological thinking begins precisely in this technique of seeing from another's point of view.[6] Crude as it may be, the imagination of a human world in miniature presents an opportunity to move beyond our instinctive revulsion towards insects, especially when they appear in our homes. Instead, with practice, we might become more empathetic towards bugs, however flawed our anthropomorphic identification may be.

And developing empathy with insects and spiders is an urgent task, given the scarcely believable rate of arthropod annihilation that has been playing out for at least half a century. As revealed in a widely reported 2019 scientific article, more than 40 per cent of insect species are now threatened with extinction and many others are declining at an alarming rate, a situation caused by habitat loss through the conversion of 'wild' land for intensive agriculture, the increasing use of agrochemical pollutants (insecticides mostly), invasive species and climate change.[7] This insect apocalypse threatens not only human concerns, such as the efficient pollination of our staple food resources, but entire ecosystems across the planet. In this context, the dangers of anthropomorphism in relation to the human imagination of insects seem massively outweighed by humans continuing to regard insects as pests. Learning to imaginatively identify with the alien in our midst – to see their microcosmos through our own eyes – is a small but important step towards valuing them in ways that might stem the tide of annihilation.

Beetle

Beetles come into buildings searching for food. Some hunt down our comestibles: these are Coleopteran specialists, often named after their desired product, including bacon, coffee, biscuits, grain, rice, cigarettes, flour, fruit and beans. Others prefer to nibble on our fixtures and fittings, whether carpets, fur or even metal cables. Still others are named after their favoured hiding places, for example larder and the now rare cellar beetles. The most feared are those that eat buildings from the inside out: timber-digesting species such as woodworm, deathwatch and house longhorn beetles. Despite the fact that they rarely build for themselves, beetles may be the most numerous of any animal species that choose to inhabit our buildings.[8]

Beetles enter unannounced and unwanted through cracks, gaps in door and window frames, or by already hiding in timber, furniture, plants and packages. The various types of beetle that feed on timber are the scourge of architectural conservationists or anyone with an old house or cherished piece of antique furniture. The larvae of the adult longhorn and bark beetles and weevils are the primary decomposers of dead trees, but they will bore channels into hardwoods too. Although they cause great consternation, the larvae often take many years to mature, with the wood being hollowed out so slowly that decades, even centuries, are likely to pass before it crumbles. Still, the presence of hidden interlopers is disconcerting. In a quiet house infested with deathwatch beetles, you can hear the adult males banging their heads against the wood in which they are hiding in order to attract females.

Given enough time, woodworm and other beetles can rip through a timber-framed building, rendering it structurally unsafe; the wood itself turns into a Swiss cheese of meandering tunnels – multitudinous, miniature tubular architectures of their own. In China Miéville's fantasy novel *Perdido Street Station* (2000), an entire district of the book's extraordinary imaginary city New Crobuzon has the appearance of a scaled-up version of architectural woodworm. Here, the larval offspring of the Khepri – human/scarab beetle hybrids – have adapted conventional tenement housing to their own needs. The roofs and exterior walls are covered in the white mucus of the grubs, 'linking different buildings into a lumpy, congealed totality'. Inside, walls and floors originally built for humans are broken apart and reconstituted as the grubs burrow their way through the spaces, 'oozing their phlegm-cement from their abdomens'. Rectilinear forms are transformed into 'twisting organic passageways' that 'looked from the inside like giant worm-tracks'.[9] The disgust provoked by such imagery has the effect of jolting us out of the miniature scale of the woodworm's architecture into that of our own habitats; we suddenly see those spaces as not just tiny tunnels inside wood, but profoundly alien worlds that somehow stick to us in their gooey viscosity.

A beetle/human meld was rendered very differently in Franz Kafka's 1915 novella *Metamorphosis*, its famous opening line seeing the unfortunate Gregor Samsa waking up one morning to find 'himself transformed into a gigantic insect'.[10] Commentators usually presume that Gregor has metamorphosed into a cockroach (an insect species closer to ants than beetles), but his convex segmented belly and rounded back (suggestive of wing cases) are diagnostic beetle characteristics. Yet his transformation is only ever partial: Gregor never discovers his wings and still possesses human features such as eyelids. Throughout the story, Gregor hears himself speak in his familiar human voice while his family hear only unintelligible hisses, and his insect body is poignantly contrasted with his quite human thoughts – of his love and concern for his family, of his inability to go to work and support them and of his bodily functions, most notably, his longing for food. The matter-of-fact way in which this fantastic transformation is described by Kafka provides a powerful and deeply unsettling insight into beetle life. Gregor's bedroom – the most intimate of domestic spaces for humans and one from which he hardly ever emerges – becomes disgusting to the rest of the family, first cleared of most of its furniture so that Gregor can scuttle more freely and then used as a dumping ground for the family's unwanted junk. In the end, the outsized beetle dies in squalor. Once his body is removed, his once loving sister is relieved, her own young body 'stretching into life' in the final sentence, her emerging beauty presented in stark and damning contrast to the dead husk that was once her brother.

Beetles are the most abundant insect, indeed any animal, species. Of all the known animals on Earth, about 25 per cent – at least 350,000 – are beetles. An average of four new species of beetle have been discovered every single day for the past 250 years, with many thousands assumed to be still awaiting identification.[11] However, like all insects, beetles are disappearing at an alarming rate, victims of human rapaciousness: whether they are regarded as enemies of agriculture and extinguished without a thought through pesticides or the destruction of their habitats, or because they are unable to adapt to anthropogenic climate change. The recent appearance of 'bug hotels' in cities such as London are modest attempts to redress this alarming decline. Bug hotels are usually unassuming box-shaped structures, their facades pierced with small cavities that mimic beetles' proclivity to burrow or hide in leaf litter and other decaying vegetation. In 2015 French artists Vaulout & Dyèvre created an upscale version of a bug hotel in a Paris park, which they titled *Insectopia*. This installation consisted of several agglomerations of tiny wooden boxes mounted on posts that only insects could inhabit.[12] Resembling the abstract cities seen in the paintings of Paul Klee, the installation invited a direct correlation to be made between the architectural form of insect colonies (nest-building species such as bees and wasps) and our own urban environments – a very different kind of metaphor than Kafka's alienated bug-human monster imprisoned in a bedroom.

More ambitious still was artist Fritz Haeg's *Animal Estates* project, which ran from 2008 until 2013 and has already been mentioned in the Introduction to this book.[13] In 2008, in Portland, Oregon, part of Haeg's installation was designed to be inhabited by snail-eating ground beetles, while in London in 2011–12 he encouraged citizens to make homes for stag beetles (the UK's largest native species) by burying decaying wood or woodchip piles in the ground. Here, beetles, as much as humans, are conceived as 'clients' in design, the architect's brief involving gaining knowledge about multi-species habitats that normally go unnoticed, and then designing and building for cohabitation. *Animal Estates* moved beyond the conventional human treatment of animals as exotic spectacles, anthropomorphized cartoon characters, friendly companions, resources to be exploited, inconveniences to be tolerated, or pests to be exterminated.[14] The wide-ranging programme of *Animal Estates* was centred on recognizing the needs of non-humans in every design and planning decision. At the same time, though, the structures built by Haeg were resolutely separated from the human domestic realm. Thus, even as beetles might be accommodated more visibly and more self-consciously in cities, their 'estates' were largely still very different from our own.

But what if, in our enthusiasm to accommodate beetles, they were able to thrive too well, to infest a place rather than inhabit it with good grace? In Henrietta Rose-Innes's 2011 novel *Nineveh*, a luxury housing development on the edge of Cape Town becomes the victim of a beetle infestation. Sited

Fritz Haeg's 'Animal Estate regional model homes 5.0', part of the *Animal Estates* exhibition held in Portland in 2008.

on former swampland, the resolutely inorganic architecture is taken over by what it has seemingly cast out – longhorn beetles swarming in the fetid, teeming swamp that lies just beyond the walls of the development. When a pest-removal specialist, the rather too aptly named Katya Grubbs, is hired to deal with the problem, she becomes increasingly aware of the infestation as a harbinger of the future destruction that awaits organic bodies and inorganic buildings alike. Putting her ear to a wall in order to listen to a beetle scuttling within, Katya realizes that all things are transient – a truth that is often displaced by the seeming permanency of the buildings we inhabit, which, after all, almost always continue to stand beyond any one human lifespan.[15] The infestation also brings to the surface a primal fear we have of insects, namely of their ability to swarm in numbers beyond either our comprehension or control. Many a childhood is traumatized by just such encounters with insects: unexpected swarms of flying ants in late summer, or a bees' nest stumbled upon by accident.

The characteristic swarming behaviour of beetles has been given a positive spin in a research pavilion built at the University of Stuttgart from

Elytra filament pavilion created by Achim Menges, Moritz Dörstelmann, Jan Knippers and Thomas Auer at the University of Stuttgart in 2013–14.

2013 to 2014 by the Institute for Computational Design and Construction in collaboration with the Institute of Building Structures and Structural Design. Involving a multidisciplinary team of biologists, palaeontologists, architects and engineers, the pavilion was developed from an intensive study of the material character of elytra – the protective shells of the delicate wings and soft abdomens of beetles. These chitin fibres embedded in a protein matrix were identified by the research team as an ideal model for a highly efficient form of construction. A double-layered modular system was developed, comprised of thin strands of resin-coated fibreglass that were woven together by two custom-built robots. The robots eventually made 36 individual elements, creating a 50-square-metre pavilion that weighed just 593 kilograms.[16] Widely celebrated as a paradigmatic example of biomimetic architecture, the pavilion's delicate materiality contrasted starkly with its structural toughness – a mirror image of the way in which the elytra of beetles function.[17]

Like many examples of architectural biomimicry, the strikingly organic appearance of the pavilion obscured its basis in wholly artificial building materials, the original inspiration being merely a fragment of the beetle isolated and probed for its instrumental use for humans. Is not a beetle much more than the sum of its constituent parts, a living being rather than just a model for a novel form of structural mechanics? Perhaps, instead, the unique architectures *created* by beetles, such as the networks of tunnels carved by woodworm, longhorn and deathwatch beetles, might also be embraced as sites where architecture can be attuned to insect life. These miniature excavations need not be feared as inevitably leading to the destruction of precious structural materials; as already stated, it usually takes decades, or centuries, for beetles to damage timber beyond repair. It is possible that wooden frames might be materially reconfigured to accommodate beetles, even to make their micro-architectures visible so they can be managed and accepted rather than feared. And, rather than a threatening swarm, the beetle hordes of *Nineveh* might be understood as creating a miraculous form of spatial knowledge, one that links us terrestrials with what lies beyond and beneath either our lived experience or our fantasies of control.

Spider

A year after exhibiting their beetle-inspired pavilion, the University of Stuttgart hosted another pavilion inspired by arthropods: a tent-like structure built by an industrial robot from the inside out, the automaton printing lines of carbon-fibre bundles onto the underside of an inflated EFTE membrane. This remarkably thin and lightweight structure was based on collaborative research into the habitat of the water or 'diving bell' spider (*Argyroneta aquatica*), which is the only species of spider known to live almost entirely underwater. This biomimetic pavilion was inspired by the spider's ability to enclose itself in a silk-covered air bubble in order to retain a consistent supply of oxygen underwater.[18] Although this pavilion, like its beetle predecessor, was limited in being merely an aesthetic representation of a natural phenomenon, it nevertheless highlighted how a construction process might adjust to local conditions as this particular spider does in its own unpredictable subaqueous habitat.

Spiders thrive in a vast array of environmental conditions, living everywhere on earth except the polar regions. The oft-quoted statistic that you are never more than 2 metres away from a rat is perhaps more truthfully

ICD/ITKE Research Pavilion, created at the University of Stuttgart in 2014–16.

applied to spiders: there are 40,000 known species (with hundreds of new ones discovered every year), and all construct some form of web to trap their prey, usually insects.[19] Although the orb-shaped web – a two-dimensional structure that looks like a bicycle wheel or dartboard – is the most commonly known, spiders make webs of many different shapes, including triangles, sheets, tangles, funnels, tubes, laces and purses. All spiders build with silk produced by a gland in their entrails connected to short spinnerets with many spigots. The orb-web, made by the *Araneus* genus of spiders, has received intense scrutiny by human observers for millennia. An *Araneus* spider first joins together two fixed points with a silk thread; next it starts to build a frame around the central point of that first thread, adding radial and spiral elements. Then the spider moves from the edge of the emerging web to its centre, spacing the radial elements closer together in order to provide additional structural strength to the web. The hub in the very centre is made of much stronger and thicker silk, this usually being the place where the spider captures and then consumes ensnared prey.[20]

As well as being admired for their engineering prowess, spiders have also given rise to a whole host of often conflicting symbolic meanings, many mediated through Ovid's famous story of the Lydian weaver Arachne in his long narrative poem *Metamorphoses*, composed in 8 CE. This story tells of how Arachne challenged the goddess Athena to a weaving contest, the enraged goddess promptly turning the human weaver into a spider.[21] A spider's web may therefore be a direct symbol of human creativity, tempered by the knowledge that much of the effort put into creative work is pointless – the work itself often frail and ephemeral. In the modern period the image of a spider at the centre of its web has symbolized both the 'ordering hand of the Great Architect' but also a snare in which the unwary may become trapped (voiced most strongly in spiders' association with the femme fatale).[22] More recently, the development of the Internet, and the World Wide Web, offered powerful technological metaphors of spiders' webs, although Sir Tim Berners-Lee, inventor of the latter, protested in 2007 against such a comparison, as his virtual web had no centre or controller.[23]

The meticulous way in which a spider constructs its web, coupled with the extraordinary structural properties of the web's silk strands (reputedly almost as strong in tension as steel), has meant that spiders have long held a fascination for human designers. German architect Frei Otto pioneered lightweight construction in the second half of the twentieth century in buildings that incorporated cable nets, tents, pneumatic structures and grid shells.[24] His buildings for the Munich Olympics in 1972 used spider-web-inspired cable-net structures to gracefully cover the sporting stadia, which, when viewed from above, resembled the sheet webs built by social species of spider. More recently, bioengineers have experimented in using spider threads as a stitching material in neurological operations to repair damaged nerve fibres, while artist Jalila Essaïdi's '2.6g 329m/s' scheme aims to implant a matrix of spider-silk into human skin in order to make it bulletproof. If these experiments might seem like a product of science-fiction scenarios, then the so-called Biosteel Goat is the fantastic made real. This is a genetically engineered goat, developed by the U.S. Army and Canadian firm Nexia Biotechnologies, that produces spider-silk proteins in its milk, which are then extracted and weaved into super-fibres for making light-weight body armour.[25]

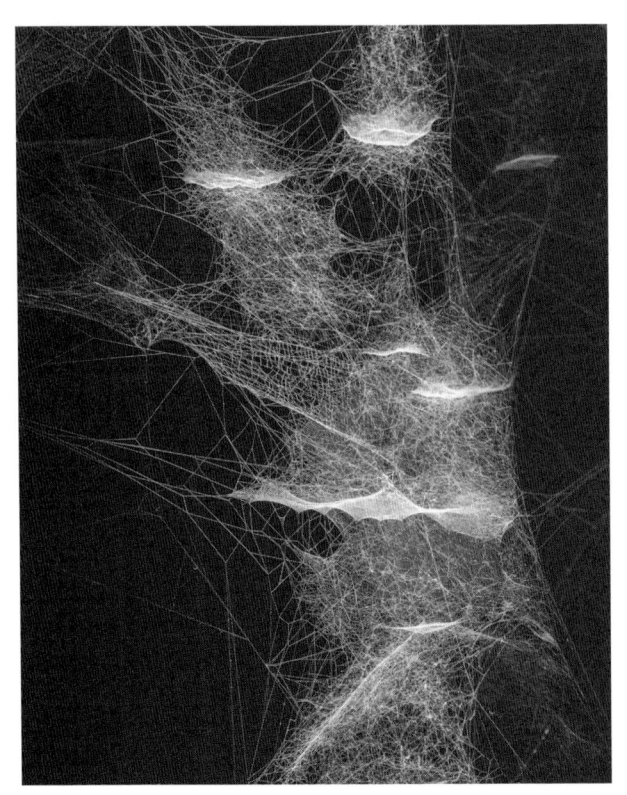

Tomás Saraceno, *Hybrid Spider/Webs* (2019), shown within Spider/Web Pavilion 7, presented at the 58th Biennale di Venezia, curated by Ralph Rugoff.

Argentine-born, Berlin-based artist Tomás Saraceno has literally co-opted spiders to build his *Hybrid Webs* series of projects. Using specially designed glass boxes, Saraceno brought together several different species of spider to collaboratively produce a three-dimensional web, which was then scanned by a machine and reconstructed as a model. For Saraceno, spiderwebs possess cosmic meaning: watching spiders at work provides both a model of 'environmental relationships and their fragility' and also of the early universe, namely in the 'analogy between cosmic filaments and a spider web'.[26] Some 76 iterations of the *Hybrid Webs* formed part of Saraceno's installation at the Palais de Tokyo in Paris in 2018. In addition, five hundred live spiders spun their webs around the vast interior of the building, stimulated into action by a vibration created by a live audio stream from the European Gravitational Observatory. This was an experiment to see if the frequencies of black holes colliding millions of years ago (detected by the observatory) could be translated into a particular kind of weaving practice by the spiders. In the same exhibition, the installation *Galaxies Forming Along Filaments, Like Droplets Along the Strands of Spiderwebs* featured a room of thin elastic cables spanning floor and ceiling. Visitors could dodge the threads or make them vibrate to form a collective piece of music.[27] This cornucopia of spider-related art was designed to encourage – indeed force – visitors to 'reflect on their place within the infinitely complex networks that structure our existence, from the minutiae of dust particles and the vibrations of spiderwebs to the collisions of galaxies in the universe'.[28]

Saraceno's immersive installations suggest that the built environment – entire cities even – might be radically reshaped and experienced as interconnected webs, with any one individual's actions always impacting on another's. This reflects a strand within twentieth-century design-thinking that saw in technology the promise of reducing the impact of human construction on more-than-human worlds. Richard Buckminster Fuller's geodesic domes were perhaps the most strident realization of this vision, but it was also present within speculative projects such as Frederick Kiesler's *Space City* (1925) and Archigram's 'Living City' exhibition from 1963. In the latter, David Greene and Michael Webb presented a colossal net-like structure, called a 'Thing', suspended above a desolate city. This triangulated space-frame, which they imagined as eventually encircling the entire planet, keyed into modernist visions of architecture freed from its basis in solid materials – a new floating built environment without walls or foundations and one that would create radical new possibilities for social life.[29]

A different strand of visionary thinking informed the imagination of Octavia, one of Italo Calvino's *Invisible Cities* in his 1972 book. In this 'spider-web city', a net spans a precipice between two mountains, and serves as both 'passage and . . . support' for the the city of Octavia. Instead of rising up from the ground, Octavia hangs beneath the net: a tangle of 'rope ladders, hammocks, houses made like sacks, clothes, hangers, ter- races like gondolas, skins of water, gas jets, spits, baskets on strings, dumb- waiters, showers, trapezes and rings for children's games, cable cars, chandeliers, pots with trailing plants'. A steampunk version of Saraceno's technologically sophisticated aerial installations, Octavia draws attention to human fragility and the uncertainty of our built environments. The residents of this chaotic spiderweb city know that 'the net will last only so long' but are nevertheless reassured in that knowledge.[30] London-based design studio Ordinary Ltd visualized Calvino's city as Arachnia, a metropolis suspended over a tectonic fault-zone. Here it is spiders them- selves that protect the city from the violence of recurring earthquakes, spinning their silk around the suspended living units, creating a vast protective web.[31]

Arachnia, created by Ordinary Ltd: a visualization of Octavia, a city in Italo Calvino's *Invisible Cities* (1972).

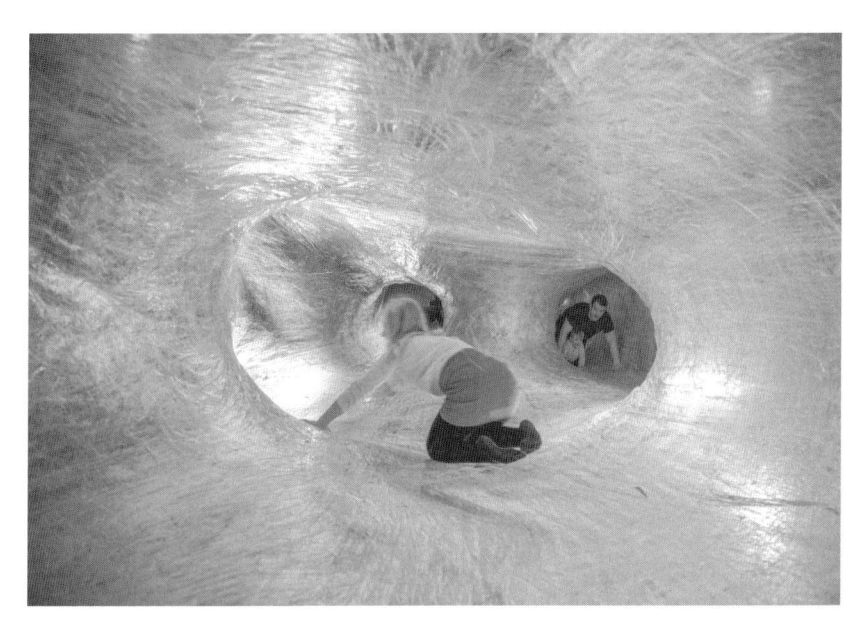

Tape installation in the Science and Industry Museum, Manchester, 2017, created by Croatian-Austrian art collective Numen/For Use.

This equating of spiderwebs with reassuring protection stands in direct contrast to their more usual association with entrapment and suffocation. Although only around two dozen of the world's 40,000 or so species of spider present a genuine danger to humans, arachnophobia is one of the commonest phobias. The widespread revulsion generated by spiders is thought to originate in the anxieties of our distant ancestors, more specifically their fear of darkness and danger.[32] Karl Abraham, a pupil of Sigmund Freud, argued that the psychological root of arachnophobia lay in the subject's fear of an enveloping and all-consuming mother.[33] Arachnophobes often speak of spiderwebs as generating images of smothering and some spider-haters obsess about the object of their neurosis returning their gaze. This has been exploited most powerfully in images of proliferating spiderwebs, to some extent reflected in how a few species of social spider actually build their webs (as sheets). John Wyndham's last novel, *Web* (published posthumously in 1979), posits a remote island overrun by such webs, the spiders themselves seemingly mutated into murderous hordes by fallout from atomic tests carried out nearby.[34] In a similar vein, the 1977 film *Kingdom of the Spiders* sees a remote desert town in America overrun by homicidal tarantulas, the final chilling sequence showing the entire valley subsumed under a vast sheet of webs, the last remaining residents of the town trapped in this enveloping structure.

Conflicting human responses to spiderwebs characterized the installation *Tape*, created by Croatian-Austrian design collective Numen/For Use and exhibited in cities all over the world from 2009 to 2019. *Tape* comprised translucent tunnels created entirely from the application of layer upon layer of sticky-tape and plastic. Each iteration of the installation was subtly different and was adapted to the space in which it was created, whether inside or outside a building. Together with my nine-year-old daughter, I experienced the version of *Tape* exhibited in an early nineteenth-century former warehouse at the Science and Industry Museum in Manchester in October 2017. A human-sized version of the structures made by funnel-web spiders, *Tape* was designed to give visitors 'an arachnid's-eye view of the world'.[35] Yet wherever it was re-created, the artists subtly altered its connotations: for example, in Vienna (2009), it recorded the choreography of a group of dancers; in Frankfurt (2010), it was meant to foster community collaboration; in Paris (2014), it represented regression into a primordial state; in Des Moines (2017), it was a parasitic organic structure in a rectilinear modernist space.[36] My experience of it in Manchester was one of both liberation and entrapment, of vulnerability and power, of security and claustrophobia. With its crude materials and method of construction, *Tape* draws us away from a celebratory focus on the rational technology of the spiderweb and back into a more ambivalent symbolic world that has been present ever since spiders chose to live alongside us. At every moment and in almost every space, spiders are building their own miniature houses of entrapment and murder, often very close by to each and every one of us.

Ant

Beetles and spiders may be the most numerous arthropods in terms of the diversity of their species, but it is ants (the Formicidae family) that are the most successful by numbers alone. The combined weight of every living ant on earth has been estimated to be half that of all insects; by another estimate, if the nearly 8 billion humans on earth weigh a combined 332 billion kilograms, the 10,000 trillion ants come in at 40 billion kilograms.[37] The tiny size of ants (individual species ranging from 0.7 to 30 millimetres in length) belies their significance as gargantuan collectives – in effect, super-organisms, the largest colonies of which comprise tens of millions of individuals, the insect equivalents of megacities.

Ant colonies are ambivalent metaphors of human societies. If some have regarded ant colonies as utopian worlds in miniature – hierarchical societies that function with almost perfect efficiency – others have seen the machine-like behaviour of ants as a mirror of dystopian nightmares of the mechanization of human life. Still others are horrified by ants' capacity to infest spaces (like beetles). Most of my early childhood memories have been lost to oblivion, but one still stands out: a scene in the 1977 TV movie *It Happened at Lakewood Manor* (also known as *Ants!*), in which three unfortunate people become trapped in a house infested with killer ants. Realizing that their attempts to remove the ants from their bodies only cause the insects to become more aggressive, they decide to sit as still as possible, breathing through long paper tubes, as the ants swarm over them.

Just like beetles, ants can draw attention to the hidden spaces within our buildings – the microcosmos that we only perceive as we imagine in miniature. In Calvino's short-story 'The Argentine Ant' (1960), a young couple with a newborn baby are seduced by the dream of owning their own house, only to discover that it is infested with tiny ants. With a dawning realization that there is no way to exterminate their unwanted house guests, the family's dream of a settled life of domestic bliss is made untenable. The house they took to be 'smooth and solid on the surface was in fact porous and honeycombed with cracks and holes'.[38] Here, the miniature world of ants reveals hidden truths about architecture itself, namely that Vitruvius' age-old ideal of 'firmness' might in fact be an illusion. Calvino's ants also break down the distinction between the inside and outside of buildings in a disturbing reversal of the harmony strived for by modernist architects: 'the insects formed an uninterrupted veil, issued from what must be thousands of underground nests and feeding on the thick, sticky soil and the low vegetation.' These are creatures that are indifferent to our architectural barriers and thresholds: 'an enemy like fog or sand'.[39]

Like termites, bees and wasps, ants are social insects that build, constructing or excavating nests that usually last as long as the resident queen ant is active (sometimes decades). Subterranean colonies can grow very large: for example, ant biologist Walter Tschinkel's plaster model of a nest

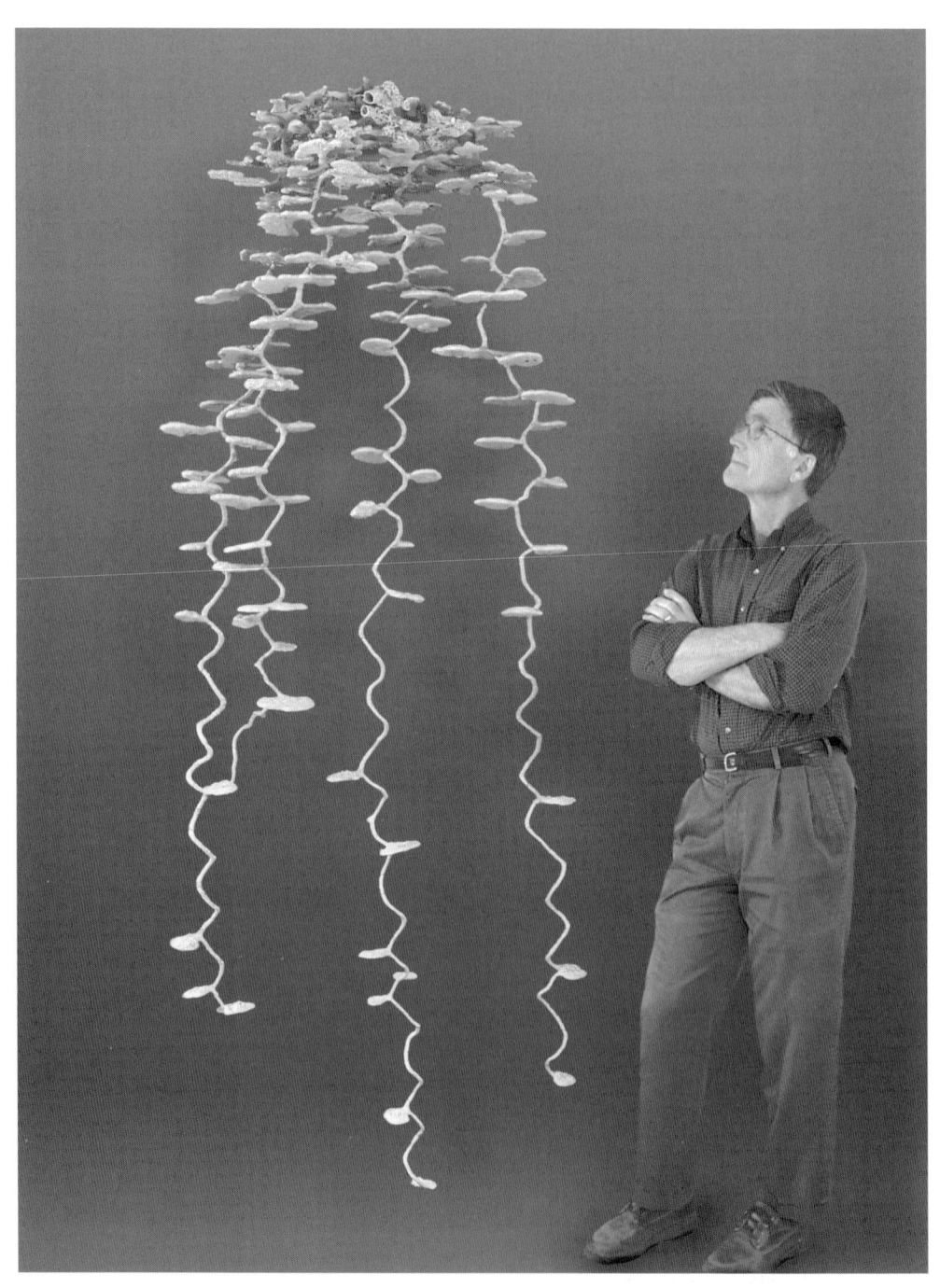

Cast made in 2006 of the nest of ant species *Pogonomyrmex badius*, with its creator, Walter Tschinkel, providing a sense of scale.

of the Florida harvester ant is taller than a man (Tschinkel using himself as a model to demonstrate this).[40] Almost jellyfish-like in its appearance, the model reveals many metres of interconnecting tunnels linking chambers for rearing larvae and depositing waste. In 2012 a vast nest built by millions of leafcutter ants in Brazil was discovered abandoned.[41] It was then filled with concrete, which was allowed to set, after which the underground city was excavated to reveal the characteristic chambers and interconnecting tunnels built by the ants. In a similar manner to the sculptures made by British artist Rachel Whiteread, it is the absent forms of architecture – the spaces in between the supporting materials – that are revealed by this casting process. Spatially inverted, the ant colony appears as a fantastical organic architecture not unlike the bone-like structures of the *Alien* series of films, conceived by H. R. Giger.

Ant architecture has often been compared to whatever is regarded as its human equivalent in terms of scale, the excavated leafcutter nest in Brazil being described as the 'ant equivalent of the Great Wall of China'.[42] Dense human settlements, particularly large cities, are often described, usually by their detractors, as human anthills; while the late nineteenth-century American naturalist Henry McCook compared ants' nests to the ancient Egyptian pyramids, calculating how the volume of each structure related to the respective size of their builders. He concluded that the structures built by ants made even our great cities look no more impressive than villages.[43]

Ants' capacity to build complex large-scale structures has led to imaginings of the possible power of their collective intelligence. Saul Bass's 1974 science-fiction film *Phase IV* draws on such diverse themes as Cold War paranoia, reverse colonization and the arrogance of science, in its presentation of ants as Machiavellian warmongers. A gigantic queen of an interspecies subterranean colony under the Arizona desert has come under the influence of an unknown alien intelligence. Her super-colony begins to attack its predators, including the residents of the unfortunately named Paradise City, a half-completed development in the desert. One of the residents, a young woman named Kendra, is able to escape and joins a two-man scientific team in a geodesic research station. This has been constructed next to a cluster of mud towers built by the ants, each of which is angled to the sky by means of a triangular, mouth-like opening. When these are destroyed by one of the scientists, the ants retaliate by constructing

Scene from Saul Bass's *Phase IV* (1974) showing towers built by ants under the influence of an alien intelligence.

mirrors that reflect sunlight back onto the research station, causing it to overheat and its scientific equipment to malfunction. It is eventually revealed that the ants' intention is to infiltrate the human mind – Kendra rising out of the sand in a chamber of the subterranean colony to embrace her new life as an alien-controlled subject. The film is remarkable for Dick Bush's cinematography, which uses macro-lenses to depict the lives of the ants themselves – we look through their compound eyes 'seeing' us, the tiny spaces they move through magnified to human proportions. The ants even communicate to the scientists through an architectural drawing created by a printer: a dot inscribed in a circle, inscribed in a square representing the human subject, the research base and the ant world beyond.

The idea that ants might be capable of producing an architectural drawing may seem absurd, but it reflects a long fascination with ants' ability to build complex structures without blueprints or centralized control. As researchers have demonstrated, the organization of construction of an ants' nest is achieved through pheromones secreted by each individual ant, which stimulate others to perform a particular task. In addition, ants use their bodies as templates to configure spaces within the nest itself. Tropical army ants use their bodies as literal building blocks – they are nomadic hordes: each night, they swarm together to create a living bivouac around the queen; they also link their bodies together to make bridges or rafts to survive flooding. Ants are also skilled at manipulating building materials, whether sand, mud or clay. Like traditional mud building in human settlements, some ants have been observed creating 'bricks', small hollow balls that are fitted together with their powerful jaws.[44] In all cases, the form of any individual ants' nest emerges through a continuous chain of communication. Thus a higher level of organization emerges from below.[45]

The social organization of ants has long fascinated children and specially designed ant farms have been popular toys since the nineteenth century (and still are in many countries). An ant farm traditionally consists of a glass-sided dirt-filled box in which ants build an artificial colony, the pathways excavated by the ants emerging before the eyes of enraptured youngsters. Ant farms have also been built by architects. For example, LYCS Architecture's *Learning from Ants* project explored how ants' emergent building practices might be applied to architecture for humans.[46] An experimental ant farm allowed meticulous observation of the ants' tunnelling behaviour, revealing the ways in which they created spaces as they were using them. This direct equating of building and inhabitation has long been the dream of architects seeking a truly organic relationship between form and function, yet it has usually led to a highly subjective and individualized way of building, completely at odds with ants' ability to build collectively from below. A more subversive interpretation of ants' building behaviour is STUDIO 1:1's *Urban Ant Farm* installation from 2015. Here,

Ant farm created by LYCS Architecture as part of their installation *Learning from Ants.*

hundreds of Spanish ants were allowed to 'hack' a scaled-map of Rotterdam, creating their own landscape of paths and tunnels through sand sandwiched between glass.[47] The ants created an anarchic 'counter-city' through the existing one – an autonomous labyrinth of pathways beyond the control of any overarching authority.

The tension between ants as a highly organized collective, a model animal society for humans to observe and emulate and an anarchic disruptor of anthropocentric building is characteristic of human engagements with these insects. Contemplating the social organization of an ant farm, children fantasize about being in charge of a miniature kingdom – the fantasist becoming, comparatively, a giant in his/her own world.[48] But ant farms also demonstrate insects' utter disregard for the order that humans impose upon the world and the fact that the human urge to expand and protect borders is mirrored in the behaviour of ants. These insects may be miniature in size but viewed close up, as beautifully illustrated in the cinematography of *Phase IV*, it is clear that, in Charlotte Sleigh's words, 'it is we who are beneath the perceptual threshold of the ant, and not the other way around. The ant burrows and spreads across a globe in which humans are too insignificant to appear in its gaze.'[49]

Colombian artist Rafael Gómezbarros has reversed the characteristic miniature view of ants in his *House Taken* series, created from 2008 onwards. These works bring together more than 3,000 giant fibreglass ants as installations on the facades of prominent urban buildings and in gallery spaces across the world. Each ant is made from two moulds shaped in the form of human skulls, the resulting swarm symbolizing the forced displacement and uprooting of human communities in the wake of globalization.[50] Together, the giant ants also bring us back to the fear of infestation that characterizes human engagement with these and other insects. They call attention to the all too common portrayal of the movement of migrants as a less-than-human infestation – an unwanted invasion. By magnifying ants and making them attack architecture, Gómezbarros also reminds us that the way humans see the world is not so much a matter of fact as one of perspective. Giant ants shake the ground of our own assumptions about the nature of space itself. They remind us of myriad invisible cities beneath the ones we can see, whether those are made by humans or other, decidedly alien, creatures.

Wasp

Ants' ability to build complex structures without hierarchical control is also characteristic of other social insects, such as bees and wasps. Although it is beehives that get the most attention in terms of their correlation to human-built structures, the paper nests built by wasps in the Vespidae family are no less magnificent in their demonstration of engineering prowess. Other, usually solitary, wasps from the Sphecidae and Crabronidae families build less complex structures with mud, creating pipes, mounds or pots to protect their offspring from predators. Many wasps' nests, whether paper or mud, are found on or inside human-built structures. Paper nests are commonly found in uninhabited domestic spaces, such as lofts or attics, while mud nests may appear on almost any available space: behind curtains, on walls, inside porches and barns, under bridges and even inside the engines of jet aircraft (known to have been responsible for several fatal crashes).

It is the paper nests created by vespid wasps that have generated most interest in terms of their construction method. An individual nest begins when a solitary queen, emerging from hibernation in the spring, searches for a suitable site on which to build. Using wood pulp that she has scraped off any available timber surface and mixed with her saliva, the queen fashions a hanging stem upon which she creates the first hexagonal cells for her initial brood of a dozen or so larvae. If the queen is extraordinarily lucky (only around 0.01 per cent of these early attempts to found a new nest are successful), the golf-ball sized structure she makes will eventually evolve into a beachball-sized nest created by thousands of sterile female workers (male offspring are far less numerous and bred only for their sperm). Unlike bees, whose colonies can last for many years, even decades, wasps' nests become redundant after six months, with most then eaten by other animals or quickly destroyed by the elements. Wasps' nests generally consist of a secure outer structure made from layers of paper with a single entrance usually located at the base, inside of which are built the hexagonal combs for the larvae. The combs are built downwards in rows and supported on columns that replicate the first example built by the queen, upon which the entire structure is secured.[51]

In 2016 Mattia Menchetti, an Italian biology student, provided coloured paper for a colony of European paper wasps to build their nest. By substituting one colour for another as the wasps completed each new row of combs, the nest evolved into a rainbow-like construction that drew attention to the incremental stages of building.[52] The different colours also gave visual form to the ways in which the wasps build as both individuals and as a collective. Individuals collect and make the wood pulp, but once they bring this back to the nest it is their sensory engagement with the nest itself that determines where and how they apply this material. It is not just the mathematic precision of the hexagonal combs that has puzzled researchers: each cell is curved according to its relative position in the nest and the overall shape of the nest is altered by workers responding to the climatic conditions outside. Animal researcher Guy Theraulaz has observed that when wasps decide to build a new cell, they make use of information provided by the local configurations of existing cells on the outer circumference of the comb, which they sense with their antennae. Identifying the rules followed by the wasps, Theraulaz and his colleague Eric Bonabeau used a computer to generate similar sets of rules for buildings, demonstrating that a wide range of architectural diversity can be created by only very small changes in the determining parameters.[53]

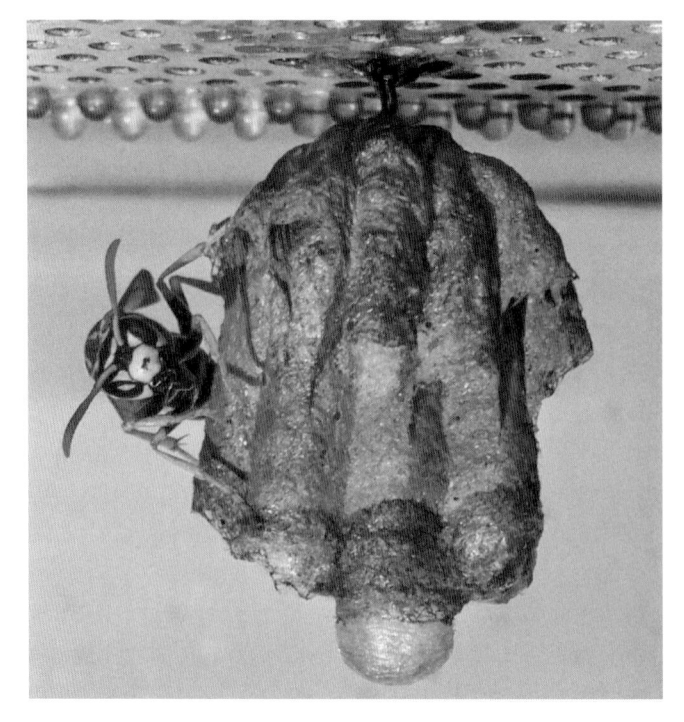

A nest being built by wasps with multi-coloured paper provided by Mattia Menchetti in 2016.

House designed by WASP, the mud walls created using a Crane WASP 3-D printer in Bologna in 2018.

This observation of wasp building behaviour, commonly known as 'swarm intelligence', suggests the possibility of an architecture that does not arise from blueprints and hierarchical forms of control, but rather emerges from the local conditions in which construction is situated.[54] Buildings would then adapt and change as they are constructed and used, allowing them to flex and morph in ways that are mostly unworkable in conventional built environments. For example, the aptly named WASP company (World's Advanced Saving Project) builds giant 3-D printers to 'fabricate' large objects such as houses. With Mario Cucinella Architects they developed a prototype tiny house that was printed with mud by a specially designed Crane WASP printer in Bologna in October 2018.[55] Taking inspiration from potter wasps, the house's curvilinear walls emerged from a computer program that optimized their shape according to local conditions. The much more ambitious TECLA project aims to use multiple 3-D printers to build entire eco-cities anywhere in the world. Printing buildings with raw earth, sourced *in situ*, is argued to be more ecologically sound than fabricating materials in advance and transporting them to the construction site.[56]

The name TECLA was inspired by one of the imaginary cities depicted in Calvino's *Invisible Cities*. This is a city that is perpetually under construction, a city of scaffolding, wooden catwalks hanging from ropes, ladders, trestles and metal armatures. As Calvino stated, a visitor to this perpetual construction site might well be confounded as to its meaning, asking why there is no blueprint that would eventually see the city completed. The answer was provided only when the work stopped at sunset: 'Darkness falls over the building site. The sky is filled with stars. "There is the blueprint," they say.'[57] Calvino's imagined city underscores the absurdity of the human desire for completion. WASP might imagine their 3-D printers to be mimicking the building behaviour of living wasps, but this ignores the all-too-human basis of machines, the fact that they are entirely controlled by human-designed programs. Assuming that a wasp is like a machine is really just a case of humans imposing their understanding on animal behaviour they ultimately cannot fathom.

A more insightful – and fantastical – imagining of wasp/human interaction occurs in E. Lily Yu's short story 'The Cartographer Wasps and the Anarchist Bees', first published in 2011. At the beginning of the story, a boy living in a village in China breaks a long-standing truce between the local wasps and humans by throwing a stone at a nest and suffering the consequences. The fallen nest, however, discloses an extraordinary secret: dipped in hot water, the wasps' paper 'unfurled into beautifully accurate maps of provinces near and far, inked in vegetable pigments and labeled in careful Mandarin that could be distinguished beneath a microscope'.[58] These cartographer wasps are revealed to be analogous to human empire-builders. When the wasps leave the village and build a new nest, they come into conflict with a nearby bee colony (cast as the animal equivalent of the *ancien régime*). The wasps issue a typical imperial ultimatum of cooperation or extinction, taking some of the bees as their slaves, and go about planning their next conquests, while training the captive bees to learn cartography in the nest's Great Library. Eventually, the wasps' domination is undermined by a stray 'anarchist' bee who smuggles his anti-authoritarian politics into the nest and proceeds to convert others to his cause. The anarchist renegades survive after the last surviving wasp nest is stolen by a local girl, the bees awakening the following spring to find another anarchist bee colony that has inscribed its words of revolution on pages sealed with wax.

The anthropomorphism in this story works quite differently from that seen in the WASP 3-D printers' mimicking of swarm intelligence. In using the lives of social insects – wasps and bees – as a metaphor for different kinds of human social organization, the story does not argue, as biomimicry does, that human products can take on the characteristics of non-human ones; rather that whatever life-world the insects inhabit is only accessible through a creative mode of imagining that fuses two starkly different realities into a new compound reality. As outlined in the introduction to this book, this stress on imagination as a tool of connection is at the heart of Object-Oriented Ontology. E. Lily Yu's story allows us to imaginatively inhabit a wasps' nest through its creation of a 'new amalgamated reality' of wasp-being and human-being. In effect, this strange story deepens anthropomorphism precisely in order to move beyond it.[59]

Metaphorical connections can also be made as a result of studying the nature of wasps' nests themselves, particularly how they relate to human spaces and structures. Queen wasps will build a nest on any surface they sense is safe from harm. In addition to their more common preference for lofts and attics, wasps' nests have been found inside abandoned cars and doll's houses and on disused beds, ladders, even on the side of a sofa.

Hornets' nest constructed beneath a sculpture of a human head, discovered in 2014.

One of the most startling examples was discovered in 2014: an abandoned hornets' nest built in a shed directly beneath a wooden sculpture of a human head.[60] Enveloping the surrounding timber, the paper nest resembles a petrified screaming human subject – as alien and monstrous as the shape-shifting Thing in John Carpenter's titular film. This particular example powerfully conveys the profoundly alien character of vespid architecture, of wasps' need for human-built spaces coupled with their complete indifference to our needs and desires. It is not surprising that images like this are often deployed by pest-control specialists as a way of selling their services to fearful homeowners. Yet there is another possible response that embraces such a melding of the human and non-human as a rich place to flesh out a different kind of relationship, however disturbing that may be for us.

Indeed, other species are not as discriminating as humans are when it comes to wasps' nests. The nests of mud-dauber wasps located on walls and under bridges in the USA are regularly used by barn swallows because of their firm attachment to the vertical concrete surfaces, while white-necked rockfowl in Ghana often build their nests directly on top of mud-dauber wasps' nests.[61] This process of accretion by difference illustrates how non-human architectures always make use of what is at hand, rather than the *tabula rasa* approach that is so characteristic of human building, particularly in the modern period. Even though it is difficult to imagine how wasps' nests might be useful to us, being more open to the fusion of one kind of building with another offers a powerful way to rethink the relationship between human and more-than-human builders.

Bee

Bees are without doubt the most esteemed of all the social insects, mainly because they have proved the most useful to humans. For at least 4,500 years humans have kept bees in artificial hives to harvest the honey that certain species produce, a form of animal husbandry known as apiculture. Alone among insects, indeed all animals except humans, bees manufacture a product from elements external to themselves. Unlike silk from a silk-worm or milk from a cow, honey is bees' own finished and complete product. It is made from gathered nectar that is passed mouth-to-mouth among individuals, a process that reduces the moisture content of the nectar in order to transform it into honey. Today, in the USA alone, there are an estimated 2.59 million artificial bee colonies, each with an average annual yield of 31.8 kilograms of honey.[62]

Apiculture has generated a wide range of structures to house bee colonies. Pre-modern hives generally took two forms, depending on the local climate. In arid regions of the world, beehives were made from materials ranging from baked mud to logs, wicker and bricks; the bees built their combs within, usually vertically from a single anchor point. Upright hives developed in the forested areas of northern Europe, where wild honeybees made their nests in hollows in tree trunks. These artificial hives were generally bell-shaped straw or wicker 'skeps': lifting the skep would enable the beekeeper to simply cut out the comb within. The great drawback of both of these pre-modern hive designs was that harvesting the honey destroyed the cells the bees constructed to house it. Left alone, in the wild, bee colonies can survive for many years, a remnant population of the hive overwintering each year in a tight ball to generate enough heat to keep the queen and, if they are lucky, themselves alive.

The modern 'rational' beehive, a box-shaped structure with suspended moveable frames and a horizontal cover, was probably invented by an American clergyman, L. L. Langstroth, in 1851.[63] This innovation not only enabled honey to be taken out of the hive without destroying the combs within, but the careful observation and tending of the entire colony so as to keep it healthy for many years – decades in some cases. Additional storeys ('supers') could also be added, leading to stacked colonies not altogether dissimilar to the metal-framed structures of skyscrapers that were developed just a few decades later in Chicago and New York.[64]

As architectural historian Juan Antonio Ramírez has argued, beehives have long inspired architects as exemplars of natural design. Indeed, some human-built structures have been literally modelled on skeps. These include vernacular cabins built by indigenous peoples in many parts of the world, the bell-shaped mud houses of northern Syria and similar stone structures in Europe and storage facilities, such as granaries.[65] The reverse is also true, namely beehives modelled on human structures. In the medieval period it was commonplace to build shelters to house multiple bee colonies with some, such as the Bee Bole at Hartpury, Gloucestershire, even featuring

A traditional skep made from coils of wicker.

architectural ornamentation.[66] Today, an entire bee village near Portland, Oregon, and Bee City in South Carolina feature beehives taking the form of typical urban buildings, from town halls to hospitals. In a different vein, architect Joyce Hwang's Hive City project in 2012 invited speculative proposals for bee towers, cubes, domes and other structures modelled on urban architecture more usually built for human occupation.[67]

There is a more nuanced apian influence evidenced in the work of such architectural luminaries as Antoni Gaudí, Frank Lloyd Wright and Le Corbusier. Gaudí's invention of the parabolic arch came from his direct observation of the way in which bees construct their hives. Since the mid-eighteenth century, treatises on apiculture have illustrated how bees, in the wild, join their bodies together in the shape of an inverted parabolic arch to 'map' the shape of the hanging honeycomb they will eventually construct. In a different vein, Frank Lloyd Wright's Stuart Richardson House (1941–51) features hexagonal elements inspired by honeycombs, reflecting Wright's belief that the origins of human building lay in our ancient ancestors' observation of animal architecture. Finally, Le Corbusier's interpretation of the beehive was more rational, for example the completed Unité d'Habitation in Marseilles (1947–72) resembled, in abstract form, a giant modern beehive. Architect Jacobo Königsberg took Corbusier's metaphor quite literally in his own unrealized translation of the *Unité* into a proposed honeycomb high-rise for Mexico City in 1958.

Architects' fascination with beehives continues today in projects that promote themselves as ecologically sensitive. For example, Luigi Rosselli's The Beehive office building in Sydney, completed in 2017, used recycled terracotta roof tiles to create a textured facade that, in a similar way to a beehive, mediates sunlight and air currents.[68] Gianluca Santosuosso's speculative HIVE project draws on the long-standing understanding of hexagonal honeycombs as the most efficient way of dividing up space into

A typical modern, upright beehive.

equal parts with minimal structural supports, an animal anticipation of architectural modernism's obsession with achieving perfect structural efficiency. Santosuosso proposed a literal translation of bee to human habitat, namely an entire neighbourhood of residential structures all based on hexagons.[69] More ambitious still is a 2017 proposal submitted to *eVolo's* annual skyscraper competition for a Honeycomb Refugee Skyscraper. This high-rise, made up of stacked hexagonal apartments, was put forward as housing for Syrian refugees who had fled to Jordan. Referencing the Middle East's native honeybee (*Apis mellifera syriaca*), the beehive tower offers a model for rebuilding a society shattered by civil war according to ecological principles: residents will learn to farm sustainably and, like their bee counterparts, build a harmonious social life.[70]

Crude as these metaphors are, they reflect a long-standing equating of bee and human social organization. Since antiquity, bee colonies have been regularly employed as 'natural' metaphors of widely varying political systems. If monarchies found their perfect analogy in the queen-centred hive (until the 1670s, actually assumed to be a king), then republics equally embraced bee colonies as models of fraternity, solidarity and equality. In the nineteenth century the British Cooperative Movement often used bees and beehives as architectural ornaments in their buildings and insignia, the beehive in this case emphasizing how a unified industrious workforce can become more self-sufficient through mutual aid, in stark contrast to the practices of their often exploitative mercantile employers. In the twentieth century beehives took on more dystopian political meanings: the oblique association of drone (worker) bees and a dehumanized labouring class in Fritz Lang's 1927 film *Metropolis* is just one of many darker intimations of the reduction of humans to machines. Today, dystopian political metaphors persist (alongside utopian models of bees as exemplar ecological architects), such as the swarms of murderous cyborg nanobots in 'Hated in the Nation' (2018), an episode of the TV series *Black Mirror*, which presented a terrifying vision of the future of terrorism.

Those who keep bees cannot afford to be ambivalent when it comes to their understanding of the hive. Apiculturists have always worked at close quarters and in a symbiotic relationship with bees, possessing intimate knowledge of the spaces of the hive. This has often led to beekeepers identifying themselves with the hive itself, perhaps most powerfully expressed in Maurice Maeterlinck's 1901 poetic prose-work *The Life of the Bee*. Here, Maeterlinck imagines what a beehive would look like to a human if they were reduced to the size of a drone. Entering the hive:

> From the very top of a cupola greater in size than that in St Peter's in Rome right down to the ground, enormous walls of wax, vertical, double and parallel, descend; enormous geometrical constructions suspended in the darkness and emptiness . . . Each one of these walls, made of a substance which is still fresh, virginal, silvery and sweet-smelling, is formed from thousands of cells containing sufficient food to feed the entire population for several weeks.[71]

Maeterlinck's miniaturization of the human subject in relation to the bee-hive creates a visceral identification between species, even as it is entirely anthropomorphic.

The Hive, Kew Gardens, designed by Wolfgang Buttress in collaboration with BDP and Simmonds Studio. It was the UK Pavilion at the 2015 Milan Expo and was installed in Kew Gardens in 2016.

In the summer of 2016 the experimental installation *The Hive* in London's Kew Gardens created an architectural equivalent of Maeterlinck's imagined human-sized hive, but in this case by reversing the process of miniaturization. This hive was a 16.75-metre-tall network of delicate steel-tube hexagonal lattices, ornamented by thousands of LED lights and filled with music inspired by the characteristic hum of an active beehive. Both lighting and music were also choreographed by activity within a nearby beehive.[72]

Artist Mark Thompson would have rejected this architectural homage to the work of bees as overly sanitized. His *Live-in-Hive* project, begun in 1976, was a radical attempt to experience life in a beehive. Thompson constructed an elaborate glass hive into which he was able to insert his head, effectively sealing himself into the bees' home. Fed through tubes and sitting on a specially adapted commode, Thompson planned to spend three uninterrupted weeks inside the hive. Unsurprisingly, he was only ever able to carry out his project for much shorter periods of time, but the photographs that record his experience are still shocking to behold, graphically demonstrating just how alien an environment a beehive is and also how painfully ill-adapted humans are to experience it directly.[73]

Architectural critic Geoff Manaugh has speculated on what might result if we deepened our relationship with bees by allowing them to contribute to the built environment itself. Drawing on real-life research that genetically modified bees to produce a new kind of biodegradable plastic, Manaugh, together with designer John Becker, imagined and illustrated a 'series of science-fictional scenarios in which a new urban bee species, called *Apis caementicium* – or cement bees – could be deployed throughout the city as a low-cost way to repair statues and fix architectural ornament'. Eventually these bees would cut loose from their human controllers and start to deposit their material autonomously leaving 'tiny fragments of concrete . . . atop plants and door frames, beneath cars and on chain-link fences, coiling up and consuming the sides of structures where they were never meant to be'.[74]

This fantastic vision of bees as autonomous architectural agents has its roots in the sense of wonder that, for millennia, humans have felt for bees' seemingly miraculous ability to build without any centralized control or blueprint. Recounting an anecdote in his 1609 treatise on bees, Hampshire

John Becker and Geoff Manaugh's visualization of bee-created ornament, 2014.

vicar Charles Butler told the story of an old countrywoman who found that her bees were suffering from a disease. A devout friend advised the woman to place a fragment of the sacred Host in the hive, which she did. Some time later she opened the hive to check on the health of her bees and discovered that not only had they recovered but they had built a chapel out of wax, complete with a tiny bell-tower (and bells). The aforementioned Host had been preserved and placed on a wax altar, the bees themselves buzzing around it in harmonious devotion.[75] This fantastic story suggests that, however much we attempt to rationalize the behaviour of bees, to draw them into our orbit, these animals will always continue to build according to their own mysterious and thoroughly alien desires.

Termite

On 23 November 2017, evolutionary biologist Richard Dawkins shared a photograph on Twitter of a termite mound that bore a striking resemblance to Gaudí's Sagrada Família church in Barcelona. He stated that the termites' magnificent miniature cathedral had been created with 'no architect . . . blueprint, not even in DNA. They just followed local rules of thumb, like cells in an embryo.'[76] Dawkins saw in this structure an exemplar of his

Termite mound resembling Antoni Gaudí's Sagrada Familia, photographed in Queensland by Fiona Stewart in 2017.

own theory of the 'extended phenotype', namely that the genes of an organism are expressed beyond its merely biological boundaries, encompassing, as the termite mound does, the environment inside and outside the body of any individual organism.[77]

What Dawkins did not know at the time was that this particular termite mound's resemblance to a renowned work of architecture was the result of an unfortunate accident (revealed by natural historian Matt Shardlow the day after Dawkins's Tweet). The mound was created by members of the Australian termite species *Amitermes meridionalis*, who usually build large slab-like structures that are aligned to a north–south axis. This particular example had probably been damaged at some point and then repaired by the termites, the tall spires at the top and pillars at the base of the mound being a result of their collective effort to rebuild their home as quickly as possible. This was, in fact, a botched job that bore little resemblance to the insects' desired ideal home.[78]

The scale and complexity of termite mounds have, for centuries, suggested many architectural analogies. Termites build the biggest non-human terrestrial structures in the world: mounds in Africa, Asia and Australia can be up to 10 metres tall. Their sheer mass of numbers planet-wide (up to a million in each colony) outweighs that of humans by a scarcely credible factor of ten to one. As with ant colonies, termite mounds have often been compared with human-built structures. A 3-metre-tall mound is equivalent to the Empire State Building and a 5-metre example the Burj Khalifa; the tallest 9-metre mounds would equal an as-yet-unrealized megatall skyscraper of the future, such as Eugene Tsui's 2-mile-high Ultima Tower, first proposed in 1991.[79] Inspired by the form and 'engineering' of termite mounds (principally their means of ventilation), Tsui's tower was designed to rehouse the entire population of San Francisco in an earthquake-proof city-within-a-city, as literal a translation of a termite mound to the human world as one might imagine.

Built from millions of tiny stacked mud balls that harden over time, the interior of a termite mound is a complex network of spaces created for a host of specific tasks. In the late 1990s physiologist Scott Turner pumped plaster into a mound created by a colony of *Macrotermes* in Namibia, revealing an intricate network of interior spaces.[80] Under the mound, in a comb-like warren of tiny rooms, *Macrotermes* cultivate a fungus that helps them digest the grass that all termites collect to eat and feed to their larvae. The bottom of the fungus comb stands on peg-like legs to facilitate the circulation of air. Above the fungus garden, the termites live in a small area comprised of nurseries for larvae and the chamber that holds the queen, who is extremely long lived but immobile with her vast, swollen egg-laying abdomen. The rest of the mound – the majority of the interior – is hollowed out into a maze of interweaving tunnels, radiating chambers, galleries, archways and spiral staircases. The role of these spaces seems to centre on maintaining the right atmospheric conditions within the mound, drawing in oxygen from the outside and expelling CO_2 in a similar way to a human lung. In addition, recent studies have demonstrated the critical role of water within the mound, the termites soaking the base of the mound to control moisture levels throughout the structure during the different seasons.[81]

It is research into the complex circulatory systems of termite mounds that has perhaps had the most significant effect on architecture, particularly in an age of climate crisis, when heat and humidity have already increased in many parts of the world. Designers are understandably looking for

Plaster-cast of a *Macrotermes* mound in Namibia, created by Scott Turner in the late 1990s.

less energy-intensive ways of air-conditioning their buildings. In 1991 Zimbabwean architect Mick Pearce was commissioned to design the country's largest commercial building, the Eastgate Centre in Harare. Working with engineers at Arup, Pearce imagined termite mounds as air conditioners, drawing up a plan for a masonry-insulated building made up of large, open spaces linked by an elaborate network of pipes and chimneys. Completed in 1996, the Eastgate Centre remains a pioneering example of biomimetic architecture that was able to regulate the building's temperature without the need for costly and energy-intensive air-conditioning units. While Pearce's understanding of the thermoregulation of the termite mound was flawed, his architectural equivalent unintentionally copied the termite's true solution, namely in facilitating a transfer of energy between the mound's permeable outer surface and the thermal capacity of the surrounding soil. So, without the architect realizing it, the Eastgate Centre's concrete foundations acted in a similar way to the fungal gardens of a *Macrotermes* colony: they were heat sinks that stored energy during the warmth of the day before releasing it at night.[82]

More holistic architectural proposals tap into the larger lifeworld of the termite and the colony as a whole. In a 2010 article in the *New Scientist*, writer Philip Ball imagined a city of the future that followed the design of a termites' mound, a vision that resembled an organic version of the Ultima Tower:

> [The city's] buttressed towers are built entirely from natural, biodegradable materials. Its inhabitants live and work in quarters that are air-conditioned and humidity-regulated, without consuming a single watt of electricity. Water comes from wells that dip deep into the earth, and food is cultivated self-sufficiently in gardens within its walls. This metropolis is not just eco-friendly: with its curved walls and graceful arches, it is rather beautiful too.[83]

Here, Ball is simply describing the features of an actual termite mound in the African savannah in anthropomorphic terms: a linguistic sleight of hand that creates a direct human correspondence between termite mound and human city. A far more mundane correspondence between termites and humans derives from the ways in which these insects build. Mound construction begins with an individual termite gathering a ball of mud, mixing it with its saliva and then dropping it on the ground. Other termites, triggered by this signal, also make mud balls and stack these on top of the first ball; eventually the collected mud balls become a wall or pillar. For centuries, millennia even, humans all over the world have built mud structures in almost exactly the same way. For example, small cob buildings in the UK and elsewhere are usually built communally, each participant fashioning and then 'throwing' a ball of clay-saturated mud to gradually construct a wall.

Viewed in this way, the difference between the supposed automaton-like behaviour of termites and mud-building humans is not so stark as Richard Dawkins supposed in his comparison of a termite mound to Gaudí's organic-looking church. Researching the building habits of *Macrotermes*, Scott Turner has come to the conclusion that one cannot separate termites and mound, or termites, mound, fungus and bacteria, for that matter. For Turner, the whole is an 'extended organism'. The termites' building behaviour, rather than being determined solely by their genes, derives from their mental 'map' of an ideal mound: 'a few breezes, the perfect concentrations of CO_2 and humidity, smooth edges and hard walls – they build a world that conforms with their cognitive picture of the mound'.[84] Although it is difficult, if not impossible, to define the nature of this cognition, since termites do

Eastgate Centre in Harare, designed by Mick Pearce and completed in 1996.

TERMES robots building a wall.

not have brains, it is clear that it is always enacted as a group: a vast collective is required before that 'map' can be activated.

Along with social wasps, mound-building termites have been studied as exemplars of 'swarm intelligence' or stigmergy, a term first coined in 1959 by French biologist Pierre-Paul Grassé, but gaining significant traction only in the 1990s.[85] Stigmergy attempts to explain how very simple creatures can produce complex structures through collective work. Although the general consensus among scientists is that termites achieve this 'communication' through a saliva scent or pheromone, it is still uncertain precisely how this results in the sophisticated architecture of the mound. This is borne out in the Wyss Institute for Biologically Inspired Engineering's research into *Macrotermes* and their subsequent development of the TERMES robot, which featured on the front cover of *Science* in February 2014.[86] By following a sequence of a hundred or so pre-programmed steps, these small robots were able to build autonomously as a group, each robot 'sensing' the local environment. The research was underpinned by a desire to find a way of building in hostile environments, for example on the surface of Mars as a prelude to human colonization of the planet. The results were startling: a group of TERMES robots can construct a basic structure, such as a wall, staircase or four-sided building, without any human intervention beyond a basic set of pre-programmed rules. However, the drawback is that the robots can only build in highly controlled environments. Unlike the termites on which they are modelled, they cannot respond successfully to the highly complex environments created by life itself.

A far more evocative, if less scientific, appreciation of the termite mound was penned in 1934 by South African naturalist and poet Eugène

Marais. *The Soul of the White Ant* is both a work of meticulous natural history and also a paean to termites and the mounds they build. It is also one of the most powerful and sustained attempts to explore the 'thoughts' of the mound itself. Reflecting contemporaneous ideas of the 'superorganism' first put forward by William Wheeler in 1911, Marais called the mound 'a composite animal', but went further than most in attributing to it a 'soul'.[87] Marais argued that 'the functioning of the community or group psyche of the termitary is just as wonderful and mysterious to a human being, with a very different kind of psyche, as telepathy and other functions of the human mind which border on the supernatural'.[88] Marais's conclusion, poetically expressed as it was, prefigured Turner's idea of the extended organism, where the mound itself is seen as possessing some kind of cognition, one that requires us to 'step out of the rules of being human' in order to grasp it;[89] or, as Marais put it, to 'unlearn' our language and listen instead to the 'A B C' of the termite.[90]

The idea of termite mounds as extended organisms has far-reaching implications for the ways in which architecture is conceived, built and used. According to engineer Rupert Soar, architecture, like termite mounds, should never be completed; rather it should be continually modified by its occupants according to their changing needs and desires, which are themselves always intertwined with the environments from which they emerge. Embracing a much more radical kind of biomimicry than is generally the case in architectural practice, Soar imagines conventional construction giving way to a discomforting 'living architecture', where people interact with the built environment like insects, 'forming social swarms that rely on bio-inspired environmental cues to build and maintain their homes'.[91] In this deeply strange insect-human built environment, anarchic self-organization would replace top-down design and planning, resulting in a wild, pulsating, constantly changing city of inhabitants entangled with architecture.

2
Aerial

In his series titled *Assimilation*, South African photographer Dillon Marsh documented the various ways in which sociable weaver birds (*Philetairus socius*) build their nests on telegraph poles in the southern part of the Kalahari desert. Like an animal version of Bernd and Hilla Becher's photographic typologies of industrial structures, Marsh's images are startling reminders that animals, and particularly birds, often make their homes quite literally on or in human-made structures, in this case the only tall objects in an otherwise barren landscape.[1]

These images also disturb anthropomorphic understandings of birds' nests as metaphors of human intimacy. The philosopher Gaston Bachelard drew attention to this in his 1957 book *The Poetics of Space*. If we imagine a bird such as a robin or a wren using its own body to form the round cavity of its nest, a direct organic relationship is set up between dwelling and building. The bird's nest reminds us of a primal architecture that protects our vulnerable bodies from external threats.[2] But for sociable weaver birds, that security comes from their encounters with a starkly different kind of architecture: the birds graft their organic assemblages of woven straw onto strictly utilitarian structures, creating unsettling hybrid constructions that call attention to the stark differences between the needs of humans and those of animals.

In this chapter I focus on six birds from different families – pigeons, falcons, swallows, swifts, crows and starlings – to reflect on Marsh's reading of birds as both familiar and alien in terms of their relationship with the human-built world. Taken as a whole, these are birds that have chosen

Collage of photographs from Dillon Marsh's *Assimilation* series.

to live alongside us; they are animals that are considered so commonplace as to be almost beneath the radar of our attention (and even falcons are increasingly becoming thus as they migrate to our towns and cities). None of these species builds spectacular nests, such as the fabulous constructions of bowerbirds, weaver birds or penduline tits that are usually drawn attention to in studies of avian architecture.[3] The saliva-and-mud-built nests of swallows and some swifts defy Bachelard's association of nests with intimacy; in making homes with their own spittle, these birdhouses make us uncomfortable. Building with one's body may be the ideal of a truly organic architecture, but that dream is surely shattered when what is inside our bodies makes an appearance in or on our buildings. This 'body' is most definitely matter of our place, turning cosy domesticity into a squalid nightmare.

The six birds considered here besmirch architecture with their presence, whether very visibly in the case of swallows and peregrine falcons, which nest on outside walls and high ledges, or by subterfuge – pigeons, swifts and starlings making their homes in any available cavity. With pigeons, crows and starlings, that dirtying is accentuated by their tendency to flock together in large numbers; their roosting activities in particular often leaving behind vast quantities of guano on the exterior walls of urban buildings they choose and the pavements and streets below. Even the totemic peregrine falcon upsets our desire for clean and decent architecture: look closely at the area of a building chosen by these birds to reside on and you'll see streaks of guano and the remains of other birds they have devoured. These excremental additions present a direct challenge to the pervasive belief that the human-built world should be cleansed of impurities, cities sanitized in the name of progress. No wonder that many of these six bird families have long been persecuted: pigeons, starlings and swallows are still regarded as 'pests' by some, their extermination justified by urban authorities and pest-control companies on the grounds of their unacceptable, prolific mess-making.

Birds also defy the neat geographical boundaries of the human world, making a mockery of our territorial borders. Migratory species, such as swallows, swifts and starlings, cover huge distances in their twice-yearly journeys: up to 22,500 kilometres in the case of swifts nesting in Britain and overwintering in southern Africa. As naturalist Mark Cocker has observed, these journeys are not just between two distant places the birds experience as 'home', but full of 'intimate fragments of individual land-scapes . . . as familiar as the tree and the immediate environs of the bird's own nest site'.[4] This dovetailing of vastness and intimacy is one of the reasons why ornithologists do not precisely know why many bird species are declining at such a precipitous rate (higher than insects in some cases). Birds are truly global citizens but, unlike humans, they do not simply accumulate more and more experiences; rather their globalized lifestyles are also extremely localized – a few key places strung out on their immensely long flight paths. Perhaps more than any other animal, birds force us to think at vastly different scales simultaneously; for to care for their well-being is, perforce, to care for the well-being of the places they call home, both near at hand and far away.

Pigeon

Pigeons are synanthropes, namely animals that live in close association with human beings because it benefits them. All species of pigeon (the Columbidae family) are descended from blue rock pigeons, cliff-dwelling birds that probably migrated with our distant human ancestors into, or rather onto, their first houses, creating their rudimentary nests on any available ledge or in hidden crevices. Their present-day abundance in virtually every city across the world reflects the fact that buildings provide exactly the kind of environment that pigeons require to thrive. Yet depending on the particular species, this family of birds elicits quite different human responses. On the one hand, doves – particularly pure white breeds – are esteemed as symbols of divinity, innocence, peace and love; on the other, their pigeon cousins, especially the 'feral' varieties in cities, are regularly cast as 'rats with wings', pests who foul buildings and streets with their acidic guano, which also harbours diseases such as histoplasmosis, cryptococcosis and psittacosis that can transfer to humans.[5]

Pigeons were probably first kept as food for humans (and their guano as an agricultural fertilizer) in Egypt from at least 3000 BCE. In the Middle East the first dovecotes were created from clay pots, which were joined together and placed in areas where pigeons already gathered to roost. From these rudimentary beginnings a widely varied building type developed: the dovecote or columbarium, as named by Roman writer Varro. In *Rerum rusticarum* (*c.* 36 BCE), Varro described various types of dovecotes located in Rome, Florence and the Italian countryside, and also referred to pigeons being kept in turrets or housed in the gable ends of houses. The most spectacular surviving dovecotes were built much later in the Middle East and South Asia, whether the large-scale, profusely decorated circular towers erected in seventeenth-century Isfahan; structures known as

Chabutro in Gujarat, India, which take the form of a timber or stone pillar topped by an ornamented open structure in which the pigeons are housed; or the mud towers of the Nile Delta in Egypt, where, in cities like Mit Ghamr, clusters of tall, tapering dovecotes still dominate parts of the urban fabric.[6]

The earliest dovecotes in Britain were circular stone towers, derived from appendages to Norman castles and built in this way to protect pigeons from predators. Yet as they developed over the centuries, dovecotes proliferated in their variety. Extant examples in the United Kingdom encompass octagonal-plan towers, square- and rectangular-plan barns, four-gabled structures and half-timbered buildings like miniature Tudor houses. Later examples, such as the nineteenth-century Egyptian-style aviary at Vauxhall Farm in Tong, Shropshire, or the Pigeon Tower at Rivington, Lancashire, built in 1910, go beyond mere utility in their design and decoration.[7] This reflected not only the esteem in which pigeons were held but the belief that they required certain enticements to remain in a dovecote, free as they were to depart at any time. The eighteenth-century naturalist Georges-Louis Leclerc, Comte de Buffon, argued that, because pigeons were 'voluntary captives' rather than domesticated animals such as dogs or horses, their dwellings must provide 'all the conveniences and comforts of life'.[8]

For centuries, dovecotes in Britain and France were only allowed by law to be erected by the gentry and nobility; this reflected the high status of pigeons as a source of food but also their tendency to cause damage to nearby agricultural land by eating grain and digging up tender plants. The practice of keeping pigeons for food and agricultural fertilizer declined in Britain from the seventeenth century onwards as cheaper alternatives to both pigeon meat and guano became more widely available. Of the 26,000 dovecotes reported in the seventeenth century, only around 1,500 remained by the late 1980s, with the majority either repurposed for other uses or abandoned.[9] In post-revolutionary France many dovecotes were destroyed because they were an architectural symbol of aristocratic privilege no longer tolerated in the new Republic.

Despite the decline of the practice of keeping pigeons for food or their guano, these birds have become useful in another way, namely for the sport of racing. This practice only began in the West in 1858, when 110 pigeons from Antwerp were released from London Bridge in order to fly 'home',

Pigeon Tower at Rivington Terraced Gardens, Lancashire, built in 1910.

but thereafter it became an important way by which people in rapidly industrializing cities could maintain a tie with a nature that was seen to be quickly vanishing. The rural dovecote was thus superseded by the urban pigeon loft, with cages or more substantial structures located on roof terraces or in backyard sheds. Pigeons have a high level of endurance, flying hundreds of kilometres up to 80 kilometres per hour; they also have a highly developed sense of direction, aided by a strong memory for different smells and a heightened sensitivity to the Earth's magnetic field.[10] Yet the homing instinct of pigeons was refined only in the second half of the nineteenth century, as humans selectively bred them for sport. The important role of pigeons as military messengers during the Siege of Paris (1870–71) and the First and Second World Wars was a consequence of this earlier human intervention. As Colin Jerolmack has argued in his study of contemporary pigeon racing clubs in New York, Berlin and South Africa, this sport has produced a unique entanglement of humans and animals – the pigeons far from being passive objects, shaping, as they did and still do, social relationships among those who keep and race them.[11]

Designer Carla Novak has recognized the significance of pigeon racing for a small community in the British town of Dover. Her 2012 project for a

Carla Novak, Pigeon Racing Headquarters, 2012.

Pigeon Racing Headquarters subverts the conventional historical separation of architecture for humans and birds. Imagining a group of pigeon enthusiasts taking up residence together in a Victorian terrace, Novak's project took the unusual step of allowing the pigeons to cohabit with their human guardians, the needs of the birds eventually becoming dominant. Here, pigeons get luxury design – soft linings, heating and feeding pipes – while the human occupants would have more basic facilities. Reflecting on the fact that in Britain today pigeons are mostly considered to be pests, Novak's project asks us to question this negative attitude, extrapolating on how an already tight bond between certain humans and pigeons might be developed as a model for bridging a species divide.[12] Indeed, in places like the so-called 'Garbage City' on the eastern edges of Cairo, such a hybrid human/non-human cityscape can already be witnessed. Here, in a tradition dating back 4,000 years, flocks of pigeons are set loose each day from dozens of rooftop timber platforms raised on stilts: not for competitive racing, but in an attempt to capture neighbours' flocks while preserving one's own. The way in which the informal structures built for the pigeons merge with the rest of the urban environment directly illustrates the nature of a city built for more than one species.[13]

Yet in most cities in the Global North, pigeons are generally not welcome, their acidic guano seen as a direct threat to the material integrity of the built environment and the sanctity of private property. In London pigeons are deterred by a whole panoply of 'hostile' architecture, as revealed by designers Selena Savić and Gordan Savičić in their book *Unpleasant Design*.[14] They illustrated a host of devices on buildings designed to deter pigeons, including metal spikes, netting, electrified wire, chimney cowls, mirrors and even fake birds of prey. In December 2017 a photograph taken in Bristol showed the branches of an entire tree covered in hundreds of spikes to deter pigeons, an image that provoked widespread outrage at such a brutal exclusion of birds from their supposed natural habitat.[15] The very qualities formerly admired or actively cultivated in pigeons – their fecundity, homing instincts and nitrogen-rich guano – have now become a source of revulsion for many urban inhabitants.

Despite widespread attempts to control pigeon populations in cities, they remain indelibly tied to certain spaces, particularly prominent public squares. Until recently a significant attraction in London's Trafalgar Square

Pigeon towers in the background rising over Cairo's 'Garbage City', 2009.

was its flocks of wheeling pigeons, and tourists were offered seeds by vendors to experience the birds at close quarters. But in 2007 the seed sellers were banned by the then mayor of London, Ken Livingstone, who held the view that pigeons were 'rats with wings'. Municipal officials in Venice have recently imposed a similar censure on seed sellers in the Piazza S. Marco, yet its pigeons have a venerable heritage dating back to 1204, when the birds were honoured by Doge Enrico Dandolo for relaying a critical message from Constantinople during the Fourth Crusade. Stone bowls were installed around the piazza to refresh the pigeons, which were long believed to protect the city from the encroaching sea.[16] The makeshift pigeon towers on the fringes of Cairo, mentioned earlier, may owe their continued existence to the direct association of the distant origins of that city with the bird: a dove's nest built on top of the tent of Amr ibn al-As al-Sahmi, the seventh-century Arab invader who brought Islam to the country, was claimed as the site on which Cairo was founded.[17]

The way in which pigeons characteristically flock in iconic urban spaces such as the Piazza S. Marco bears some resemblance to the 'swarm intelligence' of social insects discussed in the previous chapter. In 2004 the New York-based design studio Aranda\Lasch developed the Brooklyn Pigeon Project, which centred on a satellite that recorded the city through the eyes of its resident pigeons. With the birds equipped with wireless video and microphones, the satellite tracked their spiralling flight patterns over Brooklyn, challenging human citizens to think beyond the rigid grid pattern of the city's streets.[18] In London in 2016, Paris-based tech company Plume Labs developed a more instrumental project utilizing pigeon perception by attaching air-pollution sensors to a flock of racing pigeons, with the unwitting animal-researchers linked to an app that disclosed the quality of the air to individual residents on their smartphones.[19] These attempts to harness pigeon perception for human benefit might seem to provide yet more evidence of our intractable conception of animals as only of worth if they can be made useful to us; yet they also open up cities to more-than-human perceptions that mitigate against the pervasive indifference, even hostility, felt towards pigeons as one of our urban co-habitants.

In the 2013 children's book *Architecture According to Pigeons*, a pigeon named Speck Lee Tailfeather flies about the world visiting iconic works of architecture: the Colosseum, the Taj Mahal, the Sydney Opera House, the Eiffel Tower and dozens of others.[20] Conceived as an engaging way of introducing children to architecture, the book keys into a long-standing human desire to see cities from a bird's-eye view, a place above the chaos and confusion of the streets, where command and control are achieved by the individual. Yet in this book that power is bestowed upon a humble pigeon, even as the illustrations provide a vicarious experience of this avian view from above for human readers. Architects and urban planners have always used such bird's-eye views to present their visions to non-specialist audiences, but here the prowess of the designer (and illustrator) is deferred to that of the bird itself. Pigeons may be the most commonplace of our avian synanthropes, but, like all of their kind, they nevertheless hold open the promise of an emancipatory way of seeing and being in the more-than-human world.

Falcon

The 'hostile' architecture installed in many cities to control populations of feral pigeons sometimes includes living beings, namely predatory raptors, such as falcons and hawks that make their homes on the ledges of tall buildings and other structures. The most iconic of these is the peregrine falcon, the fastest animal that has ever lived, reaching speeds of 320 kilometres per hour when diving, or 'stooping', from great heights to stun and then kill its prey. In Greater Manchester, where I live, there are resident pairs of peregrines that have recently chosen to nest on the tall towers of some of the civic buildings built in the nineteenth century. When I visited the former mill town of Bolton on a murky winter afternoon during the COVID-19 pandemic, the eerie silence of empty streets was suddenly broken by the scything wail of a peregrine, the bird itself glimpsed only briefly as pigeons scattered in terror in its wake. Later that day, a distant telephoto image I took of the tower of the Town Hall revealed the resident bird, perched high on one of the building's exposed stone pinnacles.

That peregrine falcons have become relatively commonplace urban animals is a direct consequence of responses to their near extinction in the 1970s as decades of persecution, coupled with the more recent catastrophic effects of the pesticide DDT, decimated populations of these birds in the wild, where their favoured nesting sites were ledges on rocky cliffs. British biologist Derek Ratcliffe's 1963 report on populations of peregrines showed them in rapid decline, confirming the warnings about DDT first laid out in Rachel Carson's groundbreaking book *Silent Spring,* published the previous year.[21] Pioneering the captive breeding of peregrines (the birds mostly donated by falconers), Cornell University was successful in mass-producing peregrines for reintroduction into the wild in the United States. Using a process known as 'hacking', a technique developed centuries ago by falconers, young peregrines were placed outdoors in artificial eyries ('hack boxes') and fed and cared for by their human overseers until they fledged. After the United States and other countries banned the use of DDT in 1972, populations of peregrines slowly recovered. Their increasing migration to cities was an inadvertent effect of captive breeding: falcons hacked from eyries built on man-made structures were much more

A peregrine falcon (bottom left) perches on a pinnacle of the Town Hall in Bolton, Greater Manchester.

successful than those bred in 'wild' sites, probably because of the presence of year-round sources of food in and near cities (mainly the scattering pigeons that often betray the presence of peregrines).[22]

In taking up residence in cities, peregrines have brought with them a distinct kind of wildness to the resolutely anthropocentric urban world. As falconer Helen Macdonald has argued, a falcon's sensory world is 'as different from ours as is that of a bat or bumblebee'. So finely tuned are their eyes that peregrines perceive the world ten times faster than we do. They see things much closer together in time and also with much greater precision, being able to resolve tiny details at great distances.[23] If it was my high-resolution camera, rather than my admittedly short-sighted human eyes, that revealed the peregrine perched on the tower of Bolton's Town Hall, then the falcon's vision far extends and exceeds that of any human-built seeing machine, bar the most advanced satellite cameras and telescopes.

Nowhere has the perceptual lifeworld of the peregrine been more poetically expressed than in J. A. Baker's compressed account of a decade-long obsession with these birds, published as *The Peregrine* in 1967, as they were still in population free fall. As Robert Macfarlane aptly noted in his introduction to the 2005 reissue of the book, Baker's purple prose allows us to metaphorically 'acquire the vision of a hawk'.[24] In Baker's words:

> Like the seafarer, the peregrine lives in a pouring-away world of no attachment, a world of wakes and tilting, of sinking planes of land and water. We who are anchored and earthbound cannot envisage this freedom of the eye. The peregrine sees and remembers patterns we do not know exist . . . he finds his way across the land by a succession of remembered symmetries.[25]

Although the flat coastal landscapes of Essex traversed by Baker's peregrines were rural, the view from above he so powerfully conveys applies equally to the perceptual world of urban peregrines. But the cityscape that peregrines perceive is very different from that apprehended by human observers viewing the city from a skyscraper observation platform. Through the eyes of a peregrine, the city becomes a kaleidoscope of fragmented shapes, rather like a Cubist painting, as Macfarlane aptly observes. Baker's determination to self-identify with the falcon he was obsessively tracking – to see like a peregrine – did not produce a comforting sense of wholeness. Rather, his pagan form of the *via negativa* led to an obliteration of self when confronted with a thoroughly alien other. Instead of gaining mastery, Baker was humiliated, reflecting the meaning of the Latin word *humiliare*, namely to be humbled through the loss of one's identity as a separate self.

The thoroughly alien perception of the urban falcon has its obverse in the ways in which the lives of many of these apex predators have now been laid bare through webcams, the first of which was installed in 1998 in a nest box on Kodak's corporate offices in Rochester, New York. Today, with at least fourteen 'live feeds' from urban peregrines nesting in cathedral and town-hall towers in England (and many others in cities across the world), the day-to-day activities of breeding falcons have become a way of galvanizing and sustaining human attachment to these birds, creating communities of care and protection via computer or smartphone screens. Perhaps more than any other urban animal, peregrines are now the object of intense human scrutiny. These birds have also become symbols of the buildings on which they choose to establish their eyries. Skyscrapers and other tall buildings in cities have long been powerful sites for the enactment of civic and corporate power. A nesting pair of falcons is often seen as enhancing this status, reflecting centuries of symbolic associations of falcons with nobility and strength. Yet the effect goes both ways, with the actions of falcons, as protected animals, impacting the material existence of the buildings they alight on. An example was how the ongoing renovation of the clock tower of Manchester's Town Hall was interrupted by a nesting pair of peregrines in spring 2020.

In 1993, before the advent of peregrine webcams, artist Adam Kuby proposed building a sculpture on a skyscraper that would provide both a nesting habitat for peregrines and also a space for public viewing. The skyscraper's glass skin would be pierced to make room for ledges of artificial rock, around which an observation space would be created. Contrasting

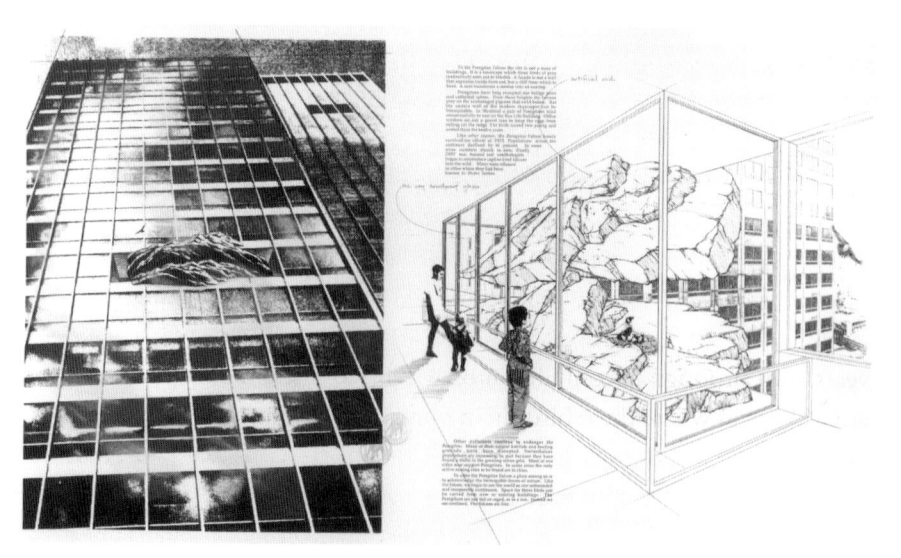

Adam Kuby's proposal for a cliff dwelling for peregrine falcons, 1993.

Webcam view of a peregrine falcon in a nest box on Ship Canal Bridge, Seattle, 2011.

his project with caged birds in zoos, Kuby allowed the falcons to remain free, while the human viewers would be the ones who would be confined.[26] In drawing attention to the strange collision of wild/domestic and natural/ artificial that captive-bred peregrines bring to cities when they choose to nest on buildings, Kuby's proposal unsettles the neat divisions we usually make when we speak of 'nature' in the city. As geographers Steve Hinchliffe and Sarah Whatmore have argued, the presence of peregrines in cities 'suggests that there is more to city living than technology and culture or, more tellingly, more to technology and culture than human design'.[27]

Falcons have been kept by humans as hunting aids for at least 6,000 years and, although falconry has mostly evolved into a niche sport, there are still places where these birds help humans hunt for food.[28] As already noted, falcons have long been associated with nobility – symbolic counterparts to humans that are privileged enough to occupy the apex of their respective social hierarchies. In the pre-modern period, captive-bred falcons were kept in the summer (their time of moulting) in enclosures known as mews, an architectural term that is more familiar today as the name for exclusive low-rise rows of houses on quiet lanes in central London. As much as they were tokens of wildness, falcons were also tamed by captive-breeding, the process of 'hacking' young birds resulting in strong lifelong bonds between handlers and falcons. As Macdonald has noted, in the Gulf States today falcons are often carried by their owners in everyday spaces, such as shopping malls and city streets, to cement these domestic bonds, while British falconer and author Phillip Glasier had a peregrine that slept on his bookshelf and jumped into his bed in the morning to wake him by nibbling his ear.[29]

The way in which humans create a bond between themselves and a falcon is known as 'imprinting'. This entails handlers assuming the role of a real falcon, bringing the bird food, making courtship noises and, most extraordinary of all with male (tiercel) peregrines, allowing them to copulate with the handler on a specially designed latex hat. The semen of the tiercel is then collected and used to inseminate an imprinted female falcon. Imprinting also applies to the way in which falcons become attached to places and is one of the reasons why captive breeding has led them to favour life in cities. But it is also due to the changing nature of cities themselves. Although peregrines were known to nest in medieval cathedral towers from the mid-nineteenth century (Salisbury Cathedral has had resident pairs of peregrines since the mid-1860s), it was only with the evolution of building technologies in the late nineteenth century that high-rise buildings proliferated, transforming more and more cityscapes in North America into habitats that resembled those favoured by peregrines in the wild. For example, in the 1940s a pair of falcons lived on the 24-storey Sun Life Assurance Building in Montréal, perhaps the first urban peregrines to be provided with a nest box.[30]

Imprinting is a human term that refers to a falcon's way of bonding with places and people. In a similar way to pigeons, peregrine falcons are 'homing' birds; even in the wild, where most peregrines are migratory in their habits, they return to the same nesting sites year after year. But the reciprocal attachment from humans is very different from the general sense of indifference we have to flocks of urban pigeons (bar their 'fanciers', of course). Today some urban inhabitants readily 'adopt' individual peregrine nests, the members of falcon families often being given names by groups of citizens. This overt anthropomorphizing of falcons might be criticized as yet another example of humans asserting their dominance over other animals, yet it also draws people in cities into new kinds of relationships with birds, buildings and other humans. A resident pair of falcons on a tall building is a kind of living ornament; they are animate symbols that draw people into a more holistic world of care, where the distinctions between what is artificial and what is natural become blurred. And there is no doubt that the falcon, too, has been changed by this attachment to cities: in many cases, urban peregrines do not 'wander', as befits the meaning of the Latin word *peregrinus*, literally 'one from abroad'. No longer tourists, peregrines are now confirmed urbanites.

Swallow

Falcons remain resolutely symbolic of wildness, despite their rising populations in cities; by contrast, swallows are emblematic of domesticity, choosing, as they have done for millennia, to build their nests and raise their young in close proximity to humans. Most species of the Hirundinidae family of birds (swallows and martins) make nests that individual pairs and their descendants return to year after year, despite the often vast distances they cover in their annual migrations. When I was a child, a pair of barn swallows (*Hirundo rustica*) chose to build their nest on the wall of an outside passageway of my family's 1950s council house in rural Northamptonshire. For my mother, the return of the swallows in the second half of April was always associated with mine and my brother's birthdays (20 and 14 April respectively). However, one year, the nest – brimful of young birds – fell off the wall. My mother rescued the almost fledged brood, rearing them by hand until they were ready to fly, but, despite her ministrations, the parents never again returned.

As heralds of spring, swallows have always been associated with the powerful symbolic charge of that season: they have been variously cast as bringers of fertility, love and new opportunities. Their presence in buildings was, and in places still is, actively courted, with the construction of a nest seen as an auspicious omen for the human occupants. But equally, the failure of a nest was a sign of bad luck, with some believing that a falling nest signalled the imminent collapse of the building on which it was constructed or a death in the family.[31] These old superstitions remind me of a much more recent story, told to me by my mother, of how her neighbours across the road decided one year to destroy all the swallows' nests constructed on the walls of their houses, the unsuspecting birds already ensconced within. Did these intolerant humans inadvertently bring bad luck upon themselves? Looking back on the avian disaster of my own childhood, I cannot recall if it foretold anything of note in the life of my family. It was accidental, yes; but was I any more protected from the Fates than those whose actions were clearly intentional?

As with pigeons, it is likely that swallows began to breed in close association with humans many thousands of years ago, when people first started to practice agriculture and build permanent settlements. The natural nest sites of hirundines are caves, crevices in cliffs, sinkholes, hollow trees and, in the case of sand martins, the mud- or sandbanks of rivers. Both swallows and house martins build their cup-shaped nests from thousands of individual pellets of mud, mixed with straw and glued together with their own saliva, and deposited on any suitable object projecting from a wall, such as a nail.[32] Martins build right up against the eaves of a roof, the entrances to their nests visible as tiny semicircular holes; swallows' homes are more open, perhaps the reason why they, rather than martins, have become so associated with human domesticity. In common with termite mounds, these methods of construction have strong links with vernacular buildings: the combination of mud and straw is seen all over the world in traditional domestic and agricultural structures and, today, increasingly in self-consciously ecological architecture. As already noted in the introduction, Vitruvius' *De architectura* cited swallows' nests as one of the inspirations for the first human shelters. Vitruvius argued that the origins of human language and building were intimately bound up with each other, the evolution of human architecture simply a continuation and development of primordial models already existent in the world of other animals.[33]

All that swallows require to build their nests is some kind of purchase on the sheer surfaces of walls as well as an adequate degree of shelter. As befits their common name (barn swallows), the birds usually prefer to nest inside barns, but they have been known to build their homes in an extraordinary variety of situations. Ornithologist Angela Turner has recorded swallows' nests built on a pair of garden shears hanging in an outhouse, another fashioned around the body of a dead owl dangling from a rafter in a barn, even some built on moving objects such as a steamship that traversed the same route every day or a train that ran 3 kilometres between two lakes in British Columbia.[34] In Ottoman Turkey, elaborate birdhouses and baths were regularly erected on the facades of mosques, madrasahs and palaces for swallows and other birds. Fashioned from stone, timber or mud, these ornamental birdhouses flourished from the fourteenth century to the nineteenth, but only a few remain extant. One exquisite work of craftsmanship in stone still graces an external wall of the Ayazma Mosque (1757–61) in Istanbul. Accommodating swallows, sparrows and pigeons, this birdhouse is a miniature replica of an Ottoman palace, complete with domes, arched entrances and a curious side building, presumably to accommodate an unsociable occupant.[35]

Ottoman birdhouse on the Ayazma Mosque, Istanbul.

The idea of constructing a bird-version of a human building in order to bestow good fortune through architectural mimicry may strike some as the very worst kind of anthropomorphism. Bird protection organizations, such as the RSPB in Britain, have warned against such provision, arguing instead for unsentimental functionalism when it comes to bird-box design. Yet, as Helen Macdonald has argued, this attitude stems more from human issues of taste (and class) than empirical evidence. In reality, the birds display complete indifference to our design ethos: the enjoyment to be had from housing birds is always ours and ours alone.[36]

Rather than being a sign of our intrinsic selfishness as a species, this kind of anthropomorphism has the potential to generate widespread cultures of care for migratory birds such as swallows and martins. In the United States, summer-visiting purple martins (*Progne subis*) are cavity nesters that rely almost entirely on human assistance for their survival. In rural areas of eastern North America, nest boxes are often provided for these avian visitors, where they are valued for their tendency to mob predators of poultry and also raise the alarm when these stalkers approach. More than a million people in the USA attract purple martins with nest boxes mounted on tall poles, some taking the form of miniature houses, civic buildings or even castles with dozens of rooms in which the birds could build their nests. This fashion was started in the early twentieth century by J. Warren Jacobs (1868–1947) and his Jacobs Birdhouse Company, based in Waynesburg, Pennsylvania, and still active today. Jacobs established colonies of purple martins at his home in 1896, building elaborate birdhouses for them, including miniature replicas of iconic buildings such as Independence Hall in Philadelphia and the state capitol in Washington, DC. His ornamental birdhouses became immensely popular, particularly after he displayed them at the Chicago World's Fair in 1933.[37] Today, the tradition continues, with ornamental birdhouses supplemented by more utilitarian structures such as the 21-metre-high tower built in Griggsville, Illinois, in 1962, which contains 562 apartments for individual pairs of purple martins. With another 5,000 birdhouses installed along the city's streets (one even named Purple Martin Boulevard), Griggsville lays claim to being the Purple Martin Capital of the Nation (a title that is not uncontested by other bird-loving communities).[38]

The kind of avian care that has developed in Griggsville and many other places in the USA is a hopeful counter to the human desire to purge nesting

Purple martin nest boxes, Lake Brandt, Maryland, 2018.

birds from their houses, a desire rooted in fear of disorder (and there are several companies that prey on this fear, advertising their services to deter what they term avian 'pests'). Yet even the nineteenth-century naturalist James Rennie regarded hirundines as 'parasitic' animals, because they seemingly got everything they needed from our human-built world without offering anything tangible in return (our enjoyment notwithstanding).[39] But there is also a positive meaning to the parasite, namely, the way a dependent species' world becomes meshed with our own, the swallows' or martins' nests not only a mirror of 'primitive' ways of human building but another kind of architecture that has become quite literally attached to our own. For the many who rejoice at the return of swallows or martins to their empty winter nests, there are others that fear them as what anthropologist Mary Douglas has termed 'matter out of place', polluting pristine surfaces with their mud and guano.[40] And even for the welcoming crowd, acceptance of another species is always highly selective, as illustrated by insects, almost invariably repulsed from buildings as invasive pests.

In 2013 the Belgian architect Vincent Callebaut presented his 'Swallow's Nest' proposal for a competition for the Taichung City Cultural Center in

Vincent Callebaut Architectures, the Swallow's Nest, a proposal for a cultural centre in Taichung City, Taiwan, 2013.

Taiwan. Probably inspired by the iconic Beijing National Stadium (known as the Bird's Nest) built for the Olympics in 2008, the 'Swallow's Nest' moniker derived from the shape of Callebaut's structure: a 'Möbius ring' created by the simple repetition of standardized sections of glass. Vaunting its impressive ecological credentials, the Swallow's Nest, if built, will feature photovoltaic cells embedded in its glass panels, sumptuous greenery on its walls and roof and earthquake-resistant supports at its base.[41] As strident a vision of high-tech eco-modernism as one might imagine, it is a far cry from both the crude mud-and-straw construction of real swallows' nests and the architectural pastiche of ornamental birdhouses. It is also characteristic of the contemporary landscape of 'green' architecture, which sees no contradiction in self-proclaimed organic design realized with artificial materials such as glass, steel and concrete, all of which are energy-intensive in their fabrication, maintenance and disposal/reuse.

Callebaut's Swallow's Nest also disavows the vibrant but disorderly lifeworld of its avian counterparts and the mess that birds bring when they choose to construct their buildings on our own, with organic mud meeting geometric brick, plaster or concrete. Sacrosanct to modernists, the ideal of purity – of form, function and occupation – remains a powerfully seductive element in many contemporary design proposals that aim to be both ecological and progressive. When selling a vision to potential investors, or competition judges, there is no room here for matter out of place, for non-human life as it really is, alien and indifferent to human concerns in architecture, whether aesthetics, cost or the wishes of clients. It is not surprising that the place where the mesh of more-than-human life can be best appreciated is in the realm of the everyday, the very idiom that modernists rejected as too prosaic, ill-defined and earthbound. As swallowphiles have known for millennia, it is in the domestic sphere that human and non-humans meet most directly. For the brief months of the year that they choose to live alongside us, swallows meld their domesticity with our own, marking the passage of time: 'twittering away at a baby's conception and fluttering over the dead at the end'.[42]

Swift

The same areas of North America visited by purple martins are also the breeding grounds of migratory chimney swifts (*Chaetura pelagica*); and, just like the martins, these birds have become dependent on human-built structures for their survival. Originally nesting in hollow trees, chimney swifts adapted to the colonization of the United States by European settlers by changing their behaviour, finding in chimneys and other manmade structures an artificial equivalent to hollow trees, many of which were felled by the colonizers. This move initially benefited the birds, their numbers and breeding range greatly expanding as humans moved westwards across the continent. Yet in recent years, as masonry towers have been capped or removed in favour of new construction, chimney swifts have been in decline and, in a similar response to the plight of purple martins, purpose-built towers are increasingly being offered as substitutes for defunct chimneys.[43]

In fact, the first example was built more than a century ago by Iowa naturalist Althea Rosina Sherman – an 8.5-metre-tall square-plan tower constructed from pine flooring, large enough to house both the swifts and a human observer. Sherman's design was resurrected by Paul and Georgean Kyle in the late 1980s, and the duo have gone on to promote designs for masonry and timber swift towers that can be built by householders with some basic experience in construction. As they describe in *Chimney Swift Towers* (2005), the birds select nesting sites very carefully. Unlike their European counterparts, chimney swifts do not abandon their nests once the chicks have fledged; they stay until the autumn, the single pair of resident swifts joined by many other birds at dusk, as nest sites morph into roosts. When a new tower is discovered in the spring by a returning swift, it completes a lightning-quick survey of the building, making passes at every conceivable angle, inspecting both exterior and interior before claiming it as 'home'. As with swallows, pairs of birds will return to the same nesting sites for many years after first claiming them.[44] Chimney swifts build cup-shaped nests from small twigs caught on the wing from the tops of trees, gluing the sticks together with their saliva.

European swifts are equally attached to human structures, returning to the same nesting sites year after year, but their annual stay is far shorter than that of their American cousins: they arrive in early May and leave for

Swift tower built by Althea Rosina Sherman in Iowa in the early 20th century, recreated by Paul and Georgean Kyle in the late 1980s.

southern Africa by mid-August. An accidental equivalent to Sherman's structure is the tower of the University Museum in Oxford, built from 1855 to 1860 as the city's natural history museum. Although the tower was not purpose-built for swifts, it seems apt that these birds should have chosen to nest in such an auspicious location, finding ideal purchase within the forty ventilation holes on the four sides of the steeply pitched tower. Since 1948 this structure has been specially adapted to act as both home for the swifts and a laboratory for observing them: first, wooden platforms were erected inside the tower; then nest boxes were substituted for the ventilator shafts, each fitted with a glass lid for observing the birds at close quarters. Visitors to the museum can now see the nests via video cameras that were installed in 1996; they can also listen to the birds using headphones.[45] In recent years the number of pairs of swifts nesting in the tower has declined, indicative of a much wider trend across the birds' summer breeding grounds in Europe and East Asia, with a 50 per cent reduction in numbers in the UK between 1995 and 2015. This decline is due to both a shortage of nesting sites – property-owners increasingly intolerant to the gaps and hidden recesses needed by swifts to build their nests – and a dramatic decline in their staple food, insects, victims of agricultural intensification,

Swift tower designed by Menthol Architects, installed in Exeter city centre in 2015.

the monoculture it has created vastly reducing once abundant insect populations.[46] Like other migratory birds, swifts have also suffered due to loss of their winter habitats, the relentless pressure on land exerted by a rapidly expanding human population.

As in the United States, attempts are now being made to redress this decline through the provision of bespoke nest boxes and towers. The former include the Ecosury swift box, a hollow brick pierced with a semi-circular entrance hole that is meant to replace two whole and two half bricks in the facade of a wall. Another is the Schwegler GmbH swift and bat box, a larger structure with three separate nesting chambers that can be inserted into a gap in the brickwork of a wall or flush with it. Catering more for the sociable nature of swifts, towers are standalone structures that have been built in urban areas to mitigate the lack of suitable nesting sites in surrounding buildings. In 2010 artists Andy Merritt and Paul Smyth (known as Something & Son) built a striking sculptural swift tower in Logan's Meadow in Cambridge, comprised of 150 agglomerated nest boxes, the whole mounted on two 10-metre-high poles. Gaps within the metal grid system of boxes provide natural ventilation to cool the nest boxes. The rainbow-like colours painted on the front of the boxes, which, according to the artists, are a pixellated version of an African sunset, were created in response to swifts' ability to see a wide spectrum of light: the boxes act like 'a code of colour' for individual pairs of birds on their annual return from wintering grounds in southern Africa.[47] The more recent towers installed in Shalford (2020), a village near Guildford, and in the centre of Exeter demonstrate two very different approaches: the former designed by artist Will Nash as a rising series of eight timber platforms,[48] the latter one of a group of similar structures created by Menthol Architects. Installed in 2015 on a roundabout in the city centre, the Exeter tower was inspired by the dynamic silhouette of a swift in flight.[49] This direct visual correspondence between bird and nest site was intended to make the function of the tower immediately apparent to (human) urban inhabitants, but also to promote community action to protect future populations of the birds. Yet in all three cases it has proved difficult to attract returning birds to these new homes: the example in Cambridge only proved successful after recorded calls of swifts were played repeatedly at the nesting site.[50]

Something & Son's swift tower in Logan's Meadow, Cambridge, installed in 2010.

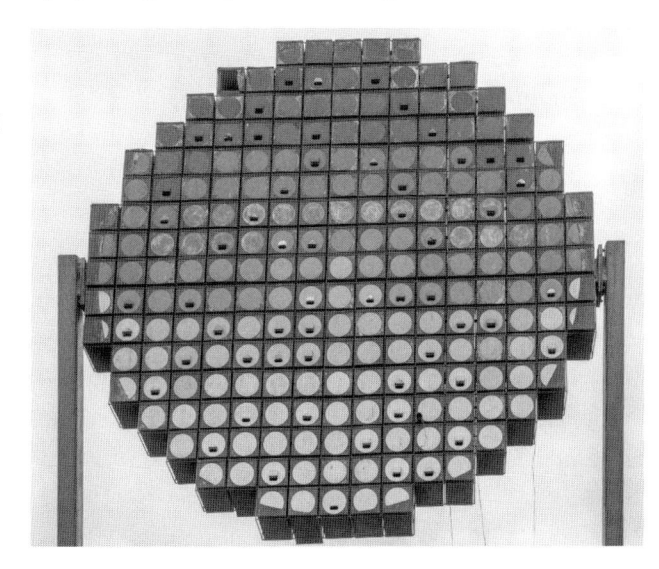

The characteristic modernity of these towers – sculptural yet also functional objects – derives from a long-standing human fascination with swifts as being the most aerodynamic of all birds. Like peregrine falcons, swifts are more often heard than seen and they are almost always seen from a distance: European swifts never touch the ground and only land on manmade structures when nesting (the three short months they visit their northern breeding ranges each year). Once the young swifts have fledged, they will never see their parents again. After taking their first flight, the young birds will not touch ground again until they are ready to breed three years later; they must also navigate the thousands of kilometres to their winter homes without any help from their parents. It is almost impossible for humans, earthbound as we are, to comprehend what such an unmitigated aerial existence means; and the historical naming of swifts as 'devil's birds' reflects their profoundly alien character as animals. Swifts also 'scream' to our ears, the wheeling parties of scissoring birds characteristic of warm summer evenings in European towns and cities. In fact, slowed down by recording devices, these screams are revealed to be trilling calls. Like the peregrine, they are animals that perceive the world more acutely and much faster than we do.[51] Giacomo Bella's 1913 painting *Swifts: Paths of Movement + Dynamic Sequences* attempted to capture the extraordinary dynamism of the swift's flight. Reflecting the Italian Futurists' fascination with speed, this is a still image of prolific movement – like a composite of many photographs that can now be taken by digital cameras, and probably inspired by late nineteenth-century studies of the motion of animals by French physiologist Étienne-Jules Marey and English photographer Eadweard Muybridge.[52] Captured in this way, flying swifts leave behind architectonic traces: a slipstream of lines and curves that are, in this painting, paradoxically frozen into static forms.

Perhaps the most extraordinary behaviour exhibited by swifts is their so-called vesper flights, a beautiful phrase that refers to their collective ascents high into the sky on warm summer evenings, as well as their subsequent tendency to sleep on the wing before returning to the lower regions of the atmosphere. Vespers are more commonly associated with evening devotional prayers, the last of the day in many Christian communities. It is still not understood why swifts engage in this remarkable group behaviour; as Helen Macdonald has noted, it is speculated that the swifts ascend to assess the state of the atmosphere, the invisible currents of up- and down-draughts 'read' by the birds at night in order to map their future flight patterns (and it is no accident that vesper flights are more common near to the time of migration).[53] It has long been known that swifts also fly around low-pressure systems to avoid inclement weather and the corresponding dip in the number of airborne insects, an activity that can see the birds cover huge distances in just a few hours. The aerial geographies of swifts alert us to the profound limitations of being an earthbound species, but also the acute perceptual abilities of other animals in being able to negotiate and in some respects master the air.

The perpetual aerial lives of swifts challenge humans to reconsider the nature of the environment above our towns and cities. In September 2020 Chinese architectural student Mengying Xie presented her final-year degree project at the Royal Institute of Technology in Stockholm.[54] This project envisioned parts of Beijing being radically reconfigured for the benefit of migratory birds, such as the species of swift named after the city (*Apus apus pekinensis*). The rapid expansion of Chinese cities since the 1990s, coupled with an equally rapid decline in urban air quality, has seen swift populations plummet – as much as 60 per cent in Beijing alone in the past thirty years. In striking perspective drawings, Xie's project imagines the construction of several different types of towers for the nesting swifts and for human observers. These towers would be nestled in green zones landscaped to encourage the proliferation of insects. Aerial elements such as telecommunication wires and elevated walkways would accommodate both swifts and

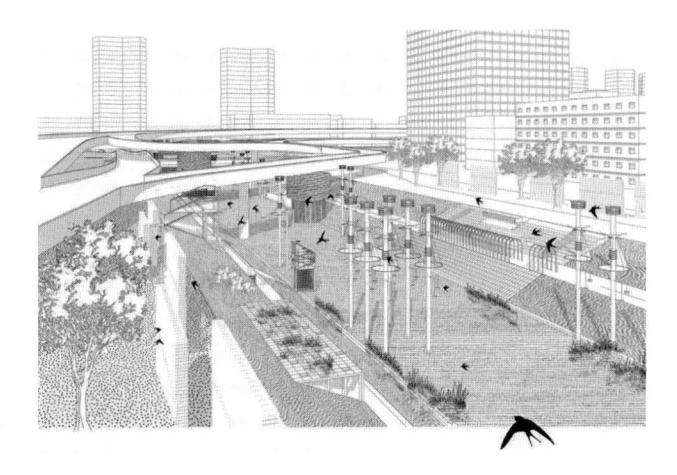

A visualization from Mengying Xie's Beijing swift project, 2020.

people together in the lower regions of the sky. This project demonstrates in a very pragmatic way how urbanization might develop in tune with the needs of a particular species and the other animals and plants on which that species depends. Here, the needs of humans and birds are not regarded as mutually exclusive, the quite literal 'bird's-eye' perspective of the drawings belonging to the perceptual worlds of both swifts and humans alike.

Crow

The seemingly miraculous ability of swallows and swifts to pinpoint 'home' on their twice-yearly intercontinental journeys is not just a characteristic of migratory birds; it also applies to year-round residents, particularly sociable species such as rooks. British naturalist Mark Cocker developed an obsession with these commonplace birds, finding in the geography of their nesting and roosting colonies an ancient avian map of the English landscape. Rookeries – agglomerations of nests of breeding pairs of rooks – are a familiar feature of the English countryside, and Cocker discovered that many of these sites are ancient in origin, with new rookeries sometimes created on sites where the birds either nested or roosted long ago. Cocker has described these rookeries as 'lodestones' in the landscape, '[places] of high trees, whose engrained familiarity conferred a deep sense of security and comfort' on the rooks.[55] Often located on well-protected private land, rookeries are also bound up with the human politics of property and class; they are 'cultural repositories' that link species together in a mesh of meanings.

Until the early twentieth century there were also rookeries in central London. A long-lived group of nests that occupied trees in the garden of the Temple church was recorded at the time of the Great Fire in 1666 and celebrated a century later by Anglo-Irish novelist Oliver Goldsmith. There was also a rookery located in nearby Chancery Lane, in London's legal district. During the nineteenth century, the inexorable outward growth of the city made it increasingly difficult for rooks nesting in the city centre to find open spaces to forage for food; the last birds disappeared from the Chancery Lane rookery in the early twentieth century.[56] But Londoners in the Victorian period would have been much more familiar with another kind of rookery, namely densely populated districts in the city that would now be called slums. It is probably no accident that Charles Dickens's novel *Bleak House* (1852–3) linked Chancery with the most famous of these human rookeries in the nearby area of St Giles, barely fictionalized in the novel as Tom-All-Alone's.[57] An area of dilapidated houses, narrow streets, hidden passageways and all sorts of repulsive sights, sounds and smells, the St Giles rookery was increasingly scrutinized by middle-class reformers in the early 1840s, determined as they were to rid London of this perceived 'plague-spot' at its very centre.[58] An attempt to clear the site with the building of New Oxford Street from 1844 to 1847 only concentrated the squalor elsewhere. In 1849, after the clearance, the *Illustrated London News* visualized a street in the relocated rookery, the cacophonous scene reminiscent of its avian namesake. Smoke-stained houses seem to literally moulder on the page, organic life of all kinds mingling in a wild confusion that would have both repulsed and excited the newspaper's upper middle-class readers.

A very different corvid-inspired structure is a 'crow's nest' on a ship, a watch-tower located at the very top of a mast, first invented by whaler William Scoresby in 1807. The naming of this structure probably reflected a much longer-standing association of corvids and ships that dates back to the biblical story of Noah's ark, when a raven was sent out by Noah to scout for dry land after the apocalyptic flood that God visited on a depraved humanity.[59] Crow's nests also referred to other human-built structures on high vantage points, including the observation platforms built on top of Westminster Abbey, St Paul's Cathedral and other church buildings for the first Ordnance Survey of London in 1848–9. Pictured in the *Illustrated London News* a year before they visualized the rookery of St Giles, these temporary structures were designed to give the military surveyors the best vantage points from which to map the city.[60] Highly visible structures that did indeed resemble enormous crows' nests, they enabled, for the first time, the accurate measurement of the topography of London's streets, a necessary first step in what would turn out to be a long process of transforming London's underground network of sewers from vectors of disease to revolutionary cleansing agents.[61] These two corvid-inspired architectures in early Victorian London could not have been more different. If the rookeries were an atavistic remnant of a medieval past, their organic appearance out of step with the march of progress, then the crow's nests of the

The rookery of St Giles, as pictured by the *Illustrated London News* in 1849.

Ordnance Survey were harbingers of rational order, the literal bird's-eye view of the city obtained by the surveyors heralding the transformation of the city into a cleaner, more well-governed paradigm of progressive modernity.

Despite the disappearance of rooks in central London, other corvid species are still commonplace in urban areas; magpies, jays and carrion crows being the most likely to be encountered in London today. The harsh chatter of magpies, in particular, is a familiar element in the layers of sounds encountered in the city. Yet perhaps the most famous corvids in London are the ravens, currently nine in number, kept at the Tower of London and long held to be present there since the reign of Charles II,

Crow's-nest observation tower constructed on top of Westminster Abbey as part of the first Ordnance Survey of London, 1848.

but actually deliberately introduced around 1883 when the Tower was first marketed to tourists as a Gothic castle, with its associations with ghosts and the romantic elements that so fascinated visitors to Victorian London. The claim that England will never be invaded while the ravens remain in the Tower dates from the Second World War, when the birds, with their more-than-human perception, were able to provide early warning of approaching German aircraft and their bombs.[62] Housed for many years in an ad hoc assemblage of sheds, in 2015 the ravens were provided with a new enclosure designed by Llowarch Llowarch Architects. Although the architects built a relatively unobtrusive and functional shelter for the birds – a series of oak-slatted frames covered in wire mesh – they nevertheless made references to the long history of the Tower in their use of timber, since the site was supposedly occupied by wooden structures before the building of the now UNESCO-protected White Tower. The ravens continue to have free range of the Tower grounds during the day, the enclosure used only at night for the birds' protection.[63] The architects worked closely with both the Tower's official keeper of the ravens (the Ravenmaster) and the Curator of Birds at London Zoo. The ravens kept at the latter were among the first animals to be provided with permanent accommodation, in the form of a cage designed by Decimus Burton in 1829 and used for 150 years before the birds were rehoused.[64]

In his story 'The Raven' (1992), American writer Russell Hoban imagined a cosmic encounter with the ravens in their modern enclosure at London Zoo. Communicating with the birds telepathically, an unnamed visitor to the zoo is drawn into what Hoban calls 'the black' – a journey to the very end of time itself, human and bird and everything else joined together 'through revolving repetitions over hundreds of thousands of millions of years' as material decay grinds them down over the aeons into sameness. Midway through the story the process suddenly reverses, with the human and raven coming back from the brink to the present moment.[65] Inscrutable in its meaning, this strange story draws on a pervasive human understanding of ravens as omens of bad fortune. Because of their uniform blackness and harsh call, both ravens and carrion crows are often considered to be harbingers of death, whereas the more brightly clad magpies and jays tell of more ambivalent fates, some good, some bad. These long-standing associations have found perhaps their most well-known expression

Llowarch Llowarch Architects' raven enclosure in the grounds of the Tower of London, completed in 2015.

in the Scottish verse that begins 'One for sorrow, two for mirth', ending with the 'Nine for hell, And ten for the Devil's own sel[f]'. Counting magpies reflects the human desire to have some measure of control over the wild varieties of fate that might befall us; it also reflects the relative tameness of these birds and their ambiguous appearance and nature.

There is no such ambiguity in perhaps the most famous use of corvids and architecture in visual culture, namely in a sequence in Alfred Hitchcock's film *The Birds* (1963), adapted from Daphne du Maurier's short story of the same name, published in 1952. As all kinds of birds begin to attack humans in an isolated settlement in Bodega Bay, California (a Cornish peninsula in du Maurier's story), Melanie Daniels (Tippi Hedren) goes to the local school to check on the safety of the children. While she waits outside on a bench, smoking a cigarette, American crows begin to assemble behind her on a children's climbing frame. After a while Daniels notices a crow flying, her gaze following it across the sky to the climbing frame, all of a sudden shockingly full of perching birds, ready to attack. The power of this sequence is also greatly enhanced by the nursery rhyme heard in the background being sung by the children, its repetitive litany of nonsense words directly keying into the image of gathering crows.[66] Both short story and film end with hordes of birds laying siege to homes, the sanctity of the domestic sphere no match for the murderous jabbing of innumerable beaks and claws. In the end, birds find the gaps that humans have been unable to secure, whether descending en masse down chimneys, smashing the glass of windows in suicidal dives, or pecking through boards of wood nailed over windows or door panels.

Just why the birds turn on humans is not made clear in either du Maurier's story or Hitchcock's film, but in both the threatening avian hordes transform the home from a place of security and familiarity into one of threat and unease. The work of British sculptor Kate MccGwire provides a similar take on crows as something ominous, her installations using the feathers of corvids to give visual expression to Sigmund Freud's notion of the uncanny (from the German *unheimlich*, meaning 'unhomely').[67] In *Enteric* (2018), crows' feathers are attached to glass and other materials in a thoroughly disconcerting rope-like form, which erupts from the floor of the Renaissance-era Chiostro del Bramante in Rome. The earlier work *Slick* (2010) featured crow and magpie feathers attached to an antique fire-basket, flowing out of the structure in a way that resembled an oil spillage. The serpentine forms that MccGwire creates seem to suggest the primal chaos of the human unconscious, but they also reference the swirling patterns of sociable corvids such as rooks when they flock together in large numbers in their nesting and roosting colonies. Bringing a sense of the avian horde into domestic space is highly disturbing: it dissolves the boundary between the human and the non-human we like to think is inviolate. But just like the monstrous hordes that break through doors and windows in *The Birds*, MccGwire's sculptures tell us otherwise.

Starling

Birds that congregate in large numbers are sometimes regarded by humans as pests: along with pigeons, this moniker has often been applied to sparrows and starlings, particularly if they are classed as invasive species or they

Kate MccGwire's installation *Enteric* (2018), in the Chiostro del Bramante in Rome.

exhibit supposedly bad behaviour, such as starlings stealing the nests of other birds or the staple foodstuffs of humans (agricultural grains mostly). Yet these attitudes always emerge from specific social and cultural contexts. In the USA, starlings are a non-native species and are widely called 'rats with wings' (as urban pigeons sometimes are in the UK). In the USA starlings have no official protection and are often exterminated in large numbers, while in the UK and Western Europe their numbers have declined to such an extent they are now red-listed in Britain as a bird of high conservation concern. The European starling (*Sturnus vulgaris*) was one of a number of Old World species deliberately introduced into the USA in the nineteenth century by so-called 'acclimatization societies' that sought to mitigate settlers' homesickness by providing them with some of the sights and sounds of their European homelands. Finding a reference to starlings in Shakespeare's *Henry IV*, New York pharmacist and prominent acclimatist Eugene Schieffelin released eighty birds imported from England into a snowy Central Park in March 1890. A century later there were more than 200 million starlings living in the USA, all direct descendants of that original group. The extraordinary success of these birds was a direct consequence of colonial expansion across the continent, with starlings preferring to nest in cavities under the cornices of buildings and roof tiles, or inside lofts and attics, their foraging behaviour well adapted to urban parks and other green spaces created or left behind by humans.[68]

One of the reasons why starling populations have recently declined in Western Europe is precisely the lack of such voids and gaps in newer buildings, or older ones that have been renovated, the holes sealed up. Starlings compete for these habitats with hirundines, swifts and pigeons, but they have the advantage over migratory species in being present year-round in some European countries (Britain, France and Spain, for example), and can thus seize the best sites early on in the year before swallows, martins and swifts return.[69]

The fact that starlings are sociable birds, nesting and foraging in small colonies, has made them one of a number of avian species that have been favoured as pets for humans; so has their extraordinary capacity for mimicry. In the first century CE Pliny the Elder kept a starling to study how the bird picked up sounds from the environment; Julius Caesar apparently taught his pet starling to speak to him in Greek and Latin. Later, most famously, Wolfgang Amadeus Mozart kept a pet starling for three years in his rooms in Vienna after he heard a bird in a pet shop repeating a phrase from his own Piano Concerto No. 17 in G, KV 453, in May 1784, a work he had completed only a month before the starling somehow learned how to mimic it.[70] More recently, in researching Mozart's starling, American naturalist Lyanda Lynn Haupt 'adopted' a baby starling that was about to be exterminated in a park near to her home in Seattle. In *Mozart's Starling* she described in vivid detail the ways in which her domesticated starling, which she named Carmen, occupied her house and developed a relationship with her. Like other social animals, starlings will readily adopt humans into their world: Haupt described how Carmen responded to different spaces in the house (a liking for her study, a fear of the stairwell), how the bird would try to involve Haupt in her games and, perhaps most extraordinary of all, how Carmen would mimic the sounds around her with such dexterity that she was able to greet humans and other animals in their own languages: 'Hi, Carmen!' learned as a greeting for the humans in the house; 'Meow!' for the pet cat.[71]

Recent research on starlings' vocalizations has shown the species capable of what American linguist Noam Chomsky termed 'recursive' language (and which he adamantly believes is unique to humans). This refers to the ability of humans to embed words or phrases within short sentences to expand their frame of meaning, a process Chomsky termed 'unbounded Merge'. Neuroscientist Timothy Gentner and others have shown that the sounds mimicked by starlings (up to thirty or more in some individual birds) are also organized in this way, rather than simply repeated one after another. Moreover, the way starlings pick up sounds has been shown to be very similar to how human infants learn to talk, from babbling to forming words to developing the latter into phrases and sentences.[72] This demonstrates that not only do starlings have a high level of intelligence, but that they relate to their environment in complex and nuanced ways that are strikingly similar to our own. For a pet starling, a house becomes a repository of familiar sounds, gleaned from its spaces and the flows of occupants, both human and more-than-human. As Haupt learned through her adoption of a starling, this complex behaviour is profoundly at odds with the bird's reputation as vermin, a consequence, perhaps, of seeing negative aspects of ourselves in the starling.

A murmuration of starlings on Otmoor, Oxfordshire, in November 2008.

Starlings and humans also meet in an another context: namely, in the winter months when the birds flock together in huge numbers at dusk before roosting. As the afternoon light fades, starlings fly in from their day-time foraging grounds in ever-increasing numbers, swirling in the sky in tightly packed groups, creating rapidly shifting patterns that are primarily meant to confuse predators such as peregrine falcons, hobbies and other birds of prey (often seen at roosting sites).[73] These starling spectacles are known as murmurations and have long enraptured human observers. The Romantic poet Samuel Taylor Coleridge witnessed a rare morning mur-muration from his London-bound stagecoach in November 1799, its 'glory' for Coleridge stemming from the way in which the whole mass of starlings seemed 'like a body unindexed with voluntary power'.[74] Today, large crowds often gather to watch evening murmurations, with as many as a thousand at prime sites such as Ham Wall on the Somerset Levels in England. Geographer Andy Morris has argued that these popular events should be thought of as co-gatherings of starlings and people, the flocking behaviour of human spectators to some extent mirroring that of the birds, the landscape around the starling roosts adapted into a space for human as much as avian conviviality.[75] Many spectators see familiar shapes in the starlings' pulsing movements. Back in 1799 Coleridge's eyes saw the birds morphing from 'a Square – now a Globe – now from complete orb into an Elipse – then obligated into a Balloon with the Car suspended, now a concave Semicircle', while in March 2020 the high-spec digital camera of James Crombie saw, for a fraction of a second, the starlings massed into the shape of a giant bird.[76]

Researchers studying murmurations around buildings in Rome (where starlings are winter migrants from Siberia) have found a much closer physiological link between human fascination with these phenomena, our ability to see recognizable shapes in their shifting movements and the way starlings actually coordinate themselves in their aerial manoeuvres. Using advanced GPS devices and accelerometers, they found that even in huge flocks of starlings, each individual bird interacts with only a limited number of its nearest neighbours, on average six or seven other birds. This means that the extraordinary coordination achieved by thousands of birds is actually the result of local interactions alone. Similar to the way in which social insects build their homes, a kind of 'swarm intelligence' is at work in a murmuration of starlings.[77] The researchers also found that the collective motion of starlings produces just a few key dynamic shapes that are also seen in other mobile animal groups, as well as many physical and chemical systems. It is hypothesized that the patterns produced in murmurations explain our fascination with the spectacle: something in the way the birds move resonates with the basic pattern language of our own bodies and minds.[78]

The resonances that starling murmurations create in human observers are striking instances of what architect Christopher Alexander described as 'a pattern language' in his contributions to the book of that title (1977), perhaps the most widely read text on architectural theory in recent decades. A pattern is defined by Alexander as a physical design that responds to human relationships, and he proposed that the human-built world at all different scales should be patterned in such a way as to promote wholeness in those who encounter it. This resonates strongly with recent architectural projects inspired by starling murmurations. In July 2020 Dutch

SO-IL, *Murmuration* installation, High Museum of Art, Atlanta, 2020.

Time-lapse image of Squidsoup's *Murmuration* installation at the Scottsdale Museum of Contemporary Art in Arizona, 2019–20.

architecture firm SO-IL installed *Murmuration* at the High Museum of Art in Atlanta, a temporary pavilion comprised of metal frames supporting a sculptural arrangement of agricultural netting echoing 'the form of a bird murmuration . . . momentarily suspended in mid-air'.[79] Also resembling the canopy of a tree, the pavilion was designed for occupation by both humans and birds, with feeders and perches included to attract the latter. These avian features were designed to stimulate awareness of the decline of many bird populations in the USA, but without any specific reference to starlings, not surprising given the birds' problematic status in the USA as an invasive species.

A very different take on the patterns generated by flocking starlings can be seen in another *Murmuration* installation that was created directly outside the Scottsdale Museum of Contemporary Art for six months from November 2019. Designed by UK artists SquidSoup, the installation consisted of seven hundred interconnected orbs, each of which emitted light and sound that created an artificial 'murmuration' as together they responded to environmental stimuli by means of electronic sensors. An intertwining ecosystem of electronic and environmental elements, this *Murmuration* mimicked the mesmeric shifts in form seen in flocks of starlings to create an ever-changing audiovisual experience.[80] It is perhaps no coincidence that both of these starling-inspired projects were exhibited during the global COVID-19 pandemic in 2020, even as they were conceived in less troubled times. In this extended period of enforced isolation for the majority of humans on the planet, being together in the manner of a starling murmuration became unthinkable and, in many countries, illegal. Both of these artificial murmurations functioned as a way of providing some much-needed connection: carefully controlled in the case of the Atlanta pavilion; at a distance in the Scottsdale installation. Meanwhile, of course, starlings themselves continued to enjoy what we were temporarily denied in our buildings and urban spaces.

3
Wild

During the first wave of the COVID-19 pandemic in Spring 2020, when national lockdowns were implemented most strongly, many cities were seemingly emptied of humans, uncannily reminiscent of post-apocalyptic scenarios in films such as *28 Days Later* (2002) and *I Am Legend* (2007). During this period, recurrent images captured by photographers were of animals roaming empty city streets: a puma in Santiago, Chile; a raccoon in New York's Central Park; a leopard in Hyderabad, India; fallow deer in London; wild boar in Ajaccio, Corsica; mountain goats in Llandudno, Wales.[1] For many, these images provided comfort in a time of great anxiety and unprecedented confinement, wild animals finding some measure of freedom in otherwise human-dominated environments. But these images were also unsettling, revealing that the spatial boundaries between humans and animals are perhaps much more porous than we generally believe them to be or, even, that wild animals were already at home in our cities, revealed to us only when we had temporarily retreated from their spaces.

This chapter focuses on six animals that probe the boundaries between human- and animal-built worlds and those between wild and domesticated animals. Beginning with rats, this chapter shows just how porous these boundaries are: rats are animals that positively thrive in cities, and yet they remain 'wild' in our imaginations, creatures that we would rather not bring to mind precisely because of their promiscuity (sexual and geographical) and their connotations with filth and disease. In a similar way, bats transgress boundaries in their thoroughly alien appearance and lifestyle, yet they also often find human-built structures conducive to their needs: the South Congress Bridge in Austin, Texas, which houses millions of migrating bats in the summer months, is one of the most notable examples. Like rats and bats, the third animals considered here – foxes – live in the urban shadows in cities as a subterranean presence that often threatens to destabilize our classifications of what, and more particularly where, 'wild' animals should be. Revealed most powerfully in the hysteria that often accompanies news reports of (very rare) fox attacks on people, the very nomenclature of the 'urban fox' suggests that this animal should really be making its home elsewhere.

There is a shift in focus in the second half of this chapter to animals that are both 'wild' and also, to varying degrees, domesticated. Here the predominant architectural focus is on the difference between the inside and outside of animal and human-built worlds. So, the section on lizards draws attention to the increasing popularity of these animals as pets, focusing on the typical homes that owners build for them, namely glass tanks or vivaria. In a completely different vein, dinosaurs, the colossal lizards of the past, occasionally appear as either literal buildings or, more often, as skeletons – animal examples of functionalist design. Similarly, today's largest living land animals, elephants, have often become architectural metaphors. There are many examples of buildings and monuments shaped like elephants that draw on the animal's long-standing association with power and strength. Finally, our closest living relatives, apes, have often been perceived of as animal embodiments of the baser human instincts – the animal in ourselves. Here, two prominent ape fictions – *Planet of the Apes* and *King Kong* – extrapolate on what apes might do to architecture and cities if humans ever lose what they generally think of as their evolutionary pre-eminence.

In both the architectural imagination and in cities themselves, what counts as a wild animal is thus open to multiple interpretations. This in itself challenges the often reductive ways in which the conventional animal categories of wild, tame and feral are presented in arguments for the restoration of supposedly pristine natural habitats. For example, British writer George Monbiot's impassioned argument for 'rewilding' in *Feral* (2013) proposed that entire landscapes devoted to sheep farming in Britain be replaced by 'natural ecosystems' of the past, allowing once endemic animals such as wolves and lynxes to return.[2] The central problem with this argument is that it rests on a presupposed separation of the human and the animal, of nature and culture and of the wild and domesticated. In the Anthropocene those distinctions have been revealed to be romantic illusions. Today, arguably the most pristine environment left on Earth – the Antarctic continent – is one of the places most affected by anthropogenic climate change, while the plastics we disgorge from our cities have ended up creating their own toxic landmass in the remotest part of the Pacific Ocean. These disturbing developments alone (and there are countless others that could be considered) forcefully remind us that there is nothing in the world that is not affected by what humans do. Perhaps, instead of lamenting this fact and believing that firm boundaries between nature and the built environment can somehow be restored, we should rather embrace their discomforting dissolution. Out of this might develop something richer and more positive, namely what, back in 1973, Ivan Illich termed 'conviviality', a living-together that refuses to turn away from the ways in which humans have destroyed so much but which also holds out the hope of the future development of healthier, more mutually supportive relationships between species.[3]

Rat

As explored in Chapter One, beehives were a powerful metaphor of ideal human societies for modernist architects such as Le Corbusier. The perceived rationality of the hive, with its densely packed hexagonal cells, together with the apparent docility of the massed bees, seemed to suggest that humans could live well enough in standardized living spaces in high-rise buildings. But, from the late 1940s onwards, another family of animals – rodents, and particularly rats and mice – were used to directly challenge this modernist idealization of standardization and densification in human habitats.[4]

Although rats and mice have been the subjects of laboratory experiments since the mid-nineteenth century, it was only in the twentieth that rodents began to be used to investigate the problem-solving behaviour of animals, with the building of mazes and puzzle boxes for experiments on rodents.[5] From 1947 until the early 1970s, ethologist John Calhoun built a series of increasingly sophisticated structures for large numbers of rats and

One of John Calhoun's 'rat cities' built at Johns Hopkins University, Baltimore, 1970.

mice to inhabit, what Calhoun described as 'rat cities'. Supported by the Rodent Ecology Project, set up at Johns Hopkins University in Baltimore in 1942, Calhoun's experiments investigated the effects of overcrowding on rodent populations. These experiments mirrored widespread fears about the long-term effects of the burgeoning human population in the post-war period. Calhoun's structures deliberately mimicked inner-city tower blocks that were built from the 1950s onwards: nesting spaces for the rats were stacked vertically, and stairwells and other spaces forced the rodents into regular contact with each other. What Calhoun found was that overcrowding caused severe behavioural pathologies in his rodent populations, which he provocatively described in anthropomorphic terms: dominant rats became 'despots'; violent younger rats were 'juvenile delinquents'; mothers attacking their young were 'child-abusers'. For Calhoun, the relevance of his findings to humans could not be clearer: modernist architectural utopias were in reality 'behavioral sinks' that would have a catastrophic effect on their inhabitants.[6]

Although it has been pointed out by critics that using just one kind of animal as a substitute for humans is deeply problematic (rats and mice represent just 0.001 per cent of the creatures that might have been studied), Calhoun's miniature urban hells contributed much to the denigration of modernist faith in beehive cities. High-rise mass-housing, in particular, was increasingly taken to task by urban critics such as Lewis Mumford and Oscar Newman.[7] Yet the recent resurgence of luxury high-rise buildings in cities across the world has, in hindsight, revealed these experiments to be grounded in a conservative, anti-urban philosophy that equated density with degeneration. Just like the modernist visions of idealized human beehives they purportedly worked against, Calhoun's experiments were similarly grounded in a desire for control, rooted in a long-standing fear that it was only the urban poor who needed to be constrained, not those who were more privileged and whom, it was presumed, would behave better.

As explored in the previous chapter, in nineteenth-century London urban slums were often seen as possessing animal-like qualities, 'rookeries' being just one kind of animal image employed. Middle-class commentators found much that was more-than-human in these environments, including real and metaphorical rodents. For example, in Thomas Beames's account of the St Giles rookery, he described the epicentre of the slum as being the Rat's Castle, a notorious public house that was a veritable 'den of iniquity', while *Bleak House* piles on the organic metaphors to nauseating effect in Dickens's descriptions of St Giles: just like urban rats, the human population there 'crawls in and out of gaps in walls and boards; and coils itself to sleep, in maggot numbers'.[8]

These deeply unsettling metaphors were not just a product of a Victorian middle-class imagination that feared, perhaps above all else, the revolutionary rising-up of the proliferating urban poor, but also reflective of much longer-standing associations of rats with disease, rapacious appetites (including cannibalism) and debased natures. Although the link between disease (particularly bubonic plague) and rats was only established conclusively in France in 1898, these rodents have long been regarded as harbingers of disease and other misfortunes, largely on account of their close reliance on humans, more specifically the wastes that we generate, increasingly so in the modern period of urbanization.[9] As Jonathan Burt has argued, rats constantly push 'at the edges of the borders set to contain them', much in the same way as middle-class observers feared the urban poor were doing in nineteenth-century London.[10] Even though the oft-quoted factoid that, in a city, you are never more than 2 metres away from a rat is probably an exaggeration, humans have long feared the unbridled proliferation of these rodents, particularly in light of their extreme fecundity (female rats are sexually mature just three months from birth and can raise multiple litters of offspring each year). For example, journalist Henry

Mayhew's *London Labour and the London Poor* (1851) introduced a long section on rat-killing and rat-fighting in the city with the alarming statement that if, in an ideal habitat, a given female rat could produce ten litters in a year, then in just four years 'not far short of 3,000,000 might be produced from a single pair'.[11]

Mayhew's voluminous account of various rat-based human activities in mid-Victorian London was at once a vigorous assertion of the close association of animals and humans in the city and also a nostalgic lament for the imminent loss of such interspecies bonds. For, just as Mayhew was researching rats, a new sewer system for London was being conceived. Eventually constructed in the 1860s, it was presumed that this sanitary revolution would destroy not only rats, who found shelter in underground urban spaces, but that it would also sweep away figures such as Jack Black, 'rat-catcher to the Queen', and nefarious activities like rat-fighting, where dogs competed to kill the highest number of rats in specially designed 'pits' in taverns.[12] But, despite widespread sanitary improvements, rats continue to thrive in even the cleanest cities. Robert Sullivan's illuminating account of his own research into New York City's resident rats in the early 2000s revealed a city teeming with these unwanted inhabitants. Ample lodging spaces for brown rats are provided by tiny gaps in the city's concrete sidewalks, the basements of older buildings, the crumbling walls of subway tunnels and narrow alleyways. These literal holes in the city are ideal rat habitats, especially when they are located near to food waste generated by humans. Sullivan argued that rats, like humans, are able to construct their own mental maps of the city. Rats become so familiar with their home territories, usually just one city block or even a single alleyway, that 'deep in their rat tendons they know history'.[13]

As Sullivan's conversations with rat exterminators revealed, these animals are intimately associated with places in cities that are neglected or overlooked – 'places with a story that had been forgotten for one reason or another'.[14] Little wonder then that rats have often featured in fictions of urban undergrounds haunted by monsters, whether metaphorically in the case of *Les Gaspards* (The Rats, 1973), a film that centres on a group of subversive utopians/terrorists living in the catacombs beneath a modernizing Paris, or literally as animal hordes signalling the presence of a monstrous human killer living under London in *Creep* (2005).

Brown rat emerging from a sewer in London.

The repulsion felt by many to the presence of rats in cities derives from the animals' ability to cross boundaries that we would rather remained inviolate: rats can literally collapse their skeletons in order to squeeze their bodies through the narrowest of cracks. Yet rats' ability to work their way into and through the hidden crevices of cities can also be read in a more positive light. Two notable fantasy novels, Neil Gaiman's *Neverwhere* (written at the same time as a BBC television series aired in 1996) and China Miéville's *King Rat* (1998), portray rats as powerful totemic animals in their subversive reimaginings of 1990s London. *Neverwhere* charts the adventures of Richard Mayhew (his surname a direct reference to his adventurous Victorian counterpart), who discovers a hidden world – London Below – of mythic humans and animals in the city's subterranean spaces. Here, rats, or rather one of them – Lord Rat – are quite literally the city's rulers: the articulate squeaks of this aristocratic rodent only understood by those who have the ears to hear.[15]

With a much darker sense of horror, *King Rat* also imagines its central protagonist, Saul Garamond, straddling the city's many vertical levels. The title of Miéville's novel references the horrific 'rat king' – a rare phenomenon in which the tails of several nesting rats (up to thirty in one known case) become permanently entangled.[16] King Rat of Miéville's novel is an altogether different kind of monster: early on Saul discovers that he is, in fact, half-rat – a member of a tribe of human/animal hybrids that have lived for centuries in the shadows of the city. Given a mission to save his kin from the terrifying villain known as The Piper, Saul discovers new powers in his rat identity – he can climb to the city's heights and descend through cracks to its depths, but always as an outcast of human society. Late in the novel Saul has a powerful sense of the built environment as porous and riddled with cracks, both literal and metaphorical. Standing on a former Second World War bomb site near Edgware Road, he feels the vulnerability of the city: 'the buildings' underbellies, soft underneath the aesthetic carapace . . . seen from behind, caught unawares, the functionality of the city was exposed.'[17]

Both novels provide a political reading of rats and the city in their equating of human and animal outcasts with the actual built environment. They picture a city that is rooted in intransigent social divisions that are seemingly hard-wired into the vertical geography of the city itself, from its high rooftops to subterranean sewers and tunnels. But this invisible city has always been known best by the rats, animals which are perhaps the most powerful urban truth-tellers, moving, as they do, in all the places – and with all the people – we would rather not see brought into the light.

Bat

If rats are the shadow animals of humans – always near to us but also just out of sight – bats might be described as our inverse species. Bats and humans are, according to anthropologist Roy Wagner, 'inside-out' versions of each other. Bats are only active at night and sleep upside-down during the day. Bats of the suborder Microchiroptera also sense the world through echolocation, emitting high-pitched sound waves that reflect off surfaces and other animals, enabling these bats to 'see' the world around them. For most animals, and humans especially, sounds are generally perceived as 'outside' the body and are processed internally; for bats, the reverse is true – they reverberate externally, their picture of the world the exact inverse of our own.[18] In addition, bats' ideal habitats are pitch-dark caves, chthonic spaces that humans have long feared, perhaps because they remind us, unconsciously, of the lives of our distant ancestors, who performed sacred rituals in these subterranean spaces as a way of appeasing their primal fears of death and the power of other creatures, whether seen or unseen.[19]

Bat caves have inspired a cornucopia of Batman fictions, from the first incarnations of this superhero figure in both Japanese and American culture in the 1930s to countless televisual, cinematic and live-action spectacles from the 1960s onwards. These range in tone from the deadly serious (for example, Christopher Nolan's celebrated trilogy of films) to the laughably kitsch (the 1960s television series).[20] In all Batman fictions, caves feature as prominent spaces that link humans and Chiroptera: in Nolan's *Batman Begins* (2005), for example, Bruce Wayne creates his bat-cave in a warren of underground spaces that incorporate the deepest foundations of his ancestral home.[21] It is here where Wayne masters his primal fear of bats, a product of a traumatic childhood that saw both of his parents murdered soon after he himself fell down a well shaft into a bat-infested underworld. In Nolan's trilogy, the bat-cave evolves into a laboratory for building technological marvels – the primal, organic space transformed into one of human domination – Prometheus not so much unbound as thoroughly mastered.

The human desire to conquer the chthonic is in essence the attempt to overthrow what is perceived to be the irrational domain of the bat: we want to put right its upside-down existence and to bring light into the dark recesses of its underworld home. But the continuing existence of real bats depends on these spaces remaining inviolate. The largest bat colony in the world, for example, roosts every summer in Bracken Cave near San Antonio in Texas: 20 million Mexican free-tailed bats (*Tadarida brasiliensis*) stream in and out of this underworld at dawn and dusk in a vast bat cloud that was captured by British artist Jeremy Deller in his films *Memory Bucket* (2003) and *Exodus* (2012).[22] Although the cave and its surroundings are now protected by Bat Conservation International, many other bat-roosting sites have been negatively affected by human development that has either disturbed subterranean roosts or destroyed trees that bats also use.

In 1925 Texan physician Charles A. Campbell argued that the bats of the Bracken and other caves were 'sanitary workers' that not only saved crops by eating troublesome insects but provided valuable agricultural fertilizer in the form of guano, which collected in vast quantities in their roosting caves (up to 20 metres deep on the floor of Bracken Cave).[23] As part of his plan to domesticate the bats and collect their 'black gold', Campbell built a monumental bat house in San Antonio in 1914 that eventually housed tens of thousands of chiropteran residents. The timber-clad truncated pyramidal structure was 6 metres high and mounted on four lofty wooden supports: a prominent cross fitted on its roof was no doubt a decorative embellishment that referenced bats' long and unfortunate association with demonic forces.[24] Campbell marketed his invention as a 'Municipal Bat House' that could be replicated anywhere; sixteen Campbell-designed bat houses followed, but the only one that remains is the so-called Hygieostatic Bat Roost (1918) near the town of Comfort, Texas, where the animals still perform their task of keeping down the mosquito population.[25]

In recent years the provision of artificial homes for bats has become an abiding concern for a select group of artists and architects. Jeremy Deller launched a bat-house competition in 2009: the winning proposal, designed by Jørgen Tandberg and Yo Murata, was constructed at the London Wetland Centre in Barnes. More architecturally sophisticated than Campbell's monumental tower, this structure is made from 'hemcrete' (a biodegradable

A contemporary reconstruction of Charles A. Campbell's 'Municipal Bat House' (1914), near Comfort, Texas, 2009.

Bat house designed by Jørgen Tandberg and Yo Murata and installed in the London Wetland Centre in 2010.

mixture of hemp and lime), the perforated patterns cut into its surfaces designed to ventilate the tower in a such a way as to maintain the roost at an even temperature (as in a cave).[26] A more literal recreation of bats' favoured habitat can be seen in the world's first artificial bat-cave, constructed for gray bats (*Myotis grisescens*) in Kentucky in 2012. Designed for winter hibernation, the structure creates a cold air trap, its internal concrete surfaces textured for gripping, with curled fan belts, metal spirals and netting attached to the ceiling providing readymade 'perches' for the bats. Monitored by 24-hour CCTV, this artificial bat roost is an attempt by human protectors to intervene in the spread of a fungus that causes 'white-nose syndrome', a condition that kills bats by causing them to awake too early from their winter hibernations and thus starve to death for lack of their staple food, insects.[27]

In the case of the South Congress Bridge in Austin, Texas, bats have chosen a human-made structure as their roost. Renovations made to the bridge in the early 1980s inadvertently provided ideal purchase for migrating Mexican free-tailed bats. In the summer months the bridge is now home to nearly one and half million of these animals; their daily exodus at sunset attracts so many human observers that the city has adopted the animal as a mascot and hosts an annual 'Bat Fest' in August.[28] Architectural students at the University of Texas at Austin have suggested building a bat observatory to accommodate these visitors. Their proposed observation platform would simultaneously accommodate bat watchers and transmogrify their environment into something resembling the spectacle they are engrossed in, a stylized bat wing that captures the aerodynamic quality of the animals in flight.[29]

A very different type of bat cloud was realized by American architect Joyce Hwang in 2012: a hanging canopy of vessels in five trees located in the Tifft Nature Preserve near Buffalo.[30] In addition to supporting bat habitation, the structures were intended to raise awareness of the critical but often unnoticed role that bats play in maintaining healthy ecosystems. Like Deller, Hwang is particularly drawn to bats, with several of her other projects centred on this animal. Perhaps most striking is her Bat Tower, built in Griffis Sculpture Park, also near Buffalo. This sculptural object is both a carefully considered bat home and striking aesthetic statement meant to garner public attention. Bats are attracted by the insects that gather over a

Joyce Hwang's Bat Cloud installation in the Tifft Nature Preserve near Buffalo, 2012.

nearby pond, while 'landing pads' installed near the top of the tower and patterns of grooves on other surfaces help the bats to climb the tower and cling to its ceiling. As Hwang has stated, the overt visibility of the tower is meant as a counter to conventional 'off-the-shelf' bat houses marketed for people to install on or in their houses, which tend to be blandly functional. Hwang sees no contradiction in accommodating the needs of two different species of animal in her bat house: the anthropomorphic elements of the design are as important as those that are overtly chiroptera-centred.[31]

But is it possible for us to know what a bat really needs? The question is particularly apposite given that it was a bat, rather than any other animal, that formed the focus of philosopher Thomas Nagel's famous 1974 essay 'What Is It Like to Be a Bat?', a work often quoted in studies of consciousness, human or otherwise, and used earlier to introduce the themes of this book.[32] Nagel's conclusion was that there is really no way of understanding what he termed the 'alien' perception of bats (or, indeed, any other animal). For Nagel, humans are intractably locked into their own subjectivity when it comes to perception and even imagination. As recounted in the Introduction to this book, novelist J. M. Coetzee offered

Joyce Hwang's Bat Tower, Griffis Sculpture Park, 2010.

a direct challenge to Nagel in his assertion that just as novelists are able to think their way 'into the existence of a being who has never existed, then I can think my way into the existence of a bat or a chimpanzee or an oyster, with whom I share the substrate of life'.[33]

There is a wonderful story of a bat/human relationship that grounds this philosophical debate in earthy reality. In his 1991 book *Raising Archie*, Australian broadcaster Richard Morecroft recounted his experience of adopting a baby grey-headed flying fox (*Pteropus poliocephalus*), a species of bat belonging to the sub-order Megachiroptera that includes larger bat species that do not echolocate but are still nevertheless thoroughly 'alien' in the way that Nagel supposed. In his ministrations as a surrogate parent, Morecroft struggled to teach the young bat to fly and, in desperation, he resorted to flapping his arms in a crude imitation of flight. This simple trick worked: Archie flexed his wings, launched into flight and landed on Morecroft's head.[34] Here, in some mysterious way, Archie recognized the image of flight being offered by a human and responded in kind. As Tessa Laird beautifully put it, in this moment the interspecies divide was crossed by Archie finding out 'what it is like to be a bat by imitating a human imitating a bat'.[35]

Fox

Animals that make their homes underground or in caves have long been powerful metaphors of unrestrained animality that human intellect and reason supposedly rise above, but in reality only suppress. In the medieval period in Europe, it was arguably foxes that embodied these forces most strongly, particularly as it was a red fox (*Vulpes vulpes*) that starred in one of the most popular mythic tales of that period, *The Historye of Reynart the Fox*. This was first published in English by William Caxton in 1481, who had translated the tale from Middle Dutch; but the story dates back to an earlier epic verse, itself based on Aesop's fables from antiquity. The fox at the centre of this multilingual story makes mischief for anyone he encounters. In order to resist capture by his enemies, Reynart constructs a castle called Maleperduys, a fantastical version of the burrows that foxes usually inhabit in reality.[36] With its labyrinthine passageways, numerous exit and entry holes, dead ends and secret chambers, Maleperduys was an architectural embodiment not only of the fox as a thoroughly secretive animal, but of his 'crooked, subterranean intelligence that enable[d]' him to 'elude his enemies and anticipate their assaults'.[37]

In reality, of course, a fox's den is a far more prosaic construction, or rather excavation: at its most basic a den consists of a hole dug into the ground that leads to a hollowed-out chamber in which the fox sleeps and the cubs are raised. But, like Maleperduys, dens often feature multiple entrances and exits: the naturalist Ronald Nowak referring to one example that had nineteen in total.[38] Den construction also demonstrates animal intelligence: foxes usually excavate a 'plumber's pipe' opening in which a tunnel first falls, then rises, then falls again to create a water stop. Some foxes will also build side passages to create more room for a large family, or excavate a right-angled turn inside the den to deter predators and mitigate flooding.[39] In the eighteenth century the Comte de Buffon regarded such design prowess as evidence of aesthetic judgement in foxes, particularly in how they fashion passageways that both conceal them and facilitate easy escape from predators. In ascribing a 'superior degree of sentiment' to the fox, Buffon went against the grain of conventional attitudes towards this animal as the embodiment of human wickedness.[40]

A red fox peers out of its burrow.

The various names given to fox burrows – dens, earths, kennels, lairs – also refer to excavations made by a wide variety of other animals, including mammals (badgers, bears and rabbits), birds (penguins and puffins), reptiles (snakes and lizards) and insects (spiders and solitary bees).[41] For animals and humans alike, underground dwelling is attractive because it is perceived as more secure than living above ground: one can protect one's home more easily from the elements and unwanted intruders, be they predators or others looking for a secure home. Although Franz Kafka did not specify the identity, or gender, of the animal narrator in his 1924 story 'The Burrow', he or she bears all the hallmarks of the vulpine intelligence admired by the Comte de Buffon. Kafka's burrow is born of intellectual endeavour, a mathematical construction designed to make the burrow undetectable by intruders. As the animal narrator explains, the big hole that gives away the entrance to the burrow is nothing but a ruse, leading to a wall of rock; inside there are multiple cells, in which the animal sleeps, and at the centre of the burrow a 'castle keep', in which precious provisions are stored. In this subterranean lair, designer and inhabitant are fused.[42] But, in the end, as Kafka's animal fears throughout the story, the 'perfect' burrow turns out to be a tomb; eventually, a ferocious predator breaches the elaborate defences of the burrow from beneath. Kafka's story demonstrates that, however secure you think your home is, you can never escape the anxieties that bubble up from within.

Kafka's burrow directly inspired another fox-like dwelling in J. M. Coetzee's *The Life and Times of Michael K* (1983).[43] The titular outlaw of this story returns to his ancestral home somewhere in the South African veld, before deciding to build his own shelter nearby between the walls of a narrow crevice, creating an invisible burrow to hide himself from the predatory world outside. Over time, Michael K increasingly behaves like a fox, becoming 'so much a creature of twilight and night that the daylight hurt his eyes'. However, unlike Kafka's anxious animal narrator, Michael K lies peacefully in his burrow, his perception slowing down as he gradually yields 'himself to time . . . flowing slowly like oil from horizon to horizon over the face of the world, washing over his body'.[44] The burrow itself is purposively 'careless' and 'makeshift' in its construction – 'to be abandoned without a tugging at the heartstrings'. When Michael K is finally discovered by passing soldiers, he leaves his burrow knowing that 'we must all leave home, after all, we must all leave our mothers.'[45] This bittersweet reading of the burrow as a temporary respite from an alienated adulthood serves to humanize Kafka's animal narrator, even as he, like the fox, remains firmly on the edges of (human) society.

In Coetzee's story, Michael K's burrow transgresses conventional forms of homemaking; yet it also taps into our deepest desires for primal intimacy. Foxes are also widely regarded as transgressive animals by humans, particularly in recent years as populations of urban foxes have increased, the animals attracted by an abundance of food in cities and readymade places to shelter. Similar to rats, foxes tend to occupy distinct territories in towns and cities; they hollow out dens beneath sheds and other temporary buildings, and they traverse the same paths every day within their territories, creating a distinct vulpine geography within the human-built environment.[46] Foxes are also notorious for turning up in places where they are least expected, sometimes with horrific consequences. On 7 June 2010 UK media outlets reported that nine-month-old twins had been seriously injured by an urban fox, the animal entering a house in Stoke Newington, London, on a warm evening after the parents of the twins had left a door open. A moral panic ensued, with dozens of media articles decrying the savage behaviour of this non-human perpetrator.[47]

As geographers Angela Cassidy and Brett Mills have argued, the UK media response to this fox attack was undergirded by the fact that this particular animal 'breached a series of societal boundaries drawn around humans, animals, and "nature"'. The fox was, first and foremost, not where it should have been: by entering a human home, a place where we should feel secure and removed from 'wild' nature, this fox transgressed a supposed inviolate boundary. In actual fact, the actions of this animal revealed that this boundary is not a 'natural' construct, but rather one that is deeply anthropocentric. The fox becomes a 'savage' precisely at the point at which it crosses a human-made threshold; at this moment, it turns from a 'wild' creature into a malicious intruder in pointed contrast to how domestic animals such as dogs never get portrayed in this way, despite attacking people (particularly children) far more often than foxes do.

There is another side to the urban fox, however, namely its capacity to open up opportunities for new kinds of interspecies connections. In early April 2021, as London was still eerily quiet during the second year

A red fox crosses a road in Berlin.

of the COVID-19 pandemic, *Guardian* columnist Tim Dowling reported on a strange relationship that had developed between his pet dog and an urban fox. In the middle of the night, Dowling awoke to the sound of his dog barking and discovered a fox waiting patiently in his garden. It turned out that dog and fox had become playmates – the fox often seen waiting beneath street lamps for the dog to emerge, even imitating its barks in order to attract its attention.[48] This remarkable coming together of species creates an uncomfortable awareness that humans might not be at the centre of things in cities, that other animal kinships are being forged without our consent.

Folk tales sometimes draw on the power of foxes to communicate and respond to other animals. In the Andes a fox is known as *Pascualito, hijo de la tierra* (son of the earth), and the indigenous peoples that live there hold foxes in high esteem because of their ability to communicate with the earth, a faculty that allows foxes to discern events otherwise hidden from humans. In this positive reading, foxes can help human communities come to terms with forces beyond their control, offering them an exemplar of what it means to live close to the earth: because the fox's knowledge lies beneath the ground, it is equated with the living power of the earth.[49] Even in cities, where the earth is mostly replaced by impermeable asphalt and concrete, what lies beneath is still what ultimately sustains life, whether human or otherwise. That underworld may be riddled with networks of sewers, pipes, tunnels and railways; but this artificial substate reminds us that our vitality, like the fox's, is dependent on what lies beneath.

Lizard

Subterranean dens are home to a wide variety of animals, including reptiles such as snakes and lizards. Cool recesses between and under rocks or hollows in the ground offer reptiles convenient places to hide from predators and regulate their body temperature. As cold-blooded animals, reptiles are dependent on the sun as their principal source of body heat, hence the common sight of lizards basking on rocks in the morning in Mediterranean locales. Dens are where lizards go to cool down in the middle of day, or to overwinter in a dormant state until the return of the sun's warmth in the spring. Lizards will claim any available cavity as a life-saving shelter, whether crevices between rocks, the burrows of other animals, gravel and sand beds, abandoned buildings, or spaces under houses and other structures.[50]

In 2012 New Zealand-based designers Renee Davies, Cris de Groot and Martin Boult designed and built what they termed Prosthetic Lizard Homes, namely artificial dens that could be integrated into green or 'living' roofs on urban buildings. In this case, the reptile client was the copper skink (*Oligosoma aeneum*), the site was a green roof on New Zealand's North Island where the lizards are endemic. The artificial dens were flattened box-shaped structures made from a ceramic/concrete mixture and partially sunk into the soil of the green roof. The interiors of the structures were hollowed out into a series of interlocking spaces that provided niches into which the skinks could wedge themselves. A roof protected the den from rain and trapped cooler air inside, and a water reservoir was installed at the base of the structure to provide drinking water for the skinks. When trial dens were installed, they not only attracted the desired skinks but burrowing insect species such as crickets. In many subterranean environments such interspecies cohabitation is commonplace, a consequence of the fact that territories below ground are usually less fiercely guarded than those above.[51]

For the growing number of people who choose to keep reptiles as pets, off-the-shelf designs for dens tend to be far less sophisticated than the Prosthetic Lizard Homes examples. A cursory Amazon search will reveal a diverse range of lizard dens offered for sale, including miniature plastic caves, halved coconut shells and tree logs, as well as kitsch structures such as tiny hobbit-homes and even artificial human skulls.[52] For a prospective reptile owner, purchasing a den would be part of the larger process of creating an artificial environment for their chosen pets, usually involving a climate-controlled glass tank known as a vivarium.[53] The reptile houses that have been part of zoological parks across the world since the mid-nineteenth century are mostly scaled-up vivaria, the emphasis in zoos being on housing a range of exotic reptiles and amphibians in individual tanks arrayed in one bespoke building. Even as the glass tanks generally form the focus for the habitats built for individual species, the reptile houses themselves have been designed in a variety of architectural styles, from the Italianate example built in 1926 at London Zoo (the third successive reptile house on this site); the dinosaur-embellished 1931 Byzantine-revival Reptile House at the Smithsonian's National Zoo in Washington, DC; the overtly modernist *acquario-rettilario* in Turin designed by local architect Enzo Venturelli; and the largest example of its kind in the world at Reptile Gardens in South Dakota, the three-storey Sky Dome, a scaled-up vivarium housing a huge range of reptiles.[54]

In Lorcan Finnegan's 2019 film *Vivarium*, the titular glass tank is not designed for tetrapods but an unsuspecting human couple. Led by a distinctly lizard-like estate agent to an American suburb where every house is identical, the couple discover that they cannot leave, the entire estate a giant vivarium seemingly enclosed within its own invisible glass walls. It is later revealed that the humans have been imprisoned here by a humanoid alien race who use them as surrogate parents for their deeply strange offspring. Although Finnegan has stated that this concept is based on the life cycle of the cuckoo, which lays its eggs in the nests of other birds, the film's title, together with the geography and architecture of the environment in which it is set, also suggest a reptilian inspiration. The film asks us

Interior of Reptile Gardens in South Dakota.

to consider the psychological effects of enforced imprisonment and endless repetition on human and non-human species, as well as the alien-like presence of ourselves as omnipresent observers peering through the transparent glass walls of real-life vivaria. This species role-reversal is doubly uncanny because it also equates bland suburbia with the most destructive kind of imprisonment we impose on non-humans and, indeed, on ourselves.

The reptilian character of both aliens and humans in *Vivarium* derives some of its potency from the once popular notion of the 'lizard brain', a theory that the evolution of the brain in vertebrates has been by accretion over aeons. Developed in the 1960s by Paul McClean and popularized by Carl Sagan in *The Dragons of Eden* (1977), this concept rested on the idea that the first layer of the brain to be created was the 'reptilian complex', namely the part responsible for aggression, territorial behaviour and the desire for dominance (the other two layers being successively 'civilizing' in adding the potential for more complex emotions, thinking and behaviour). Thus, the most brutish human behaviour – whether seen in warfare, terrorism, or other kinds of violence – was blamed on the 'lizard brain', reptiles being cast as primitive proto-human beings in their limited cognitive abilities and instinctive viciousness. Even as this concept has now been discredited – lizard intelligence being recognized by scientists as far more complex than this reductive model suggests – it remains a potent metaphor in the popular imagination. One example was a Texan traffic sign temporarily hacked in protest of the election of Donald Trump as u.s. president in 2016, declaring that 'Donald Trump is a shape shifting lizard!' Indeed, the notion that our leaders might in fact be alien reptiles disguised as humans remains a popular if incredible example of a modern-day conspiracy theory, popularized by the former bbc sports commentator David Icke in his 1999 book *The Biggest Secret*.

When J. G. Ballard published *The Drowned World* in 1962, the lizard-brain theory was still a novel concept. It powerfully undergirds not only this novel, but much of the rest of Ballard's oeuvre. *The Drowned World* presents a hallucinatory vision of a future London that has been sunk beneath vast flood waters created by the melting of the polar ice sheets, the latter caused by rapid global warming that resulted from a sudden increase in solar radiation. Rather than offering salutary warnings about the devastating effects of climate change, Ballard's novel uses the extreme transformation of the urban environment as a mirror of the psychological regression experienced by its leading protagonist, Kerans. Presenting a direct metaphor for this reversion to the 'lizard brain', Ballard imagined the former office blocks of London filled with giant iguanas, reptiles that presage the return of the earth to the conditions experienced by the dinosaurs. Lounging impassively in what were once boardrooms, the iguanas are the animal-successors of the human bosses who once ruled the city from these corporate spaces.[55]

Ballard's vivid evocation of a future world that comes to resemble an ancient pre-human past has always been an important part of the appeal of dinosaurs, still popularly understood as gigantic lizards, even as scientists now consider them to have been a distinct order of reptiles that have much more in common with birds than any other living species. In 1854, soon after the term Dinosauria was first coined by palaeontologist Richard Owen in 1841, dinosaurs were brought vividly to life by sculptor Benjamin Waterhouse Hawkins.[56] Recently restored and still in their original location in Sydenham, Hawkins built fifteen life-size models of extinct fauna, including an 11-metre long iguanodon using an iron frame infilled with cement, tiles and stone. This particular model was also used by Hawkins for an unusual event: a dinner for 21 eminent Victorians, including Richard Owen, held inside the iguanodon sculpture on New Year's Eve of 1853. Represented in the *Illustrated London News*, this publicity stunt was not atypical for its time, with a characteristically Victorian mixture of science and showmanship. It uniquely demonstrated the colossal scale of dinosaurs, their clear relationship to present-day animals and their all too obvious evolutionary failure. By dining inside the animal, humans brought

A dinner for 21 eminent Victorians inside Benjamin Waterhouse Hawkins's iguanodon sculpture, *Illustrated London News*, 31 December 1853.

their civilizing presence to the inert remains of what was once one of the earth's reptile overlords.

Architectural historian Nathaniel Walker has drawn attention to the way in which Hawkins compared his dinosaur sculptures to houses, their iron columns and cement render equivalent to the 'bones, sinews and muscles' of the extinct reptiles.[57] From the mid-nineteenth century onwards cast and wrought iron and, later, steel, often in combination with glass, created increasingly 'skeletal' structural systems; Walker focused his attention on the interior court of the Oxford University Museum, built from 1855 to 1860. Its iron-and-glass roof canopy was an architectural mirror of the reassembled bones of extinct fauna that were housed within it. French architectural theorist Eugène-Emmanuel Viollet-le-Duc would explicitly reference dinosaur skeletons as an inspiration for modern iron engineering; and the ensuing emphasis by modernists on structural integrity and the stripping away of historical styles increasingly made many buildings resemble gigantic skeletons, most recently evident in the work of Spanish architect Santiago Calatrava.

However, as Walker argued, this skeletal analogy was predicated on a half-truth: the fossilized skeletons of dinosaurs were only partial remains. As scientists now know, back in the Palaeocene the skin of these giant lizards would have been a riot of ornamental colour, much as it still is today in many reptiles and especially in birds.[58] Even Frank Lloyd Wright called for 'plasticity' to remain a key part of any 'organic' architecture, as 'seen in the expressive flesh-covering of the skeleton as contrasted with the articulation of the skeleton itself'.[59] The fact that architectural modernists singled out bones rather than skin as their inspiration seems in hindsight like crude reductionism, a sign of their lack of willingness to embrace the full complexity of what it means to be a living, rather than just a dead, lizard.

Elephant

The structural analogy that many have seen in the bones of extinct dinosaurs reflects a longer-standing reading of gigantic animals as suggestive of architecture. When, in 1758, Charles-François Ribart de Chamoust proposed building his *L'Éléphant Triomphal* (Triumphal Elephant) on the Champs-Élysées in Paris, he was drawing on the colossal size, strength and power of the earth's largest living land animal to make a direct association with the power of France's then King Louis xv, recently victorious in the War of the Austrian Succession. In the mid-eighteenth century, before the establishment of state-organized zoological gardens, elephants were rarely seen in Europe. This proposal for a multi-storeyed, elephant-shaped building reflected the animal's exoticism and rarity; the few that entered Europe from their native habitats in Africa and Asia were highly prized by royal and imperial collectors.[60]

Ribart's elephant was both monument and inhabitable building. Ostensibly a triumphalist celebration of France's monarchic power, and the nation's imperial ambitions, the interior spaces of the elephant were envisioned as a fantastical melding of the artificial and natural. Ribart's drawings showed a dining room that resembled a tropical forest (reflecting one of the native habitats of elephants), a ballroom adorned with mythological figures and allegorical murals, and a subterranean cloister under the gigantic plinth on which the elephant would have stood. Although Ribart's proposal was never executed – the Arc de Triomphe was the eventual choice of monument for this site in 1836 – the idea was later revived by Napoleon Bonaparte in 1810 as a tribute to his own imperial power, in particular his Egyptian campaign (1798–1801). Planned as a monument to the emperor on the site of the former Bastille prison, a full-scale 12-metre-high plaster model was constructed and stood on the site until it was demolished in 1846.[61] While the model was provisional, its colossal scale attracted a great deal of attention, perhaps most notably from Victor Hugo in his 1862 novel *Les Misérables*. Hugo retrospectively described the monumental elephant in architectural terms similar to those perceived in Hawkins's iguanadon: the elephant's legs were 'like temple columns', its interior spaces like the inside of a 'huge skeleton'. But this monument was also disturbingly organic – its gradual slide into dilapidation a melancholy reminder, for Hugo at least, of France's loss of power after Napoleon's defeat. For Hugo, the crumbling plaster left 'wounds in its flanks', 'cracks in its belly', the elephant itself sinking into the ground 'as though the earth were subsiding beneath it'.[62]

These 'phantom' elephant architectures are redolent of a time of unabashed imperialism that, today, seems anachronistic; but other, more whimsical elephant buildings have found a place in a variety of contemporary settings. For example, the giant mechanical elephant constructed by

Sectional view of the Triumphal Elephant, published in Charles-François Ribart's *Architecture Singuliere : l'éléphant Triomphal: Grand Kiosque a la Gloire du Roi*, 1758.

designers François Delaroziere and Pierre Orefice for the Les Machines de l'Île theme park in Nantes is a steampunk kinetic sculpture that variously references the giant sculptural elephant that used to be located outside Paris's Moulin Rouge, the industrial history of Nantes, the novels of Jules Verne and Leonardo da Vinci's drawings of human-machine hybrids.[63] Carrying up to fifty passengers on 30-minute excursions, *Le Grand Éléphant* is a timber-and-steel construction powered by an electric motor, its interior featuring stairwells, a sitting room and, outside, a roof terrace. Equally outlandish is Lucy the Elephant, a 20-metre-tall wood-and-tin pachyderm located on the shoreline of Margate City, New Jersey. It was built in 1888 by property speculator and engineer James Lafferty as a means of luring potential property buyers to the site: the internal staircase leads to an observation deck located in the tower (known as a howdah) built on the elephant's back.[64] The fact that Lucy has survived for more than 130 years is testament to the building finding other uses: variously a tavern, summer rental home and, today, a limited-term Airbnb that pays for Lucy's upkeep as a National Historic Landmark (designated in 1976).[65]

That such an outlandish building as Lucy the Elephant could be realized reflects the way in which the seaside became a site of pleasure in the nineteenth century, allowing for the creation of architectural frivolities that would not be considered appropriate in workaday urban environments. Indeed, Lucy is the only surviving example of a trio of elephant-shaped seaside structures designed by Lafferty on the Northeast coast, the other two being the Light of Asia, a 12-metre-tall elephant that stood from 1884 to 1900 at Cape May, New Jersey, and the Elephantine Colossus at Coney Island, which was destroyed by fire in 1896 just two years after completion. This short-lived monster elephant was a scarcely credible 37 metres tall, within which were seven floors of exhibition and entertainment spaces.[66]

While Napoleon's monumental elephant stood in Paris, the first zoological gardens were finding ways to house real elephants imported to Europe from new colonial outposts. The first was the Elephant Stables designed by Decimus Burton for the Zoological Society of London in 1831. Even as Burton took his inspiration from the British Raj and domesticated elephants of India, this structure referenced the architecture of then-fashionable picturesque gardens of England, creating a hybrid mixture of styles characteristic of early nineteenth-century architecture. Later examples, such as the elephant house in the Berlin Zoological Garden, built in 1873, would reference more directly their 'Orientalist' predecessors, in this case the Royal Elephant Stables of the Gagan Mahal Palace in Vijayanagara, an Indo-Islamic building dating from the fourteenth century. The twentieth-century replacements for both the London and Berlin elephant houses ditched historicized symbolism in favour of a modernist agenda. Sir Hugh Casson's elephant and rhino house at London Zoo (1962–5) was built in the New Brutalist style. Its brick pens, clad in pick-hammered concrete and topped with conical copper roofs, have been described as 'zoomorphic' because they mirrored the shape and texture of the animals they housed. Yet this formal similarity betrayed a lack of engagement with the needs of the elephants, who were relocated in 2001 to much larger premises at Whipsnade Zoo in the Bedfordshire countryside, their London house now occupied by a family of East Indian bearded pigs.[67]

Lucy the Elephant, Margate City, New Jersey, built in 1888 by James Lafferty and pictured here in 2019.

The roof of the former elephant house at London Zoo, designed by Sir Hugh Casson and built 1962–5.

Even as the rationale of zoos has shifted from imperial celebration to conservation and education, these institutions still struggle to replicate the 'natural' habitats of their captive animals. With elephants this is particularly problematic. African elephants range over enormous areas in their native savannah and even the most extensive captive enclosures (namely wildlife reserves) can become stretched if elephant populations get too large. The design solution offered by both Foster & Partners and Markus Schietsch Architekten for their respective elephant houses at Copenhagen and Zurich zoos is to trick the elephants into thinking they are living in a natural forest rather than a prison. Foster's building resulted from careful consideration of the needs of the captive elephants. It created a large enough space for the animals to sleep together (as they would in the wild), maximized thermal insulation for the elephants' physical well-being and recreated familiar natural features, such as scattered pools of water and mud and natural shade. In addition, the glass dome covering the enclosure was ornamented with computer-generated leaf patterns, and the branches

Elephant house at Copenhagen Zoo, designed by Foster & Partners and opened in 2008.

and sand hills at ground level were remodelled each day to keep the elephants interested in wandering.[68] In a similar way, the Kaeng Krachan Elephant Park compound at Zurich Zoo is topped by a 6,800-square-metre timber roof pierced by 271 apertures, giving the dappling effect of a tree canopy. This sense of openness, however, is offset by the steel-reinforced, concrete piers that support the roof – massive structural members designed to prevent the elephants (who can move objects weighing up to 6 tonnes with their heads alone) damaging or even breaking out of the enclosure.[69]

It is provocative to compare these Eurocentric designs for elephant enclosures with a recent architectural project located in the natural habitat of the animals, namely Elephant World in Surin Province, Thailand, designed by Bangkok Project Studio and completed in 2020.[70] Although the project's title makes it seem like an animal theme park, Elephant World is, in fact, a radical attempt to meld the needs of elephants with those of

Elephant playground structure, part of Bangkok Project Studio's Elephant World in Surin Province, Thailand, completed in 2020.

144

humans. The three principal structures – a brick observation tower, an elephant 'playground' and elephant museum – were built as a response to the centuries-old association between elephants and the local Kui people, where 207 domesticated elephants are owned by mahouts (the name given to elephants riders, trainers or keepers throughout South and East Asia). It has been estimated that, of the approximately 50,000 Asian elephants left today (from a population that used to number millions), at least one-third are domesticated, the majority of these now used in the tourism industry or for ceremonial purposes.[71]

The designs for Elephant World take what, in the West, would be regarded as an intractable problem – the distance between elephants and humans – and turn it on its head. Here, as in zoos, the structures are designed for occupation by both humans and elephants, but in Elephant World that cohabitation extends to the entire lifespans of both species. In the centuries-old interactions between elephants and humans in this district of Thailand, 'people believe that elephants are family members and treat them accordingly as if there were some kind of sacredness residing in them.'[72] The elephant playground structure in particular straddles both elephant and human worlds; it is comprised of a vast timber canopy supported on slender concrete pillars that freely mingle design elements for both species – more shelter than enclosure. The observation tower, on the other hand, is meant for human occupation alone, a high vantage point for people to appreciate the interconnectedness of the landscape below. Finally, the museum building speaks more metaphorically of elephants to humans: it tells stories of the local interspecies relationships in history and also offers a place for reflection on the future of these relationships.

What this project challenges is both a reductive understanding of animals as either irrevocably separated from humans ('wild' creatures) and also a simplistic reading of human-animal relations. The fact is that, for centuries, elephants, and many other animals that we would generally like to think of as 'wild', have become hybrid species that are neither wholly wild or fully domesticated. It may be argued that using elephants as a tourist attraction is no better than using them as beasts of burden, or, as was the case further back in history, as agents of warfare; but what is the alternative when there is now no longer a clear distinction between wild and domesticated elephants? Elephant World proposes that design can be a tool to mediate these intractably muddied boundaries between species; indeed, it argues for *more* not less muddying, a full embracing of another animal as already thoroughly entwined with us. Here, architecture decentres the human by intensifying the complexity of a particular interspecies relationship. It is only a shame that we cannot really know how the elephants feel about this.

Ape

It is often pointed out that the eyes of elephants offer compelling evidence of their emotional intelligence; we meet their gaze and find some form of kinship. Yet, looking into the eyes of our closest animal relative, a great ape (whether gorilla, chimpanzee, bonobo or orangutan) can be a profoundly discomforting experience, especially when it occurs in a zoo. Meeting the gaze of an ape in its enclosure, we sense the porous boundary between species, and yet we are also acutely aware of the animal's imprisonment, the hard boundaries of zoo enclosures a stark reminder of our unwillingness to entertain richer forms of kinship. Only those with the necessary expertise – the Dian Fosseys or David Attenboroughs of our species – can breach that boundary, and only with great patience and privilege.

Despite being mostly employed to imprison primates, architecture, in other contexts, can be a fruitful way of framing the connections between humans and apes. Many architectural critics and historians in the nineteenth century were concerned with tracing the origins of the most tectonic of the human arts, especially in light of theories of biological evolution that emerged in the work of Jean-Baptiste Lamarck and Charles Darwin. In 1851 German historian and architect Gottfried Semper argued that human construction evolved from the techniques used to create textiles, the very first walls and roof coverings developed from woven fabrics and wickerwork, as opposed to assemblages of blocks of materials.[73] What Semper did not know was that weaving has a much longer evolutionary history among the great apes. As primatologist Fiona Anne Stewart has outlined, it was only in the early 1930s that it was discovered that all great apes build structures called nests or beds in which to rest and sleep.[74] As far as is known no other primates, apart from humans, build like this. Furthermore, unlike other animal architects – insects and birds – that build structures in which to

Nest created by a Bornean orangutan.

raise their offspring, apes do so simply for their own comfort and protection and, possibly, to exchange information with other members of their social group.

Apes make their nests by bending and breaking tree branches over a foundation of stronger tree limbs, interweaving these smaller branches to create a rigid structure and folding smaller twigs under the edges of the nest to form a secure rim. These circular or bowl-shaped nests are mostly used only once, new nests being constructed every day (Stewart estimated that, on average, a great ape might build 19,000 of these structures over their entire adult lives).[75] Drawing on research carried out in the 1990s, Stewart pointed to a clear link between shelter construction by early humans and nest-building by apes.[76] With hindsight, this research clearly strengthens Semper's earlier thesis, namely that human construction originated in the weaving of materials gleaned from the environment, rather than the building blocks that have so dominated architecture from antiquity onwards.

Anthropologist Tim Ingold has argued that differentiating between weaving and building blocks in architecture is not merely a technological nicety; rather, it involves 'the much more fundamental question of what it means to make things'. On the one hand, if we conceptualize building as the assembling of preformed 'blocks' into larger wholes, then architecture originates in an image of the finished product, a plan or blueprint, manifest today in the panoply of digital images made by designers of buildings to come. On the other hand, architecture conceived as weaving implies a building emerging from the construction process itself, that is, 'within a field of forces . . . established through the engagement of the practitioner with materials that have their own inclinations and vitality'. What Ingold sees in Semper's insight is a mirror of the way in which life itself comes into being through processes of growth and movement. Can it be that the woven nests of the great apes point us towards a radically different way of conceiving and making buildings, a pre-human world that, in Ingold's words, 'is knotted rather than block-built', and where construction is always enmeshed in the world out of which it emerges?[77]

Transpositions of ape and human cultures were and still are a popular theme in both literature and film, many examples of which have used interspecies contrasts as a way of drawing attention to human foibles.[78] Franz Kafka's 'Report to the Academy', published in 1917, is notable for taking a Victorian entertainment – apes dressed up as or performing for humans – and turning it into a highly charged reflection on the author's own tortured identity as a European Jew. Kafka's ape, named Red Peter, was captured and brought to Europe to either perform in music halls or be incarcerated in a zoo; the ape decides to make a virtue of necessity and becomes a great performer by adopting human characteristics, including the capacity for speech. Yet in becoming a socialized human-like being, Red Peter forfeits his right to reproduce: he chooses to become a sterile hybrid – an evolutionary dead end.

The question of interspecies evolution that Kakfa raised to reflect on his own fragile human identity became the focus of a long-running franchise of films beginning in 1968 with *Planet of the Apes,* directed by Franklin J. Schaffner. Based on the 1963 novel by Pierre Boulle, *La Planète des singes* (translated as *Monkey Planet* in 1964), the success of the first film initially spawned four sequels. The entire series was resurrected by Tim Burton's lacklustre remake of *Planet of the Apes* in 2001, and this was followed after a decade by three prequel films at three-year intervals. The central premise is the same in both the original novel and two film series: in the far future, apes have evolved as the dominant species on earth, humans becoming what the apes once were to them, namely, brute beasts that are captured for use by the more evolved species. The 1968 original remains the most significant film in terms of its development of an ape society and it included the construction of an entire Ape City by the film's art director, William Creber. Departing from the modernist-style ape-constructed buildings that Boulle imagined in the source novel, Creber and production illustrator Mentor Huebner produced a series of extraordinary sketches of structures inspired by the organic forms of the Early Christian cave dwellings in Cappadocia and the outlandish Art Nouveau buildings of Antoni Gaudí.[79]

One of Huebner's sketches pictured a structure that closely resembled Gaudí's unfinished Güell Crypt (Colònia Güell), its organic, arborescent forms seemingly hewn from the inside of a gigantic lump of rock; another depicted tulip-like towers, ape dwellings perched on their splayed tops – futuristic versions of the nest platforms real great apes build. Although these extravagant designs were significantly scaled back by mounting production costs, the completed Ape City maintained something of this organic character. The rock-hewn structures, elevated walkways and classical public spaces convey a unique kind of primitive futurism, a settlement where treetop dwelling has been translated into a new kind of architectural language that also seems prehistoric. The melding of old and new architectural forms in Ape City reflected the film's central ruse, namely that the supposed alien planet of the apes is in fact a future earth.

The meeting of the primitive and the modern also formed the central theme of the *King Kong* series of films, from the first in 1933 to, at the time of writing, the latest blockbuster monster-fighting spectacle that is *Godzilla vs. Kong*, released in May 2021.[80] A giant ape's confrontation with the technological city is at the heart of these fictions, climaxing in spectacular scenes of urban destruction and, in the case of the original film and its two remakes, King Kong scaling the city's tallest building. In the 1933 and 2005 versions, this was the Empire State Building, completed in 1931; in the 1976 remake, it was one of the twin towers of the World Trade Center, inaugurated in 1973. Peter Jackson's 2005 remake was created as a homage to the original film: the entire skyline of Manhattan, including the Empire State Building, is a CGI recreation of the 1930s city seen in the original film.[81] The effect of this entirely virtual New York is to distance viewers from the otherwise visceral quality of the film's climactic sequence with Curtiss Helldiver biplanes attacking and killing the giant ape. This may be taken as a response to the still-raw collective memory of the destruction of New York City's tallest buildings by terrorists on 9/11. But resonances nevertheless remain, not least if one also considers the same sequence of events portrayed in the 1976 film, when Kong ponderously scales one of the towers of the World Trade Center. Comparing both sequences, the structural detailing of the Empire State Building clearly made it more amenable to climbing than the blank modernist facade of the World Trade Center, while the tapering spire of the Empire State Building enhanced the drama of the final ape/human confrontation in a way that the flat-roofed World Trade Center does not.

The enduring appeal of both the *King Kong* and *Planet of the Apes* stories demonstrates the way in which apes have come to stand in for what has been repressed by humans; they are avatars from the past that threaten to destabilize the perceived civilized order of Western modernity, which remains most powerfully expressed in metropolitan architectural icons such as the Empire State Building. In light of the horrifying reality of 9/11, the repeated playing out of Kong's eventual defeat by human technologies reads like an increasingly vain attempt to keep those primal anxieties at bay, even as they have so obviously come out into the open already. Perhaps it is time for a new kind of imaginary great ape that makes space for rather than continues to repress those anxieties: a primal ape as a bridge to rather than destroyer of human worlds. I imagine a new version of the film where, instead of rampaging against the city, Kong instead weaves a giant nest between two of New York's skyscrapers, offering a startling simian counter to the human propensity to build up – a living architecture of knots rather than inert blocks.

4
Aquatic

Some 3.7 billion years ago the very first life forms (microbes) emerged in the world's oceans. From then on, until roughly 500 million years ago, the evolution of life continued in this aquatic milieu. Thus, for the majority of evolutionary time, aquatic life was the only life on earth. It is no coincidence that the embryos of many different land-based creatures still look like sea creatures. Tortoises, chickens, pigs, cows, rabbits and humans – to name but a few familiar terrestrial animals – all begin their lives as tiny aquatic embryos with long tails and nodule-like limbs. For humans and most other mammals, aquatic existence comes to an abrupt end at birth, our deep connection to liquid remaining as a strong affinity for or fear of water. In developing lungs, humans have forsaken the life aquatic for a different kind of territory, terra firma, as we like to think of it. But now, with the prospect of a significant rise in sea levels across the planet by the end of this century, that habitat is threatened, not least because we have built so many of our cities close to the sea or alongside tidal rivers.

The principal architectural materials of modernity – iron, steel and reinforced concrete – are highly vulnerable to decay if exposed to water for any length of time, and particularly saline water. The infrastructures of water management (irrigation, dam construction, sewer systems and water pipes) tend to centre on human mastery of this element, the most obvious examples being the rapid growth of desert cities such as Dubai and Phoenix. Reappraisals of indigenous architecture, from Bernard Rudofsky's 'Architecture without Architects' exhibition in 1964 to Julia Watson's 2019 best-selling book *Lo-TEK*, have questioned this arrogant attitude towards water. These counter-modernist voices have demonstrated the ways in which many indigenous peoples have learned to accommodate rather than shun water in their buildings, from the floating islands of woven reeds made by people in Peru and Iraq, to semi-aquatic settlements of houses on stilts in shallow coastal seas and lakes in Lagos, Benin, Myanmar, Chile and the Philippines, to name but a few.[1]

This chapter asks what architects might learn from aquatic animals; it immerses us in this hostile element to think with six animals that, each in their own way, have developed what might be termed a watery intelligence in relation to building. To begin, two very different animals – turtles and oysters – point us to the value of defensive architecture in shielding soft-bodied animals from predators; these two animals also provide insights into the origins of human settlements. The middle part of the chapter focuses on two aquatic animals characterized by both their intelligence and their alien-like quality for humans. First, the soft bodies of octopuses point to a completely different kind of intelligence and agency in both bodies and

Floating reed buildings constructed by the Uros people on Lake Titicaca, Peru, 2015.

buildings; while the companionable nature of dolphins has long been viewed as an opportunity to forge interspecies kinship, often using buildings of one kind or another to house human/dolphin interactions. The final two animals – salmon and beavers – move the focus to fresh water – to the role of streams and rivers in both animal and human-built worlds. Most wild salmon are now dependent on human-built structures, such as fish ladders, to enable them to pass our own edifices (dams, principally), while beavers, reintroduced with great success after being hunted almost to extinction by the end of the nineteenth century, demonstrate the power of more-than-human agents in landscape engineering: the dams, lodges and canals built by beavers are second only to our buildings in terms of their environmental impact.

Perhaps more than any other animals, those that live in water demonstrate that more-than-human life makes worlds 'for itself' and not 'for us'. Aquatic animals also show that land and water are not as disconnected as humans tend to imagine. The Haida people of northwest British Columbia tell of how Raven stole salmon from the Beaver people by rolling up their stream like a carpet. The Beaver people tried to stop Raven by gnawing down the trees he perched in, the bird dropping some of the fish as he was forced to flee. Those discarded salmon formed the great salmon rivers of western Canada, the Columbia, Fraser and Skeena.[2] This story imagines aquatic animals transmogrifying into the very element that brought them into being, an evolutionary reversal that serves to remind us that water and the animals that live in it are inextricably bound to the land in a reciprocal relationship that both nourishes and destroys. As scientists now recognize, aquatic animals that move between the realms of water and land are key to this process of exchange: they transport vital nutrients back and forth as well as often carrying unique ecosystems of tiny plants and animals on their shells or skins. Recognizing the reciprocity of land and water means thinking anew about what we imagine to be the edges of our buildings and cities.

Turtle

Apes may have passed on their nest-building skills to our closest evolutionary ancestors, but other animals also demonstrated ways of building to early humans. In Vitruvius' *De architectura* (*c.* 15 BCE), tortoises, along with swallows, featured as an important inspiration for the first human dwellings. Vitruvius imagined our distant ancestors constructing a shelter around four evenly spaced trees in a forest: the gaps between the trunks infilled with sticks, woodchip and mud to build up the walls of a high dome, the roof of which was covered in leaves and more mud.[3] This 'tortoise style' of building, as Vitruvius termed it, reappeared in the last of his ten books on architecture as a model for the first military structures, which he claimed were square-plan shelters developed to protect soldiers from assaults on their fortified settlements. These tortoise-like huts were imagined as pyramidal structures mounted on wheeled posts that lended them mobility on the battlefield.[4]

Vitruvius' focus on tortoises as embodying a defensive model of architecture reflected the way in which the shells of these animals are perhaps the epitome of defensive construction in the natural world. Tortoises are land-dwelling turtles; many of the 356 known species of turtle bridge both land and water in their life cycles, and they are also extremely long-lived (as I write this in 2022, the oldest known land animal is a 190-year-old tortoise named Jonathan). Turtles are among the most ancient of reptiles and they shared the world with dinosaurs more than 200 million years ago.[5] All turtles have bony shells that are attached to a backbone. Most are polygonal structures comprised of two distinct plates: an upper carapace and a lower plastron. In most species of turtle these two plates are linked together by a supporting structure known as a bridge. The irregular polygonal units of the outer surface of the shell are called shuts and they are made from keratin. Like the shells of molluscs, the soft bodies of turtles are directly connected to their hard shells, the latter having a blood supply and neural network, the whole shell capable of growing and changing over time.

Although turtle shells are primarily defensive structures that allow the soft head and limbs of the animal to be drawn in for protection against predators and the elements, they are also an important source of minerals for the animals, allowing them to regulate the chemical makeup of their bodies during long underwater sojourns.[6] Recent research has revealed turtle shells to be finely tuned defensive structures made up of three distinct layers: a soft outer coating of keratin protects layers of collagen and bone beneath by absorbing shocks from outside, rather like the bumper of a car.[7]

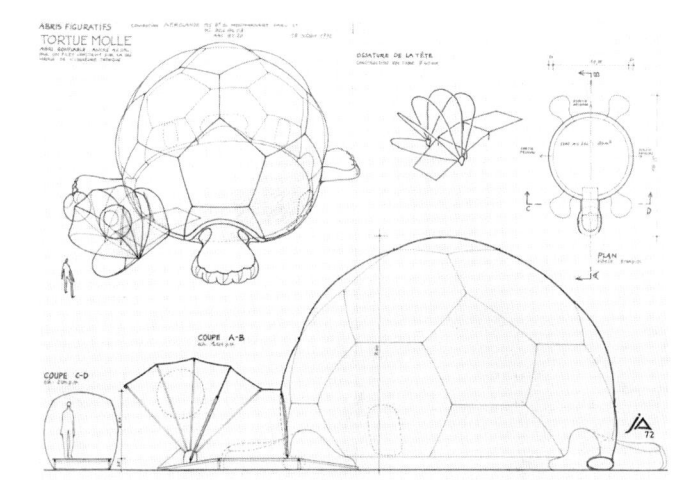

Jean Aubert's *tortue molle* drawing of an inflatable, turtle-shaped structure, 1972.

The subtle interplay of soft and hard materials in the shell of a turtle have a striking human parallel in the work of the Aérolande group of architects, made up of Jean Aubert, Jean-Paul Jungmann and Antoine Stinco. Linked in the late 1960s with the radical left-wing French artists' group Utopie, Aérolande specialized in the design and construction of inflatable structures, many of which were inspired by animals, including turtles.[8] For example, a 1972 drawing by Jean Aubert, titled *tortue molle* (soft-shell turtle), drew on the contrast between a materially fragile, lightweight and easy-to-assemble structure and the perceived hardness and slowness of the turtle. The project's title referred to a family of turtles with soft shells, namely fresh- and saltwater animals that have pliable carapaces that allow them to move more easily in open water.

Pneumatic buildings were a revolutionary departure from late 1960s architectural modernism that was characterized by hard materials (concrete and steel) and dogmatic functionalism. Once the radical fervour of that period had subsided, Aérolande developed a practice that drew on other aspects of turtle symbolism derived from Aesop's famous fable of the tortoise and the hare. Like Aesop's tortoise, the group adopted a slow, incremental method of design, drawing by hand, and developing a poetic approach that drew on mythic images of tortoises as powerfully linked to the ancient past.[9] Aubert's unrealized design for an inflatable turtle building was resurrected in 2018, three years after his death, namely in a proposal for a pavilion for the 16th International Architecture Exhibition in Venice.

This structure was to house exhibits that would tell the story of inflatables in architecture from the 1960s onwards. The giant tortoise would have been inflated inside the pavilion, the soft materiality of the structure questioning the conventional order of human architecture, with lightness, airiness and pliability subverting architecture's 'solid classical shell'.[10] Sadly, the proposal was not commissioned: and Aubert's turtle building remained on the drawing board.

Like elephants, turtles have also been translated more literally into architecture as turtle-shaped buildings. One historical example is the Fukusai-ji Zen temple in Nagasaki, founded in 1628 but reconstructed in the shape of a turtle following the U.S.-led destruction of the city by an atomic bomb on 9 August 1945. Inspired by the eighteenth-century turtle-back tombs in Okinawa, the temple was rebuilt as a mausoleum for Japanese soldiers killed during the Second World War. Here, the long-standing human association of turtle shells with protection was given a literal

Fukusai-ji Zen temple in Nagasaki, built in its present form in the late 1940s.

architectural interpretation. The reconstructed temple was intended to be a fortress of memory that stood against both the U.S.-led attempt to annihilate the city and the subsequent risk of forgetting the terrible human sacrifice of war.

In our contemporary era of ecological crisis, it is unsurprising that turtles have been co-opted as symbols of respect for and conservation of the natural world, perhaps most notably in Legacy Entertainment's vast turtle-shaped aquarium built at Phu Quoc Island in Vietnam in 2020. The building's supposed 'authentic' reference to the historical significance of the turtle in Vietnamese culture is at odds with both its materiality (concrete walls are hardly the epitome of ecological sensitivity) and its function as a place of incarceration for aquatic animals that are treated as objects for humans to 'consume'.[11] Yet, on a superficial level at least, it does reflect the long-standing cultural significance of turtles across East and South Asia. For example, one creation myth in Hindu mythology conceives of the world being carried on the back of four elephants, the elephants in turn supported by the shell of a colossal turtle. This image was adopted by Terry Pratchett for the Great A'Tuin in his Discworld series of fantasy novels. In China, some ancient myths have imagined the turtle as a metaphorical image of the universe itself: the animal's upper shell representing the heavens, its lower the earth, the turtle thus mediating these two cosmic realms just as real-life turtles mediate land and sea.[12]

In the West, the shape of the turtle's protective shell has inspired the design of some military structures, in effect following Vitruvius' association of turtles with defensive architecture. The world's first submarine, developed by David Bushnell in 1775 for use in the American Revolutionary War, was named the *American Turtle* on account of its resemblance to the titular animal.[13] In a different vein, during the early days of the Cold War, American schoolchildren were instructed by an animated turtle named Bert to *Duck and Cover* – namely, to seek shelter in the event of a nuclear attack by the Soviet Union. In the same way that Bert retreated into his protective shell when confronted with danger, it was naively assumed that children would be saved from the monstrous power of an atomic blast by hiding under tables and chairs.[14]

The turtle as the epitome of defensive architecture may have become tragically laughable in the face of the horror of contemporary warfare, but

Aerial view of Yongtai in northwest China's Gansu Province.

it remains a powerful way in which these animals have continued to be imagined by humans. The city of Yongtai in northwestern China, built during the Ming Dynasty (1368–1644), survives today as a reminder of this age-old association. Despite being mostly abandoned, its turtle-shaped ground plan, marked out clearly in its defensive walls, demonstrates quite literally the symbolic power of this animal in conferring a sense of security on a human-built settlement. Today, Yongtai's designation by the Chinese government as a 'cultural relic' protects it against invasive property developers.[15] In the West, that association has resulted in a very different kind of cultural product: the Teenage Mutant Ninja Turtles, which first appeared in 1984 in a comic created by Peter Laird and Kevin Eastman. Originally intended as a gritty satirical take on the clichéd superhero trope, the Teenage Mutant Ninja Turtles became a phenomenally successful global franchise, spawning a long-running cartoon series (1987–96), six films (both live-action and animated), numerous video games and a whole array of merchandise. The four titular turtles inhabit the sewers of New York, having mutated into human-reptile hybrids after a fishbowl containing baby turtles fell into a drain and came into contact with a broken canister of radioactive material.[16]

Absurd as the premise is, the Teenage Mutant Ninja Turtles nevertheless provide an unusual take on what were, by the mid-1980s, pervasive spatial tropes that dominated the imagination of American cities, particularly New York. As literary historian David Pike has elucidated, the underground spaces of the American city were conventionally cast as the natural habitat of monsters, whether animals, such as the giant sewer-dwelling alligator of Lewis Teague's unimaginatively titled film *Alligator* (1980), or 'degenerate' humans, the criminal gangs of Walter Hill's *The Warriors* (1979) being just one of many examples.[17] In the first film adaptation, *Teenage Mutant Ninja Turtles* (1990), comedy largely replaced fear as a response to the urban underground, with the turtles still resolutely social outcasts, but more in the mode of subversive enjoyment than dark deeds. Since 9/11 the American urban underground has once again become a site of cultural anxiety, the satirical edge of the original mutant turtles now seeming rather hollow in the face of the most recent incarnation of the enemy-from-within, even though the film franchise has had another reboot with *Rise of the Teenage Mutant Ninja Turtles: The Movie* on Netflix, released in summer 2022, and further animated features in the pipeline.[18]

Oyster

In 2001 British artist Stephen Turner made a series of cairns out of discarded oyster shells, which he titled *Grotta*. These were located in Whitstable, an English seaside town in Kent famed for its oyster beds since Roman times. Lit by single candles, the grottoes evoked the long history of oysters as an important source of food for humans, evidenced in ancient shell middens left behind by our distant nomadic ancestors and oyster-shell structures built by enterprising street children in Victorian London during the city's annual oyster feast on St James's Day (25 July).[19] Turner's luminous oyster cairns were a reminder that animal architecture might come into being as an unintended consequence of human activity: oyster building as waste dump or the result of inventive child's-play.

Although shell middens still exist today, mostly as waste left by industrial-scale oyster farming, only rarely do the carapaces of these molluscs become incorporated back into human-built worlds. One such example is Fadiouth, an island south of Dakar, Senegal. Formed over thousands of years by the

One of Stephen Turner's *Grotta* sculptures, created in Whitstable in 2001.

accumulated shells of dead or discarded mangrove oysters, Fadiouth and associated smaller islands are environments where the human and the natural are enmeshed in a remarkable way. Unsurprisingly, the local economy has long been centred on oysters. Residents of the archipelago travel in canoes from one island to the other to fish for the oysters that fill the surrounding lagoons. Houses on the principal island, which is joined to the mainland by a footbridge, are embedded with oyster shells, the island's streets lined with them. In addition, sea defences are built out of oyster shells, while bodies in the communal cemetery are interred under oyster-shell mounds. The 'natural' elements of this environment too have become dependent on oysters: the baobab trees that grow there mine the calcium contained in oyster shells to ensure their healthy development.[20] Places like Fadiouth demonstrate that there need not be a clear distinction between the worlds made by humans and those created by other animals, even ones that seemingly have virtually nothing in common with us. The fleshy bodies of oysters possess no recognizably human features, while the animals pass their adult lives in complete seclusion inside their self-constructed gnarly shells – sheets of tissue or mantle grown by oysters to protect their vulnerable flesh. Pre-dating the emergence of humans by hundreds of millions of years, oysters are also extraordinarily ancient animals; as a species they have inhabited the kind of deep time humans can barely imagine.[21]

Despite their alienness, oysters are now being co-opted by humans in their attempts to mitigate the likely future effects of climate change. In 2010, landscape architect Kate Orff, founder of the Manhattan-based practice SCAPE, exhibited her self-penned 'Oyster-tecture' as part of the Museum of Modern Art's 'Rising Currents' exhibition.[22] This was a speculative design project that proposed using oysters to clean the heavily polluted Gowanus Canal in Brooklyn, eventually enabling the growth of new eco-systems of both marine and human life. Oysters would become the 'keystone' species that would attract many others, while their presence would reinvigorate the local human population to reconnect with nature. The oysters would also once again become a food source for the city that historically had been abundant in New York's harbour until pollution and overfishing rendered its waters uninhabitable for oysters.[23] Orff's speculative proposal gained a lot of attention in 2010, but its rationale was transformed in the wake of Hurricane Sandy in 2012, which revealed in stark terms New York's

Oyster-tecture, developed for the Museum of Modern Art exhibition 'Rising Currents' (2010) by SCAPE in collaboration with Bart Chezar, Hydroqual Engineering, MTWTF, the New York Harbor School, NY/NJ Baykeeper, Paul Mankiewicz and Phil Simmons.

extreme vulnerability to the likely future effects of climate change. Thereafter, Oyster-tecture became about protecting the city from future storms, a 'living infrastructure' that would supplant conventional methods of building coastal defences.[24]

In its transformation from Oyster-tecture to a Living Breakwater, Orff's proposal has also moved from concept to reality: the project has been awarded $60 million of funding from the u.s. federal government and will eventually create defensive chains of artificial oyster reefs in New York's harbour. The Billion Oyster Project has teamed up with Orff to grow hundreds of millions of oysters in artificial tanks, many of which will be overseen by children attending some of New York's high schools. In addition, millions of discarded oyster shells collected from the city's restaurants will be used to form a substrate on which the living oysters can attach themselves. It is hoped that a robust reef system will be well underway by 2025.[25] The scale of the project has also generated other architectural spinoffs, including the Billion Oyster Pavilion, winner of the 2015 City of Dreams Pavilion Competition, and built to be disassembled and turned into an oyster habitat, and a proposed headquarters for the Billion Oyster Project, a building that literally straddles human/oyster worlds – at once office, research facility and educational space where cultivated oysters can be studied.[26]

In co-opting oysters to become 'living infrastructure', Orff's project transforms conventional notions of infrastructure as the artificial bedrock of entirely human-centred activities; here it is oysters, rather than humans, who will build part of the city's infrastructure; moreover, oysters, in fact, *are* the infrastructure itself. Yet in the project's conception, oysters remain thoroughly instrumentalized by humans; sustaining animals is really about sustaining human life. As Stephanie Wakefield and Bruce Braun argue in relation to the project, 'what matters today is not what oysters are – their texture and taste – but what oysters *do*, individually and collectively.'[27]

But what, for humans, *are* oysters? From antiquity onwards that question has tended to focus on human observers trying to imagine what life would be like inside a shell, what Gaston Bachelard has described as a particularly intense but happy kind of solitude.[28] Scottish naturalist Edward Forbes offered a philosophical reading of the oyster's interior life in 1852 when he described an undisturbed oyster bed as 'a concentration of happiness in the present', the 'soul' of each individual oyster 'concentrated on itself . . . its whole body throbbing with life and enjoyment'.[29] Such enjoyment, what Forbes termed 'the beatified existence of an Epicurean god', has also been, for many humans, a key part of the experience of eating oysters. For example, Seamus Heaney's 'Oysters' (1976) describes how the poet's sense of space expands as he gorges himself on raw oysters: his tongue 'was a filling estuary', his 'palate hung with starlight' as he imagined the ocean pouring through 'millions of [oysters] tipped and shucked and scattered'.

The paradoxical expansion of the human imagination in the face of the closed-in life of the oyster was also characteristic of French writer Francis Ponge's prose-poem *Le Parti pris des choses* (Siding with Things), first published in 1942.[30] Anticipating the methodology of Object-Oriented Ontology mentioned earlier in this book, Ponge aimed to reinvent language by returning afresh to everyday objects, to open up human understanding to the singular existence of things themselves, animal or otherwise. For Ponge, the act of eating an oyster was both brutish – prising open the closed world that held just a morsel of food – and suggestive of an entire phenomenological world. The vulnerable oyster, with the protection of its shell, lives 'under a firmament (strictly speaking) of mother-of-pearl, the heavens above sinking into the heavens below'.[31]

Returning to architecture through an imaginative anthropomorphism invites us to go beyond conceiving of oysters as simply a novel kind of infrastructure that ultimately serves only our needs. In the mid-sixteenth century French ceramicist and landscape architect Bernard Palissy designed a series of shell-like chambers to be built in gardens as places of retreat, and which 'should not seem to have been man-built'. Taking inspiration from oysters, Palissy envisaged the exterior walls of these chambers as rough and rocky surfaces; their interiors, by contrast, 'as highly polished as the inside of [an oyster] shell', the latter effect attained by building up layers of enamel and then melting the material to fuse it together as one piece.[32] As elucidated by Bachelard, Palissy's imagined oyster-tecture centred on the human desire to live in a shell: '[Palissy] wants the walls that protect him to be as smoothly polished and as firm as if his sensitive flesh has come in direct contact with them.' This, according to Bachelard, is 'inhabiting in terms of touch', expressing a human sympathy with a being that already does this.[33]

Construction from within (the mollusc's motto, according to Bachelard) means living to build a house, rather than building a house to live in. Yet oysters also need something to build *on*, a material substrate on which the innumerable tiny shell-less young oysters, known as 'spat', can get a secure purchase. Over time that original substrate becomes the oyster shells themselves – the resultant 'reef' the living infrastructure envisaged by the Oyster-tecture project. In cultivated oyster beds across the world, the materials used to create these first substrates are dictated by local environmental conditions: lime-coated tiles are used in France, submerged bamboo wigwams in Japan, bundles of birch twigs in Norway.[34] But these substrates can be any suitable object. In the mid-nineteenth century a certain Mr Payne of Blackheath assembled a collection of objects on which oysters had grown, including an 'old-fashioned champagne-bottle' salvaged from the wreck of HMS *Royal George*, which sank in 1782, and a Chinese teapot without a spout dredged from the River Fal in Cornwall.[35] In a different vein, in 2000 artist Philip Ross assembled a 7-metre-long metal frame, which he sank in Tomales Bay, California, in order to grow an oyster sculpture. The finished artwork, completed in 2003, is startlingly different from what confronted Ross when he hauled up the metal frame in 2002. The cleaned-up sculpture is bone-white, with the dead oyster shells joined together to form a structure resembling a gnarly spinal column sprouting numerous legs. What first emerged from the depths, however, was a fleshy monster: the oysters were covered with thick oozing seaweed that the artist thought 'reminiscent of something internal, bodily . . . all pink and orange and fleshy and drippy'.[36]

That fleshiness is a reminder that oyster-tecture can never be separated from the teeming aquatic environment in which it is formed and sustained. Oysters quite literally live and breathe their medium: water. Their hard shells are not a protection against the world but rather a means by which they can live more comfortably within it, ceaselessly sloshing and shucking the medium in which they dwell. And just as climbing plants, lichens and mosses will take over human-built walls if allowed, the outside of an oyster shell itself provides a rich substrate on which other life forms can proliferate.

Octopus

Some 600 million years ago, long before the dinosaurs ruled the earth and when the ocean was still the only place where life fermented, an evolutionary fork developed that separated vertebrates from molluscs and arthropods. Until recently it has been assumed that intelligent life evolved on just one side of this fork, the branch that would eventually lead to humans, mammals and birds. It is now known, however, that it did so on the other branch too and today it is generally accepted by marine biologists that cephalopods – octopuses, squid, cuttlefish and nautiluses – are not only the most intelligent invertebrates, but probably as intelligent as any other animal in the sea and many on land. With the exception of nautiluses, cephalopods either internalized or lost their shells completely during their long evolution, probably in order to improve their ability to hunt for prey. At the same time, though, their soft bodies became much more vulnerable to predation. Thus cephalopods needed brains – the wherewithal to outwit predators – to stay alive. The result is that, over immense periods of time, intelligent life has evolved at least twice by very different means.[37]

The body of an octopus is what makes it such an alien creature to humans; with almost no hard parts at all, bar a 'beak' hidden by tentacles, the octopus has a body of 'pure possibility' – the creatures transform their body shape almost continuously and can squeeze into the tiniest of spaces, as well as changing their colour at will as a form of camouflage or mimicry.[38] Octopuses have brains (not in their heads but in their throats), and they also have a separate nervous system in each of the eight tentacles attached to their heads; the dozens of suckers on each tentacle directly and independently perceive the world through a highly developed nervous system. It is no wonder that the bodies of octopuses, and particularly their tentacles, have often led humans to imagine them as extraterrestrials, from the inscrutable but friendly heptapods in Denis Villeneuve's 2016 film *Arrival*, to the monstrous shape-shifting Thing that terrorizes a group of men in the Antarctic in John Carpenter's 1982 film.

To compensate for their lack of protective body architecture, octopuses spend most of their lives hiding in dens, usually holes or crevices in rocks and other hard objects. Such is their attachment to their dens that, for millennia, fishing for octopuses has required no bait: from at least Roman

Still from *My Octopus Teacher* (2020) showing a common octopus constructing a defensive shelter from discarded shells.

times, fishermen around the world have simply dropped empty clay pots to rest on the sandy bottom of the sea, each attracting an octopus that then refuses to leave, even when hauled up by the fishermen.[39] Octopuses have also been observed building dens on the hoof – at the beginning of the documentary film *My Octopus Teacher*, filmmaker Craig Foster discovers a common octopus (*Octopus vulgaris*) in the shallow seas off the South African coast covered in an array of shells that the animal had assembled to disguise itself from a predator. In another case reported in Indonesia in 2009, an octopus was observed carrying two halves of a coconut shell, which it assembled into a hide when threatened. This ability of octopuses to assemble and disassemble objects and put them to use is a remarkably human-like skill and one that is extremely rare in other animals of any kind.[40]

The two hundred or so known octopus species vary greatly in terms of their respective sizes: the smallest is just 2 centimetres across, the largest, the giant Pacific octopus (*Enteroctopus dofleini*), over 6 metres. When humans imagine octopuses, such as the mythic kraken, they are often very large indeed; scaled up to a colossal size, the natural intelligence of octopuses is almost always subsumed by their monstrously destructive behaviour. Since the 1920s an extraordinary number of pulp comic books have featured on their covers malign octopuses (alien or otherwise) attacking humans,[41] while science-fiction and horror cinema have often featured giant cephalopods as incarnations of destructive chthonic powers. In cinema these range from the literal – *It Came from Beneath the Sea* (1955), where an American atomic bomb test inadvertently creates a giant octopus that wreaks havoc on San Francisco – to the metaphorical, the tentacled alien of *The Untamed* (2016) bringing both sexual pleasure and destruction upon a couple in a troubled marriage.[42] Key historical reference points for these numerous portrayals of octopus-like monsters are Victor Hugo's 1866 novel *Les Travailleurs de la Mer* (The Toilers of the Sea), which was an international bestseller in both its French and English-language editions; and the Norse myth of the kraken, an undersea monster of colossal size and cephalopod-like appearance, most famously brought to life in Alfred Lord Tennyson's eponymous 1830 poem (but also described as a real creature in antiquity by Pliny the Elder).[43]

Monstrous octopuses have also been readily employed as metaphors for human endeavours that become unbridled in their ambition or geographical scale. In the United States a range of monopolistic companies, from the Steel Trust to John D. Rockefeller's Standard Oil, were sometimes represented by their opponents as outsized octopuses wrapping their tentacles around iconic American buildings, such as the Capitol. In Europe political opponents were occasionally pictured as voracious cephalopods: imperial Russia, for example, was the 'Black Octopus' for some in Britain. In 1898 the French military were pictured in the American magazine *Puck* being led by a monstrous octopus, a comment on the alleged corruption and antisemitism of the institution at that time.[44] In Clough Williams-Ellis's 1929 book *England and the Octopus*, the titular animal was London in the 1920s, its tentacles the city's arterial roads and mushrooming suburbs that threatened to consume the English countryside. The cover of the first edition depicted a bowler-hatted octopus wrapping its tentacles around a picturesque English village. It is the unbounded body of the octopus, the proliferation of its grasping limbs, that offers such a powerful image of aggressive expansionism of human-built empires, whether political, monetary or territorial in nature.

The sense of the octopus's body as 'pure possibility' has led some to try to imagine an architectural equivalent of such boundlessness. H. P. Lovecraft's most famous short story, 'The Call of Cthulhu' (1928), introduced an octopus-like creature that has become an influential precedent for fantasy writers such as China Miéville (his 2010 book *Kraken* bringing together Lovecraft and ancient myths centred on the giant squid). Lovecraft's story charts the accidental emergence of the ancient god Cthulhu, a monster that is part octopus, part dragon/reptile and part human, from the depths of the South Pacific after an earthquake disturbed its underwater kingdom. The sailors who stumble across the site see parts of a 'nightmare corpse-city' called R'lyeh emerging from the sea, before catching a glimpse of the horrific Cthulhu creature itself. They describe a city where 'all the rules of matter and perspective seem upset': a 'non-Euclidean' architecture of distortions, 'crazily elusive angles' and dimensions that did not correspond to any human unit of measurement. Architectural forms that first appeared to be convex suddenly became concave, while the positions of normally stable objects – sea, sun and sky – suddenly became 'phantasmally variable'. No wonder then that this sudden eruption of a thoroughly alien city drove a great architect mad as he experienced visions of this city far away in his dreams.[45]

In Lovecraft's story, pure possibility in architecture has no positive outcome: the tentacular alien god and his non-Euclidean city are harbingers of primal chaos, thankfully returning to the bottom of the ocean but nevertheless always threatening to re-emerge again. Yet, the alienness of the

'The peril of France – at the mercy of the octopus', *Puck*, 1898.

Installation by Group X, Filthy Luker and Pedro Estrellas in an abandoned warehouse in Philadelphia, 2019.

octopus body, and its intelligence, might generate more positive correspondences, the writing tentacles of cephalopods seemingly invitations to connect with myriad life-worlds beyond our own. A very literal architectural interpretation of this is found in the creation in 2017 of a 24-metre steel-framed octopus (inspired by the kraken myth) that was mounted on top of a dilapidated u.s. Navy fuel barge, which had survived the Japanese attack on Pearl Harbor in 1941. This ship/octopus hybrid was purposefully sunk in a bay in the British Virgin Islands in 2017 to provide a substrate for the growth of a new coral ecosystem, while also acting as an education centre for marine researchers and local students from the surrounding islands. In effect, the sculpture will be completed by the marine life it is intended to attract, including coral, sea sponges, sharks, turtles and octopuses, who might find ideal dens within the folds of the steel kraken itself.[46] Even though this project has a strong sense of the corporate about it (it was kickstarted by billionaire Richard Branson), looking beyond its surface spectacle reveals a potent and accessible vision of architecture melded with the environment in which it sits.

In fact, it is now fairly commonplace to encounter octopuses in architecture. Every Halloween some companies offer giant inflatable octopus tentacles for property owners to fix on their buildings to suggest a kraken-like invasion. One such example with twenty giant tentacles, conceived by art collective Group X and made by British street artists Filthy Luker and Pedro

Estrellas, was installed inside an abandoned building in Philadelphia in 2019. It is considered to be the largest example to date of such tentacular architecture, the spectacular effect of the artwork deriving from the straight-forward formal contrast between the right angles of the building and the writhing tentacles, and also between architecture's hard, static surfaces and the soft, undulating octopus limbs.[47] It is an unsophisticated spectacle, to be sure, and one that has been commercialized to such an extent that the powerful visual effect has been somewhat hollowed out over time. But read in purely architectural terms, it flags up quite literally the way in which the 'body' of architecture generally conceived by humans is so limited and bounded compared to that of an octopus. Letting the tentacular body into the hard carapace of architecture might yet free it up to explore less fixed ways of being in the world.

Dolphin

Octopuses demonstrate how a high level of intelligence can evolve in bodies and minds very different from our own; another, more charismatic aquatic animal, the dolphin, shows how the evolution of brainpower has occurred in yet more animal pathways. Around 35 million years ago, the animals we now call dolphins abandoned the security of life on land for one entirely in the ocean. Mammals like ourselves – air-breathing, warm-blooded, birthing live offspring and equipped with complex brains – dolphins (the Delphinidae family of Cetaceans) were once hairy quadrupeds, fishing for prey in rivers and shallow seas. Around 15 million years after returning to the sea, they had acquired the form we would recognize today: an aerody-namic body shape, almost hairless rubbery skin, flippers (the evolutionary successors to limbs) and a dorsal fin for ease of swimming.[48] Many dolphins seem to smile, lending them an animal charisma that is bolstered by their reputation as being friendly towards humans.[49]

Casting aside this benevolent image, it is worth considering just how alien a mammal a dolphin is, a consequence of its evolutionary path being so different to most other mammals. Science-fiction writer Jeff VanderMeer captured this alien-quality in a chilling image in *Annihilation* (2014), the first of his Southern Reach trilogy. On an expedition to Area X, a for-bidden zone in Florida where an alien intelligence has caused all DNA to spontaneously mutate, the female protagonist witnesses a pair of dolphins breaching in a canal, one of which rolls and looks at her 'with an eye that did not, in that brief flash, resemble a dolphin eye to me. It was painfully human, almost familiar.'[50]

VanderMeer's disquieting image works against the grain of the human imagination of dolphins that is rooted in numerous ancient myths about their helpful actions towards people. When Plutarch observed that dolphins seemed to offer us friendship without asking for anything in return, he was drawing on the myth of the musician Arion, who was thrown into the sea by sailors intent on stealing his earnings, only to be rescued by a dolphin who heard him playing an ode to Apollo on his lyre. In Greek mythology Apollo had once transmogrified into a dolphin to secure a cohort of priests for the temple of the Oracle at Delphi. These classical dolphin myths grew out of the geographical setting of ancient Western cultures, namely the shores of the temperate seas of the Mediterranean. They were reflections of human encounters with these animals that captured their perceived sociability, intelligence and interspecies friendliness. They probably also reflected early examples of 'mutualistic' behaviour between humans and dolphins, first described by Pliny. From antiquity, dolphins have been taught by humans to herd fish in return for a meal of their own.[51] Ancient dolphin myths have also been captured in architectural form in Michael Graves's postmodern Disney World Dolphin Resort (1990) in Florida, the characteristic, but anatomically inaccurate, historical image of the dolphin scaled up into a gigantic ornament.

In the 1960s American neuroscientist John C. Lilly began exploring the potential for genuine interspecies communication between humans and dolphins. A prolific author and subject of two Hollywood films, *The Day of the Dolphin* (1973) and *Altered States* (1980), Lilly had first studied dolphins at Marine Studios in Florida, the first aquarium where cetaceans had been successfully kept in captivity (since 1938).[52] In 1960 Lilly purchased a property on St Thomas in the u.s. Virgin Islands, which he then converted into a house for both humans and dolphins, living there with his family and visiting researchers, including, for a time, renowned anthropologist Gregory Bateson. Although essentially captive animals, the three dolphins that lived alongside Lilly and his team – named Peter, Pamela and Sissy – were housed in a sea pool that was cleansed by the tides, with the research

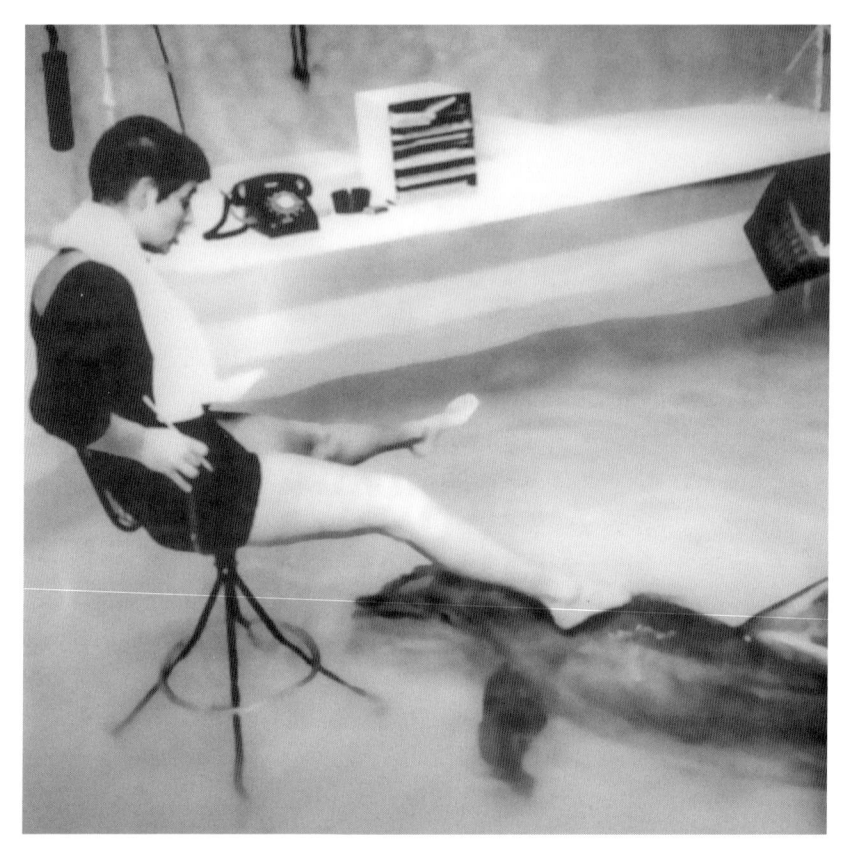

Margaret Howe Lovatt and Peter the dolphin in John Lilly's dolphin lab in the 1960s, as seen in *The Girl Who Talked to Dolphins* (2014).

laboratory situated above. One of the visiting researchers, Margaret Howe Lovatt, recounted how she lived with Peter in a room deliberately flooded so she could always be close to the animal, even when she was asleep. Most controversially, the sexual encounters she initiated with Peter were later sensationalized by *Hustler* magazine in the 1970s. Despite her radical immersion in Peter's daily life, the many attempts to train him to understand and respond to human language all failed. The laboratory closed in 1966 and the dolphins were transferred to appalling conditions in Miami. Nothing is said about what happened to Pamela and Sissy, but it is claimed that Peter took his own life by simply ceasing to breathe.[53]

An architectural project that was directly inspired by Lilly's unconventional research was American collective Ant Farm's unrealized Dolphin Embassy, conceived and developed between 1973 and 1978, after which the collective – Chip Lord, Doug Michels and Curtis Schreier – dissolved following a disastrous fire that destroyed their studio and most of their archive in San Francisco.[54] A strong zoological thread runs throughout Ant Farm's work, from the group's name that evoked the 'underground' collective work of insects to the inflatable structures they built in the form of snakes and turtles. Dolphin Embassy was their most ambitious attempt at creating an interspecies architecture.[55] Curtis Schreier's ebullient drawings show a mixture of biomorphic structures that would be inhabited by both humans and dolphins: sail-like wings that would propel the vessel; multilevel waterways for the dolphins to swim in and interact with humans; and underwater 'steerable foils' that resembled cetacean flippers. At the centre of the mobile structure was the 'Brain Room', the technological heart of the project where humans and dolphins would interact through computers, video recordings and sonar-recognition software. The Dolphin Embassy was effectively John Lilly's human/dolphin habitat scaled up and injected with a heady dose of the psychedelic drug culture that Ant Farm had embraced in the late 1960s.

Schreier's drawings include the evocative motif of an entwined human and dolphin, a mark of the project's debt to the extreme lengths to which Lilly, Lovatt and other researchers went in their attempts to communicate with dolphins. Like Lilly's laboratory, the Dolphin Embassy dissolves the objective distance of the scientific process. It also works against normally comforting realizations of domestic space; here, according to Tyler Survant, an environment is created 'in service of radical diplomacy with "alien" life'.[56] There's also a strong political dimension to the Dolphin Embassy in that it moves away from conventional anthropocentric notions of diplomacy towards the cultivation of interspecies friendship. The project is also 'siteless' in its unspecified oceanic location, lying outside traditional territorial boundaries and very much in line with the way that humans have often imagined life on the oceans to be socially and politically liberating.[57] This may presume a certain arrogance on the part of humans – the sea as frontier for radical experimentation – but it is nevertheless grounded in an emancipatory politics of inclusion, the human and more-than-human both transformed in the process of cohabitation.

Given its radical credentials, it is unsurprising that the Dolphin Embassy was never built, although a small-scale version of the project was almost

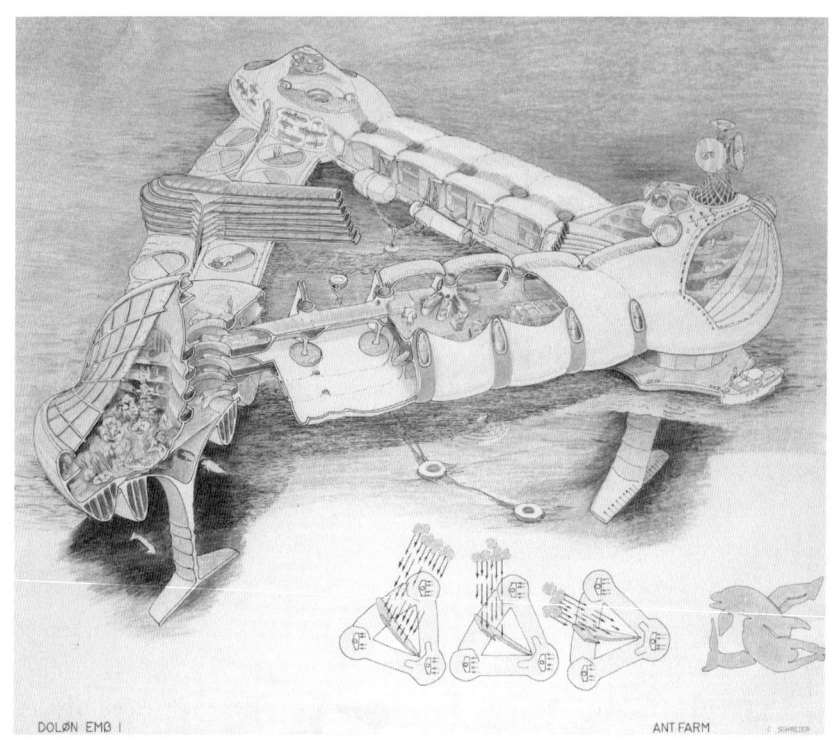

Ant Farm, Dolphin Embassy (drawing by Curtis Schreier), 1975, hand-coloured brownline.

given the green light in Australia, after Ant Farm visited the country in 1976.[58] But the project's core principle of cohabitation with dolphins remains a powerful way in which humans continue to imagine life with these animals, and nowhere more so than in the now controversial 'petting pools' included in many aquariums around the world. These are shallow pools where visitors can approach and stroke captive dolphins, which is probably highly stressful for the cetaceans but regarded as a beneficial form of therapy for developmental disorders in humans, such as autism. Here, the connection between dolphin and human is seen as offering some form of healing, a therapeutic effect grounded in human ideas of dolphins as innately intelligent, spiritual and friendly creatures.[59]

More often, though, the two hundred or so oceanaria worldwide that keep dolphins do so for the animals' spectacular displays of swimming, diving and leaping, often precisely choreographed by their trainers. Although dolphins have been kept in captivity for public display since 1938, the past few decades have witnessed a transformation in aquarium design that has seen ever-larger tanks being constructed to satisfy demand for ever-more spectacular cetacean displays.[60] This has resulted in an extreme disconnect between the avowed ecological credentials of aquariums (and their role as places of research and conservation) and the carbon-guzzling infrastructure that is required for dolphins to live and perform in artificial environments. Perhaps it might be better for aquariums to be designed with their infrastructure made visible, as indeed they often were when first constructed in the nineteenth century (albeit, then, without resident dolphins). Instead of masquerading as 'wild' spaces, aquariums might openly display their innumerable pipes, pumps, filters, humidity controllers and lighting systems to demonstrate the technological basis of dolphin husbandry. Then visitors would understand the life-support systems required not only by captive dolphins, but by all animals that live in artificial structures, ourselves included.[61]

Increasingly, though, there is a sense that keeping dolphins in captivity is in itself inherently problematic, not least because no artificial tank, however large, can come close to the unbounded ocean (and dolphins cover vast distances in their lifetimes). In tandem with initiatives to outlaw human contact with dolphins, some existing aquariums are planning to return their captive animals to the sea. In 2014 Baltimore's National Aquarium commissioned architects Studio Gang to design a seaside sanctuary to replace the city's urban aquarium.[62] The plans were unveiled in 2016 but, as of 2022, no progress had been made in the transfer of habitats. A 2016 rendering of the proposed sanctuary, however, shows the dolphins still performing for

Studio Gang's proposed National Aquarium project for the relocation of Baltimore's existing oceanarium.

a group of tourists, accommodated in the new sanctuary on piers and viewing platforms. In maintaining the centrality of spectacle, this proposal falls far short of the embodied engagement that would have been demanded by the Dolphin Embassy. The notion of returning captive animals to the wild may be seductive, fulfilling, as it does, the human desire for some kind of restorative ecology; but in reality, for any animals that humans choose to engage with, and particularly those we prize so highly for what we regard as their companionable natures, there really is no hard boundary between the domesticated and the wild – in our very act of engaging with dolphins, we change them as much as we change ourselves.

Salmon

Interspecies thinking has been central to the cosmologies and everyday lives of indigenous peoples across the world since time immemorial. In the First Nations of the North Atlantic and North Pacific, the keynote species was salmon: early nineteenth-century accounts by colonial travellers revealed entire cultures steeped in what was then a superabundant resource. On the Snake and Columbia rivers in present-day Washington State and Oregon, these travellers found a panoply of structures and materials centred on salmon, including wooden scaffolds built at Celilo Falls to gain safe access to the swirling waters in order to catch the fish; numerous barns where dead salmon were hung up to dry; even sheets of the fish's scaly skin lining baskets to make them waterproof.[63]

Today, although those cultures and the fish they depended on are mostly gone, destroyed or displaced by the ravages of colonization and the despoliation of rivers by pollution and hydroelectric dams, there is a growing feeling that salmon could once again become the keynote species in the Pacific Northwest. In 2003 Portland-based company Ecotrust formed Salmon Nation, an organization inspired by the 1999 book *Salmon Nation: People, Fish, and our Common Home*, edited by Edward C. Wolf and Seth Zuckerman. Transcending national borders, Salmon Nation is defined by salmon, rather than human, geography, stretching all the way down the Pacific coast from Alaska to northern California and inland to the fish's spawning grounds hundreds of miles upstream. United by a desire to build a bioregion 'where people, culture and nature all thrive', Salmon Nation promotes community storytelling and skill-sharing and has, to date, established a widely distributed network of participants from both indigenous and non-indigenous communities.[64] Key to the venture is the desire to bring resources, from food to finance, back into common ownership, with the geographical reach of the salmon itself pointing to a different kind of organization of human-occupied territories.

Architect Yongwook Seong's 2018 student project, Becoming Salmon, provides a local realization of Salmon Nation values in an imagined future Vancouver that has sunk beneath rising seas caused by global warming. Partially returned to its First Nation inhabitants, this sunken city of the future is also inundated by salmon, seen swimming between submerged skyscrapers in one of Seong's visualizations. Annual parades, marking the time each year when salmon head upstream to spawn, would see people dressing up as salmon, while helium-filled salmon-shaped balloons tethered to outsized fish eggs would float above the city.[65] This radical vision of a city reshaped in the image of salmon has been realized in a very different form on the shoreline of Seattle. The redevelopment of the city's Elliott Bay Seawall, partially completed in 2016, has attempted to reconnect salmon with their 'highways', namely the rivers to which the adult fish return from the ocean to spawn (almost always to the same place where they were hatched). Seriously disrupted by the industrial development of Seattle's waterfront, the salmon now have a refuge. The project involved raising the local seabed using a habitat bench made up of sand and gravel cushions stacked alongside the base of the seawall. The cantilevered promenade above was surfaced in glass blocks to allow sunlight to penetrate the waters below, encouraging plant growth and helping the salmon to better navigate the waters.[66] In very different ways, both of these projects have attempted to reintegrate salmon back into urban life by opening up spaces for them to coexist with us, and not just as a source of food, but also other more intangible forms of nourishment.

Another way of making room for salmon in the human-built world is to mitigate the disruption of the fish's life cycle that has come in the wake of the human transformation of rivers. Although spawning salmon have had to overcome man-made obstacles in rivers for many centuries (principally weirs), it was only with the construction of large-scale waterwheels and dams on rivers from the nineteenth century onwards that irrevocably disrupted the salmon's ability to move upriver. Fish ladders, or fishways, are design interventions that allow salmon and other spawning fish to pass otherwise insurmountable barriers such as dams, locks and weirs. The first modern fish ladder was built in 1830 by Scottish engineer James Smith on the River Teith to enable salmon to safely pass the waterworks of a cotton mill. This consisted of a series of low steps cut into the river that controlled the velocity of its water to enable fish to pass.[67] By the 1950s these structures had grown to enormous proportions: for example, the concrete steps of the fish ladder at Bonneville Dam on the Columbia River in Oregon span 60 metres in vertical height. A variety of designs now facilitate the movement of salmon up and downriver: baffle fishways are symmetrical closed-space baffles inserted into a channel to redirect the flow of water; fish elevators literally pick up salmon from a collection area and lift them upstream to

An image from Yongwook Seong's Becoming Salmon project, 2018, showing a parade held in honour of salmon in a future Vancouver.

Fish ladder constructed at Lopwell Dam, Devon, 2010.

continue their journeys; while fish cannons use a pneumatic tube to suck in salmon and gently propel them upstream. The drawback of most of these design solutions is that they do not address other problems associated with the construction of hydroelectric power stations, such as the many fish killed by underwater turbines. Fish ladders are also often ill-equipped to deal with migratory species other than salmon, particularly sturgeon and bass that do not have the ability to surmount these obstacles as easily as salmon do. Research has found that by far the best way to help migratory fish species is to remove dams and power stations altogether.[68]

Fish ladders are built to help wild salmon maintain their intergenerational attachment to specific places; the salmon eaten by humans are mostly a very different kind of fish, namely one that is farmed – today, almost a separate species from wild salmon. In the nineteenth century the first attempts were made to spawn salmon in purpose-built hatcheries, but it was not until the 1960s that the full life cycle of the fish was successfully accommodated in human-built structures. Norway pioneered these fish-farming technologies, building floating pens anchored by cables in sheltered sea fjords; while Scotland followed suit in 1969, the USA and Canada in the 1980s and '90s and, more recently, Chile.[69] In July 2021 the Norwegian government unveiled its new aquaculture strategy, which aims to produce 5 million metric tonnes of farmed salmon and trout by 2050, almost five times the volumes in 2022.[70] This would require almost every suitable coastal site in Norway to be exploited, as is already the case in much of western Scotland. Although farming salmon seems to be an ideal way of mitigating the dwindling numbers of wild fish, it comes with many problems, including the proliferation of diseases and parasites in cages packed with fish, as well as the huge quantities of salmon faeces that leach into surrounding waters. Some farmed salmon inevitably escape their pens, leading to increasing prevalence of disease among wild fish, particularly the deadly fungal infection furunculosis.[71] Design solutions now involve building land-based closed tanks for the salmon, an expensive alternative to current practices but one that is driven by the developing technology of closed-loop aquaculture systems, which raises smolts (young salmon) in secure pens before transferring them to sea cages as adults.[72]

With growing concern being expressed about the environmental impact of intensive farming, it is no surprise to find architecture being coopted as a public relations tool for fish farming. September 2022 saw the opening of a high-tech visitor centre, the Salmon Eye, at seafood company Eide Fjordbruk's fish-farming site in Hardangerfjord, Norway. Designed by Danish company Kvorning Design & Communication, the Salmon Eye's biomorphic form, as might be expected, is inspired by close-up photographs of a salmon's eyeball, while the hexagonal metal cladding panels resemble the scales of the fish's skin. Inside, visitors see the farmed salmon swimming around the glass walls while learning about the ways in which they are farmed, experiencing aquaculture, according to the designers, in 'an interactive and sustainable way' while also engaging in debates about the future of fish farming.[73] Given the Norwegian's government's current plans to massively increase salmon farming, the familiar rhetoric of sustainability in the promotion of the Salmon Eye rings hollow. Biomimetic design is problematic when the supposed naturalistic forms of the building serve to distract from the very real environmental problems caused by the practices it celebrates. There is a clear danger here of architectural 'greenwashing', the process of conveying a false impression or providing misleading information about how a company's products are more environmentally sound than others.

There is, however, another way in which buildings might take their inspiration from salmon. In the native villages of Russia's far east and in northern Japan, indigenous peoples have been curing salmon skins and making clothes from their leather for centuries. Meanwhile, this particular human use of salmon has added a novel element to European fashion design, despite having only limited success to date. In the early 2000s the Irish Salmon Skin Leather Company began marketing a range of bags, belts and wallets made from salmon skins. At the high end of the market, the Chilean designer Claudia Escobar, who now lives in Scotland, established the SKINI brand for a range of salmon-leather jeans and bikinis, worn by such celebrities as Kim Kardashian West.[74] There was even a salmon-skin sporran. These products were made from salmon skins that would otherwise be discarded in processing plants, since they are usually an unwanted part of the fish when it becomes human food. Although there is a world of difference between clothing and architecture, it is possible to imagine discarded fish skins as the basis for a new range of textiles and upholstery that sees architectural fixtures and fittings quite literally becoming salmon, the iridescent fish skins creating dazzling ornamental surfaces. Instead of covering over the uncomfortable truths about our relationship with these fish, salmon architecture would instead draw attention to them, reminding us in the intimate spaces of our homes that animals from outside are still present, the waste of what we have consumed turned into shimmering silver.

Beaver

It is not only human-built structures that obstruct migrating salmon moving upstream: so do beaver-built dams. Beavers construct dams in order to transform rivers and streams into the habitats they desire, namely deep, still ponds that surround their lodges – the beaver's home, a mound structure built from countless tree branches that are secured with mud. Only accessible underwater, the lodge is the protected centre of the animal's self-made world – beaver pairs remain together for life and, if possible, will hand down their lodge to successive generations of offspring. To create the still waters they desire, beavers sometimes build several interconnecting dams as well as canals that link their ponds to new sources of timber and food. In short, beavers are landscape architects; it is said that the sound of running water triggers beavers to build – an environmental cue that activates cognitive processes within the animals that manifest physically in sticks, mud and water as beavers repair leaks, create short-cuts in meandering waterways, or mend broken dams. As with termite mounds, a beaver's self-built world has been described by Richard Dawkins as a powerful example of the extended phenotype, namely a way in which the genes of an organism exert their influence beyond merely biological boundaries. In the case of beavers, that extension of influence often reaches many miles outside any individual animal's body.[75]

Beaver architecture only gained sustained attention after the colonization of North America by Europeans from the seventeenth century onwards. By then the Eurasian beaver (*Castor fiber*, a different species from the North American beaver, *Castor canadensis*) was in rapid decline. Eurasian beavers had been prized since antiquity for both the supposed therapeutic qualities of their powerful musk (castoreum), and also their fur, regarded as without peer in the creation of hard-wearing, wide-brimmed hats. North American beavers were equally valued for their skins and the westward colonization of the continent quite literally followed the animals as they retreated to escape slaughter. Early settlers believed that beavers built in teams that were sometimes hundreds strong, the animals working together in complete harmony. This was a powerful projection of the settlers' desire to build a perfect society, the beavers seemingly offering a pre-existing model for the settlers to emulate.[76] Nowhere was this beaver utopianism expressed more strongly than in Lewis Henry Morgan's book *The American Beaver and His Works* (1868). A railway lawyer by training and best known for his ethnographic studies of the Iroquois Native Americans, Morgan became fascinated with beavers in the early 1860s after visiting a new stretch of railway near the southern shores of Lake Superior that was being built for the company of which he was a director and shareholder. The illustrations that accompanied *The American Beaver* revealed hitherto unknown levels of beaver ingenuity: in the 124 square kilometres studied by Morgan were an extraordinary 63 beaver dams, ranging from 15 to 150 metres in length, the resulting ponds covering anything from 0.1 to 64 hectares, interspersed with many lodges, burrows and artificial canals.[77]

Morgan not only disproved the idea that hundreds of beavers were involved in the construction of dams (it is just one family that builds in any given territory); he also revealed the architecture of beavers' social relationships. Even as the animals were being relentlessly exterminated by trappers – the very railways Morgan invested in only perpetuated the animals' desperate retreat westwards – they were also elevated to intelligent beings motivated by more than instinct alone. According to Morgan, unlike social insects (bees, wasps, ants and termites), beavers were not driven by a 'struggle for existence', but rather to enhance their own well-being and sense of contentment: 'When a beaver stands for a moment and looks upon his work, evidently to see whether it is right, and whether anything else is needed, he shows himself capable of holding his thoughts before his beaver mind; in other words, he is conscious of his own mental processes.'[78] In attributing self-awareness to beavers, Morgan explicitly challenged the long-standing Eurocentric view of animals as 'brutes' that operated according to innate instincts rather than conscious agency.[79] He also went further, arguing that beavers learned their building skills through experimentation; Morgan discovered that every single beaver lodge, dam or canal was different, each structure a considered response on the part of a beaver family to the local environmental conditions. Morgan's conclusion was a strident challenge to human exceptionalism: if humble rodents were capable of creating extraordinary works of engineering, how much more might human designers

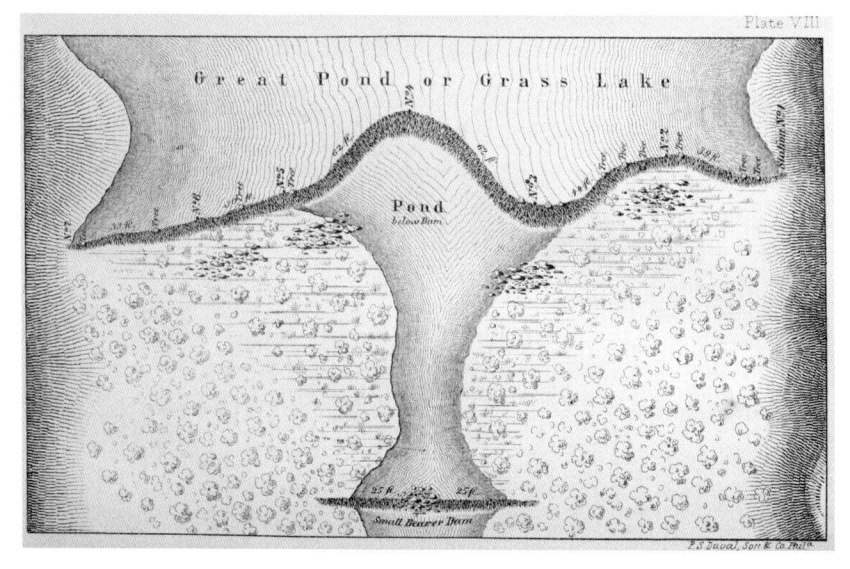

Map of dams constructed by beavers near Lake Superior in Lewis Henry Morgan's *The American Beaver and His Works* (1868).

Still from *Grey Owl's Strange Guests* (1934) showing a beaver's lodge built inside Grey Owl's cabin next to Lake Ajawaan, Saskatchewan.

accomplish? More than a century later, Austrian-American architect Bernard Rudofsky would resurrect Morgan's beaver-reverence in his call for architects to rediscover their animal instincts to counter the straitjacket of modernist dogma and technological progress. Rudofsky recast instinct as a positive virtue for both animal and human builders alike, offering as it did a way back to spontaneity, play and intuition in architecture that modernism had seemingly expunged.[80]

Canada also had its own famous beaver aficionado: Archibald Stansfeld Belaney, better known as Grey Owl. He was the country's original 'pretender', a faux-Native American who was born in England and emigrated to Canada in 1906, where he subsequently reinvented himself as Grey Owl. Subject of a number of films in the late 1920s and early 1930s, as well as an author and lecturer in his own right, Grey Owl drew on the romantic traditions of Henry David Thoreau and Ralph Waldo Emerson in casting himself as a voice of the wilderness. In the 1930s Grey Owl was recruited by the Dominion Parks Branch (today Parks Canada) to work as a caretaker in Prince Albert National Park in Saskatchewan. He was tasked with introducing a colony of beavers there to highlight the virtues of a simple life spent close to 'wild' nature.[81] The 1934 documentary *Grey Owl's Strange Guests* presented the startling image of a beavers' lodge constructed half inside and half out of Grey Owl's lakeside log cabin, the everyday life of this particular animal and its partner (named Jelly Roll and Rawhide) bound up with that of Grey Owl himself.

The film's narrative of cosy domesticity, with the beavers presented as the embodiment of gentle innocence, contrasts sharply with this discomforting image of cohabitation.[82] Beavers and humans may share many behavioural characteristics, but their architectural tastes are clearly starkly opposed; the thoroughly organic mound of sticks and mud that straddles the inside and outside of the rectilinear cabin is a stark reminder of the human propensity for neatness and order in architecture, particularly when it comes to our homes. Beaver architecture, by contrast, is highly mutable, forever accommodating destruction, abandonment and renewal in a way that human-built structures rarely do (unless, of course, they are already in ruins).[83] In a digital image published in March 2019, satirical online journal *The Onion* pictured a beaver dam built in the style of modernist architect Paul Rudolph, its stacked rectilinear agglomerations of sticks and mud an absurdist swipe at the fetishizing of geometrical purity by many an architect, and particularly those, like Rudolph, who fully embraced modernism.[84]

Today, beaver populations in both Eurasia and North America are healthy and increasing, a consequence of widespread reintroduction programmes from the 1920s onwards.[85] Biologists now regard beavers as keystone species, ecological engineers that can increase biodiversity, especially populations of aquatic insects, amphibians and birds. For so-called beaver believers the animals can do substantially more, namely mitigate the worst effects of global warming. Beavers' dams retain and slow the flow of water, giving it time to soak into the ground; this helps to put a brake on flash floods, the increasing incidence of which is firmly linked to anthropogenic climate change. Beavers have even been reintroduced into urban waterways; the first animals were spotted on the Bronx River in New York City in 2007 after a two-hundred-year absence.[86] This recent view of beavers as ecological saviours tends to underplay their autonomy as builders: in reality, the areas flooded by beaver dams can disrupt human activity, the beavers being indifferent to our desire to control their behaviour for our benefit. Elaborate devices that minimize the sound of running water are sometimes employed to fool the beavers into *not* building, a strange but entirely predictable consequence of our instrumental thinking when it comes to animals.

Perhaps, as the OPSYS design group proposed in 2018, we should instead allow beavers full autonomy to build as they please. In their speculative proposal for a 'decolonized' future Manhattan, Central Park has been taken over by beavers.[87] Seeing the iconic park as a monument to colonial power, OPSYS's radical proposal would allow beavers to 'hijack' New York's waterways and decolonize the park as it is returned to the indigenous peoples who first inhabited the site centuries ago. In this project, the flooding caused by beavers works as a powerful metaphor for the overturning of a colonial history characterized by the extermination of humans and non-humans alike. Even putting to one side the overtly political implications of this proposal, it is clear that current notions of 'reintroduction' are deeply flawed. Beavers build in a way that is contrary to the human valuing of constancy and linearity; they also always build beyond the control of humans, despite our attempts to trick them into becoming our agents. If we are to live alongside beavers in the future, we will need to come to terms with *their* agency as builders, with all the mess and uncertainty that this entails.[88]

OPSYS's speculative proposal for the re-wilding of New York's Central Park, *Damn It: A Beaver Manifesto*, collage adapted from original base infrared photograph by Paolo Pettigiani, 2018.

The 'Woman-Beaver' myth of the Haida Nation of the Haida Gwaii archipelago, separated from the coast of British Columbia by the Hecate Strait, tells of an interspecies encounter where it is a human and not a beaver that is transformed. In this story, a young woman marries a great hunter, whose long absences lead the woman to spend more and more time swimming in the pond beside their wilderness cabin. Eventually, she and her children are all transmogrified into beavers, the returning hunter searching in vain for his family until he realized that his wife has become an animal: her long hair turned into luxuriant fur and her domestic apron a beaver's tail. This story speaks of the porous boundary between humans and other animals. It reflects something about the way beavers, like many other animals, seem to mirror our own behaviours; in the case of beavers, building and maintaining a home while ensuring its viability for future generations. The Woman-Beaver story uses anthropomorphism as a way of identifying with, rather than bringing to heel, animals; just like humans, beavers build to satisfy their own needs for comfort, peace and shelter.[89]

5
Domestic

Colombian pop star Shakira was walking in a Barcelona park in September 2021 when she was attacked by a pair of wild boar. Fortunately she was able to fend off the animals without sustaining any injury; the boar, it seems, were only after the contents of her handbag.[1] Shakira was but one of an increasing number of people in Barcelona and other cities in the Global North that have been confronted by these aggressive animals in recent years. This is a consequence of urban growth, of cities butting up against mainly non-human habitats: in the case of Barcelona, this is the Serra de Collserola Natural Park. As urban sprawl drives some species out of their dwindling habitats, others, such as wild boar, take advantage of the proximity of humans, venturing into the unfamiliar urban environment to scavenge our superabundant wastes.[2] The increase in confrontations with wild boar in cities, most recently resulting in the imposition of 'curfews' on residents in parts of northern Rome after a spate of attacks and a fear that victims might not be found before they came to any harm,[3] is but one instance of a strange reversal of the general tendency of human-animal relations in cities in the Global North. The history of modern cities has been marked by the gradual removal of animals from the streets and the imposition of increasingly hard boundaries between what count as domestic and wild animals. Today, in some U.S. cities, even as you might encounter a wild boar, neither cats nor dogs are permitted to roam freely, a situation that was very different only half a century ago.

This final chapter focuses on a range of animals that are now classed as domesticated, moving from what would generally be termed pets (dogs and cats) to livestock (horses, cows, pigs and chickens). More than any other type of animal, domesticated ones are imbricated in human-built worlds. The majority of pet-owners may not build houses for their dogs or cats (those 'shelters' are mostly reserved for unwanted animals), but they nevertheless allow these animals to share their domestic and urban spaces, to a greater or lesser extent depending on personal preferences or local legal codes. As we will see, dogs and cats make sense of human-built worlds in ways that force us to question whether we really know our pets beyond our characteristic tendency to anthropomorphize their behaviours.

When we consider livestock, these relationships to architecture are much more direct. In the case of horses, this principally means their housing (stables) and spaces and structures associated with horse-riding. Now mostly straddling the border between pets and livestock, horses were once the most numerous non-human animals that lived and worked in cities, in their role as the principal method of transportation of both people and goods. As the chapter will show, the radical change in the status of horses is reflected in concomitant changes in the housing built for them. The final three animals – cows, pigs and chickens – chart the relationship between architecture and animals that we consume (and, in the case of cows and chickens, the animals' own bodily products). Unfortunately, this amounts to an increasingly depressing litany of architectures of incarceration, especially in what is now the predominant factory-farm system developed for livestock husbandry. For animals destined for human consumption, their lives are usually very short and generally bleak, with every aspect of their environments controlled by humans, from their housing to the architecture of their genes. Mostly kept well hidden from the public eye, the lives of these animals are often characterized by almost unbelievable levels of suffering, stemming ultimately from humans regarding them as solely utilitarian units for their own consumption.

In considering livestock and architecture, this chapter tries to mitigate a highly dispiriting reality with a focus on alternative ways of housing livestock, whether that means a return to small-scale husbandry or the development of more awareness and positive responses to animal welfare. I would not go so far as to argue that the only humane response to animal welfare is to become a vegetarian or vegan (even though, in my case, as a result of writing this book, both meat and poultry have become distinctly unappetizing); rather, there is a more general point to be made about trying to see livestock as much more than simply utilitarian objects for human use. The long history of human domestication of animals arguably began with a very different kind of set-up, namely a symbiotic relationship between humans and wolves that was as much about what the wolves gained from humans as the reverse. Being open, through a sympathetic imagination, to unexpected connections with familiar animals can be a far more effective tool in promoting care for livestock than the shock tactics of animal-rights activists' exposées. To truly build *with* animals in mind means much more than simply turning one's back on them as livestock, however well-intentioned that action may be. Rather, it means holding out hope for co-creation in a world where we are already intractably entwined with the lives of so many animals, whether we like it or not.

Dog

Dogs and humans have lived alongside one another for at least 12,000 years and certainly before humans first began to practice agriculture and live in permanent settlements.[4] Thus, humans and dogs have effectively co-evolved. Although this interspecies relationship is always asymmetric – namely, human owners/subservient dogs – it nevertheless offers opportunities to encounter animals as partners, albeit ones that are 'significantly unfree', in Donna Haraway's words. In her 2008 book *When Species Meet*, dogs are portrayed as simultaneously willing companions to human partners (in all forms of play, particularly), captive lab subjects, 'designer' pets, therapeutic extensions of disabled humans and competitors in sports events. Disrupting commonly held views of dogs as essentially tamed wolves (and therefore inferior to them), Haraway offered a provocative and disquieting sense of dogs as bound to humans in all sorts of conflicting ways; humans and dogs as not really separate species at all but rather thoroughly entwined.[5] The earliest archaeological evidence of the emergence of the domesticated dog is a poignant confirmation of this: a 12,000-year-old stone tomb in what is now northern Israel containing a human skeleton with one hand resting on the skeleton of a puppy.[6]

To a large extent, Haraway's research was based on her own relationships with dogs and most dog owners (in the UK in 2021 this represented about

26 per cent of adults, with 9.6 million dogs between them) would likely confirm her findings, albeit without the insights from academic critical theory. Excepting the relatively few dogs that are confined to kennels, the overwhelming majority of pet dogs live in their owners' homes, sharing as much space (and as many furnishings) as they are allowed. It is perhaps unsurprising that the growing list of accessories for pet dogs now includes a huge variety of miniature homes, human-designed canine architectures that range from mass-produced beds and baskets to architect-designed dog-houses. The long-running travelling exhibition 'Architecture for Dogs' (2012–), together with spinoffs such as the Dogchitecture Expo in Mexico in 2013, have showcased dog houses designed by such high-profile firms as MVRDV. Many of the exhibits were illustrated in the popular 2018 book *Pet-tecture*; a few designs are available to download by dog-owning readers.[7] Most are formal variations on the kennel, orthogonal structures that tend to reflect long-standing anthropomorphic readings of dogs as essentially miniature humans (and therefore desiring small-scale versions of our dwellings). A few of the designs, however, question this human-centred approach by fusing human and canine habitats: for example, Seungji Mun's Pet House (part of the architect's Pet Furniture Collection) is a gable-roofed dog house that sits in between two sofas.[8] In a different vein, 07BEACH's Stairs for Dogs provides two parallel sets of stairs – one for a small dog, the other for the dog's owner – in a house in Ho Chi Minh City.[9]

As acknowledged in *Pet-tecture*, architects' involvement in the design of dog homes stems in part from the burgeoning commercial market for pet accessories, especially in the USA, rather than as a direct response to the actual needs of dogs themselves.[10] Indeed, observation of the habits of my own pet dog Charlie, acquired as a puppy in March 2020, reveals a quite different canine relationship with domestic space. Unlike many puppy owners, we chose not to force Charlie to sleep in a crate. As a consequence, he generally finds little pleasure in occupying spaces or structures apart from our own (and it may be argued that habituating a puppy to a crate is in fact an anthropocentric projection designed to impose strict boundaries between human and dog spaces in the home). Charlie chooses to occupy the home entirely as a consequence of our actions, seeking at all times to remain close to whoever happens to be around at the time (but he invariably prefers the company of my wife). His designated spaces are therefore entwined with

07BEACH's Stairs for Dogs, 2012.

ours, excepting a pet-shop-acquired bed that he only sleeps in when a human is nearby (he is sleeping in it as I finish this sentence). While some dogs seem to feel safest in a den-like space, reflecting their habits in the wild, most are content with a very loose design intervention, for example a special rug spread over a favoured spot on a bed, carpet or sofa.

Philippe Rahm's *Maison dédomestique* (unhomely house) short film from 2011 provided a more nuanced take on architecture for dogs than the mostly conventional kennel-like homes featured in *Pet-tecture*. In this film, Rahm focused on the difference in the average body heat of dogs and humans, offering a bespoke sleeping space for a dog above a human bed, a space with a lower air temperature for the comfort of the dog.[11] Although this proposal enacts a spatial segregation of pet and owner, it does so here not to assert human control over dogs, but rather in response to the differing needs of two species, a design that is unusually sensitive to the actual physiology of dogs. In calling this project an 'unhomely house', Rahm also drew attention to the ways in which the animal needs of dogs disrupt those of humans. As I discovered myself, allowing or preventing those disruptions is very much

Image from Philippe Rahm's short film *Maison dédomestique*, 2011.

Sir John Soane's design for a dog house in the form of a classical temple, 1778.

part and parcel of what it means to own a dog, especially one that is acquired as a puppy.

Housing dogs that are not domestic companions has a much longer history than the trendy dogchitecture of recent years, for it was only in the twentieth century that dogs were largely separated from the utilitarian work they have undertaken for humans ever since their domestication more than 12,000 years ago. Dogs' powerful sense of smell (at least 100,000 times more sensitive than humans') has long made them especially useful aides for hunting other animals for food and, later, for sport. Dogs are also pliable animals, meaning that they can be trained for a large variety of tasks, particularly the herding and guarding of livestock (and even, in one case in the film industry, flying an aeroplane). Architecture for working dogs generally takes the form of kennels, which are enclosures for housing individual dogs or packs. In the eighteenth century many elaborate kennels for hunting dogs were constructed on the estates of the aristocratic classes in England and France. These were often designed in the manner of garden follies (known as *ferme ornée* in France) to fit with the tradition of picturesque landscape design that emerged in this period.[12] Surviving examples in the UK include kennels resembling castles, Gothic chapels, Palladian houses or rustic Italianate buildings.[13] In 1778 eminent architect Sir John Soane designed an extravagant dog house for his friend, the Lord Bishop of Derry. Although unexecuted, this grand classical building nevertheless embodied what many completed kennel buildings of that period sought to achieve, namely a powerful status symbol for the dogs' aristocratic owners (arguably just what today's dogchitecture does for wealthy dog owners). Soane's design also featured a central rotunda that was a common spatial feature of animal enclosures of this period: the classical Doric order of the dome's supporting columns 'civilized' the animals, as well as arranging their individual homes in such a way as to facilitate surveillance by their handlers.[14]

As architectural historian Sandra Kaji-O'Grady has observed, domes still feature prominently in architecture for dogs that are used by humans for purposes other than companionship, a prominent example being the Mars Petcare Global Innovation Center near Nashville, USA, completed in 2014. A nutrition research facility, the 180 or so dogs kept in this centre live in groups of 24 in each of the complex's seven circular buildings; every individual dog pen includes an inner area for sleeping and eating and an outside pen accessible through a dog flap. The architectural emphasis on transparency has been interpreted by O'Grady as not simply a means of exerting human control over the dogs, but rather of the human handlers (one per dog) too. The handlers must be continually attuned to their canine charges and sensitive to any change in the animal's well-being. The behaviour of the dogs, in turn, directly affects the training plans developed by their handlers. The canine-human relationship here is far from equal – clearly the dogs have very limited say in the organization of their lives – but it does demonstrate that the work done here is a product of dogs and humans quite literally living together in shared spaces.[15]

Something very different happens when dogs escape the confines of domesticity, whether that is a home, laboratory or research facility. According to the Dogs Trust Stray Dogs Survey report in 2018, 56,043 feral dogs roamed built-up areas and the countryside in the UK, this in a country where stray dogs are barely tolerated.[16] In cities in India and the former Soviet Union, free-ranging dogs are a serious problem, spreading diseases to humans through their bites and faeces. Even in the USA, with its strong cultural taboos on feral dogs, hundreds of thousands of strays are euthanized each year due to a lack of space in dog shelters and those willing to adopt them as pets.

Two recent films demonstrate what is proving to be an ongoing cultural preoccupation with feral dogs: *White God* (2014, dir. Kornél Mundruczó), a fictional account of dozens of stray dogs rising up against cruel people in modern-day Budapest, and *Stray* (2020, dir. Elizabeth Lo), a documentary film centring on a group of stray dogs in Istanbul. Both films attempt to capture canine perception, mostly by means of very low camera angles, subtle use of focus and careful attention to sound design. In both films, it is the marginal spaces of cities – brownfield or construction sites, alleyways and ruins – that provide necessary places of respite for what are precarious canine existences lived mostly at the very edge of human tolerance. There is also a poignancy in the feral dogs' ability to find succour in the most unlikely of places: for example, in one scene in *Stray*, a dog sleeps on the edge of a busy traffic intersection in Istanbul, cars beeping at the seemingly oblivious animal. Both films also make links between stray dogs and human outcasts in cities: in *White God* this is implicit, the army of brutalized strays a mirror of the negative policies towards migrants enacted by Hungary's authoritarian prime minister Viktor Orbán; in *Stray* it is explicit, a group of teenage Syrian refugees adopting the dogs as they eke out a desperate existence in the ruins of the rapidly changing European/Asian metropolis.

Despite their often brutal depictions of human mistreatment of stray dogs, both films end with affirming if enigmatic images of interspecies connection: in *Stray* the principal canine protagonist howls in harmony with the early-morning Azhan being proclaimed from a nearby mosque;

The final scene in *White God* (2014).

while the group of revolutionary dogs in *White God* are soothed by a plaintive tune played on a trumpet by a teenage girl: the final aerial shot reveals dozens of dogs resting peacefully in front of the girl and her father, who both mimic the dogs' poses by lying face down in the street. These tentative but striking images hold out the hope of interspecies care in the face of everyday brutality; they suggest that connections can be found and nurtured between what humans despise and what they love. Those connections go wider too, breaking down the often entrenched divisions that humans living in cities are generally apt to make between nature and culture, art and life and wildness and domesticity.

Cat

The documentary *Stray* was made in part due to the success of an earlier film, *Kedi* (2017, dir. Ceyda Torun), which centred on the lives of seven stray cats in Istanbul. While the dogs in *Stray* are explicitly linked with the city's human outcasts – homeless Syrian refugees – the felines in *Kedi* are, in stark contrast, esteemed by a wide range of urbanites they cross paths with, including shopkeepers, cafe and workshop owners, artists and children. These seven cats (just a tiny proportion of the thousands that have roamed free in Istanbul for hundreds of years) are valued in *Kedi* as totems of human attachment to the city. As the opening narration states, they embody 'the indescribable chaos, the culture and the uniqueness that is the essence of Istanbul'. Such a symbolic identification of animal and city extends to the ways in which cats occupy Istanbul's spaces: in *Kedi* there is a distinct emphasis on verticality: skilled climbers, these feral cats traverse the vertical layers of the city at will; they also find shelter beneath its surfaces, whether in crevices under pavements or in dark corners of buildings (also the favoured habitats of the rats they predate). In contrast to the camerawork of *Stray*, which stays hunkered to the ground, the cinematography of *Kedi* often lifts us above the streets to convey a sense of animal freedom, the cats' acrobatic abilities reflecting a human longing for liberty.

This is undoubtedly a romantic view of feral cats. *Kedi* is unabashed in its celebration of these urban animals. In more overdeveloped countries, quite the reverse is often true. For example, in some cities in the USA cats are required by law to be kept permanently indoors (although there is enormous variation in cat ordinances across the country).[17] Even so, it is estimated that there are between 25 and 80 million feral cats in the USA (compared with more than 58 million felines there that are classified as pets).[18] In recent years the dominant policy adopted towards feral cats has been Trap-Neuter-Return (TNR), which its proponents argue is a humane way to gradually reduce their numbers (as opposed to simply killing them). The Los Angeles-based 'Architects for Animals' initiative has, since 2010, raised the profile of TNR programmes by asking architects to design shelters for feral cats in both Los Angeles and New York City, and exhibit the resulting structures at the charity event FixNation, the proceeds of which fund TNR projects. In contrast to the fanciful dog homes illustrated in *Pet-tecture*, the cat shelters designed for 'Architects for Animals' are generally characterized by a raw aesthetic that befits the environments in which stray cats generally live. For example, in 2017, d3architecture exhibited their 'Alley Cats' shelter, a 2-metre-square steel frame infilled with discarded heating, ventilation and air conditioning units, with a sheltered wooden box positioned at its centre.[19] In 2019 the same design team welded together an assemblage of discarded food crates to create another shelter for feral cats. The utilitarian aesthetic of these structures reflects the problematic status of feral animals – as opposed to sequestered pets – in many U.S. cities.

In *Kedi* the residents of Istanbul seem much more tolerant of the fluid boundaries between domestic and feral animals. Some have built shelters of their own for the city's stray cats, ranging from discarded cardboard boxes temporarily housing newborn kittens to makeshift shelters built by local people on green- and brownfield sites scattered around the city. Since cats are much more sensitive to places than dogs (the latter generally attuned to people first and foremost), they require safe, secure and warm spaces in which to sleep and, more importantly, to raise their young (whether they are domesticated or feral). Also in contrast to dogs, cats have retained much of their wild behaviour despite thousands of years of domestication. Part of the reason for this is cats' intractability. It is much more difficult to train a cat than a dog: this stems from the fact that the principal use of cats to humans (rodent control) does not require a great deal of evolutionary change on the part of the cat. Thus the shelters that today's cats need are still closely tied to those they fashion in the wild, variations on the nests in which kittens are always born, whether wild, domesticated or feral. Of course, this has not prevented commercial exploitation of all kinds of products for pet cats but, unlike those created for dogs, these tend to be designed to accommodate cats' unique behaviour as animals. Examples illustrated in *Pet-tecture* include numerous scratching posts (sometimes incorporated into shelters), structures featuring built-in thread for feline play and furniture designed to accommodate both cats and humans. LYCS Architecture's CATable 1.0, for example, features hollow

d3architecture, Alley Cats shelter, 2017.

Takeshi Hosaka Architects, Inside Out house, Tokyo, 2010.

spaces cut into a wooden table that are designed to satisfy feline curiosity as its human user carries out his or her daily tasks.[20]

In some cases, entire rooms – even whole houses – have been remodelled by architects to serve such interspecies needs. Cats that are kept permanently indoors must adapt not only to much smaller territories than they would normally have if allowed outside, but a lack of stimulation for their heightened senses. The six 'cat-friendly' houses illustrated in the online magazine *Dezeen* in 2016 featured an array of design features, including elevated walkways, stepping-stone shelving and dedicated doorways for feline occupants, to offset feline stress.[21] The Inside Out house in Tokyo, designed by Takeshi Hosaka Architects for a couple and their two pet cats, attempted to bring the lost outdoor environment back to the sequestered cat.[22] The house is comprised of a fully enclosed series of living spaces surrounded by a porous outer shell: the walls and roof are pierced with openings that allow light, wind and rain to enter, nourishing the needs of the pet cat as well as the plants that grow inside.

Owners of cats are often quick to acknowledge their entanglement with their pets. Indeed, some will scoff at the very concept of cat ownership, such is the animal's perceived independence from humans. Cats are regarded as highly self-contained and self-assured animals, quietly pursuing their own agendas that are inaccessible to human perception but nevertheless powerfully evident. Historically, these feline characteristics have readily been associated with human femininity. And just as male commentators have often been troubled by what they perceived as women's spatial transgressions, particularly in cities, so analyses of cat behaviour often centre on their territorial nature, perhaps most graphically in the BBC documentary series *The Secret Life of the Cat* (2012–13), in which fifty pet cats in a village in Surrey were fitted with GPS collars to track their movements, which were visualized as lines on digital maps. These maps revealed a complex but well-ordered network of mostly very small individual feline territories (usually extending no more than 100 metres from their respective homes, less in cities). The TV series also revealed just how tenaciously cats patrolled and defended their individual patches. The maps visualized an entirely separate feline geography existing alongside our own, one where property boundaries imposed by humans, such as garden fences and walls, are completely ignored by the cats.[23] Indeed, for cats, walls and rooftops are not boundaries at all, but rather the feline equivalent of our pavements and roads. Individual cats reduce the likelihood of conflict with other animals by each moving outwards from their homes in different directions, the pattern of the collective territories resembling the petals of a flower, the lines of feline movement like the mesh of string that gets formed between two human hands in the children's game cat's cradle.

In some cities where free-roaming cats are accepted, design has played a role in helping cats move around more easily. Researched and documented by photographer Brigitte Schuster, cat ladders are scaffold-like constructions – variously taking the form of ramps, steps, even spiral staircases – that are attached to the facades of apartment blocks and which facilitate the movement of pet cats from their homes to the streets below (and vice versa).[24] Some of the ladders are standalone structures constructed by a single cat owner; but many others are interconnected, some even straddling four or five storeys of individual buildings. Most cat ladders are informal additions outside of the remit of planning authorities. As Schuster discovered, the many cat ladders in Bern are also highly varied in terms of their methods of construction: some are structures worthy of inclusion in *Pet-tecture*; others are fashioned from repurposed materials, incorporating existing features such as windowsills, postboxes and tree stumps into the resulting

A cat ladder in Reykjavik, 2016.

makeshift structure.[25] Schuster's documentation of the Swiss cat ladders is meant to inspire others to create feline-friendly architecture in cities, which actively helps cats negotiate what is, from an evolutionary standpoint, a thoroughly alien environment for them.

Design interventions for urban cats can draw attention to the ways in which humans and cats share urban spaces, even if the cats in question are feral. As part of the second Concéntrico architecture and design festival held in Logroño, Spain, in Spring 2016, the city's school of design installed street furniture in the courtyard of the La Rioja museum, which is also home to a colony of feral cats.[26] This was a multi-level structure made from interconnected, open-frame, plywood boxes, some of which functioned as cat shelters, others as feeding or watering stations for the animals. Unlike the shelters created for the 'Architects for Animals' initiative, this installation did not promote a particular approach to controlling stray animals; rather it offered local inhabitants the opportunity to experience urban spaces they share with other animals but of which they may not have been aware. In simply revealing the presence of feral cats, the project offered a much more open interpretation of their status than that presented in 'Architects for Animals'.

Installation created by the Rioja School of Design in Logroño, Spain, for the Concéntrico architecture and design festival, 2016.

Such openness also characterizes two other cities where feral cats have long been associated with distinct locales. In thirteenth-century Cairo a cat-loving Mamluk sultan founded a garden (*gheyt el-kuttah*) to house and feed strays. Situated near the sultan's mosque in the north of the city, people still bring food to the site today to feed the stray cats that have congregated there for nearly eight hundred years.[27] In a very different urban context, poet T. S. Eliot was inspired to write his interwar collection *Old Possum's Book of Practical Cats* after coming across a colony of feral cats living in Fitzroy Square in the heart of London's Bloomsbury district. Eliot's poems served as the basis for Andrew Lloyd Webber's 1981 musical *Cats*, which ever since has been running as a phenomenally successful stage production in London and elsewhere (this, in turn, inspired the much-maligned 2019 film adaptation). Even as the association between London and free-roaming felines lives on, the original physical connection has been lost, the feral cats that inspired Eliot long since evicted from the heart of the city.

Horse

It is highly unlikely you will ever see a feral horse in a city; in contrast to cats and dogs, they are just too large and unruly to be considered an acceptable presence, unless, of course, they are supervised by humans. You might, however, see horses or ponies tethered in the most unlikely of places. In 2003, while walking near the Thamesmead estate in southeast London, I saw a single white pony grazing on a small patch of grass in front of the estate's vast concrete walls. And, in several recent ostensibly realist films, including *Fish Tank* (2009, dir. Andrea Arnold), *The Selfish Giant* (2013, dir. Clio Barnard) and *Concrete Cowboy* (2021, dir. Ricky Staub), horses are seen inhabiting cities as talismans of wild nature, representing human longings for freedom in otherwise oppressive and deprived urban landscapes (respectively, in these three films, the eastern fringes of London, Bradford and Philadelphia).

As incongruous as the presence of horses in cities now seems, they were once the most common domesticated urban animal. In the nineteenth century, as industrialization stimulated the rapid growth of cities in Europe and, later, North America, horse populations exploded. Until the widespread adoption of motorized vehicles in the early twentieth century, horses were,

Horse (and cat) with a view of St Paul's Cathedral from a multi-storey stable built in the 1920s.

in effect, living machines that hauled the vehicles (cabs, omnibuses and trams) that carried people, goods and materials and also powered the heavy equipment that was used to construct and maintain urban infrastructure. For example, in London in 1897, with the human population approaching 6.3 million, there were 11,490 licensed horse-drawn cabs operating in the city (with only eighteen motorized equivalents at that time), more than 3,500 omnibuses (each drawn by up to three horses) and countless other horse-drawn carriages and trams. The hundreds of thousands of horses that lived in late nineteenth-century London all required feeding and housing in stables, not to mention the millions of tonnes of horse dung that was either cleared or left to accumulate in the city's streets.[28] Housing for horses in nineteenth-century cities generally meant, in Britain, utilitarian stables built behind terraced housing, known as mews, and accessed by an alleyway; in the USA, stables were built adjacent to houses or in a nearby side street. In addition, livery stables were purpose-built structures erected in cities where horses, riders and carriages could be hired, and where privately owned horses could be temporarily housed.[29]

The generally functional character of accommodation for horses in Victorian cities represented a stark departure from the equine architecture of previous times. From the mid-fifteenth century onwards, stable buildings had begun to take on a decidedly architectural character, particularly in

Renaissance Italy where powerful elites (rulers, both secular and religious, and aristocratic families) sought to draw attention to their humanist values through grand building projects. Between 1506 and 1510 architect Donato Bramante designed the stables for the papal palace in Viterbo, which comprised a large vaulted hall flanked by a colonnade. Luxurious rural villas built by Andrea Palladio later in the century often included *barchesse*, namely service buildings with colonnades that were often used as stables.[30] After Europe's first riding school was set up in Naples in 1532, a fashion for horsemanship spread throughout the continent, and stables of increasing architectural prominence became an essential element of large rural estates. The forerunner of today's dressage, showmanship in horse-riding became, in effect, a common sporting language adopted across Europe. It offered a powerful and universal image of nobility that asserted not only a strict human hierarchy, but regarded the horse as the most esteemed of all domesticated animals.[31] It was therefore unsurprising to see equine architecture sometimes matching the quality of homes built for humans, a few prominent neoclassical examples being Jules Hardouin-Mansart's Royal Stables at Versailles (1679–82), which is considered the largest housing for horses ever undertaken; Jean Aubert's Grands Écuries at Chantilly (1721–35); and the vast stable block built at Blenheim Palace (1705–22) to designs by Sir John Vanbrugh.

Perhaps the most extraordinary example of equine architecture – and one that survives today, albeit reconfigured for human use – is the Brighton Dome. Designed and built by William Porden for the Prince of Wales from 1803 to 1808, the decorative scheme of this palatial stable building was inspired by the Mughal architecture of India; its technologically advanced timber-framed, glazed dome, however, was modelled on the Halle aux blés, a corn market in Paris that was originally completed in 1766 and covered with a dome, originally of wood, in 1783. The Brighton Dome housed 44 stables, five coaching houses and two harness rooms, with twenty bedrooms in the upper floor for the accommodation of ostlers, stable boys and grooms. A riding house was also built on one side of the stables, lit by numerous scallop-arched windows. Measuring 53 metres long, 17 metres wide and 10 metres high, it was the largest building of its type in England. Both stables and riding house drew on an Indo-Islamic style of architecture that was characteristic of the orientalism that flourished as the British empire grew in importance; and the buildings went on to inspire an even more extravagant architectural expression of this in the Brighton Pavilion, designed by John Nash and constructed from 1815 to 1822 for the prince, whose earlier residence in Brighton had been dwarfed by the stable complex. In 1823 the riding house was incorporated into the pavilion by means of an underground tunnel, meaning that one could remain on horseback entirely under cover.[32] In 1934 the interior of the stables was reconstituted as a concert hall, for which it remains in use today as the Brighton Dome.

The twentieth century saw both the end of horses as beasts of burden in cities and also a democratization of horse ownership for leisure. Many stable buildings have, like the Brighton Dome, been converted for other (human) uses: some as private houses, the grander examples often as heritage buildings in the grounds of stately homes. The eighteenth-century stables at Dunham Massey in Greater Manchester, for example, are now owned by the National Trust, and they house a restaurant and toilets for visitors. Writing in 2014, architectural critic Jonathan Foyle lamented the lack of architectural finesse in contemporary equine architecture, seeing a long decline in quality that mirrored changing social values as European nations modernized. He singled out specialist design companies such as Equibuild as offering stable designs 'without aesthetic pretension or permanence', the more sturdy historical examples being turned into apartments with a quality of design now almost absent in most of their new counterparts.[33]

Foyle would perhaps be heartened by the recent reinvigoration of equine architecture, illustrated most strikingly in the 2020 book *Stables: High Design for Horse and Home*, which featured 25 examples of stables built within the last decade. Situated on private rural estates, these designs are generally for housing highly valuable racehorses, as is reflected in the luxurious treatment often given to the buildings. An example is the stables Estudio Ramos created in 2017 for the Argentinian polo star Nacho Figueras and his prized horses in the flatlands of La Pampa: the pronounced horizontalism of the design melds the 'Prairie Style' architecture of Frank Lloyd Wright and the high modernism of Ludwig Mies van der Rohe. The design features stalls for 44 polo horses as well as accommodation for the animals' grooms, and is striking in the way in which its flat concrete roof seems to emerge directly out of the ground; covered in turf, it also functions as an extended grazing area for the horses.[34] In a different vein, Matias Zegers's MSsporthorses complex,

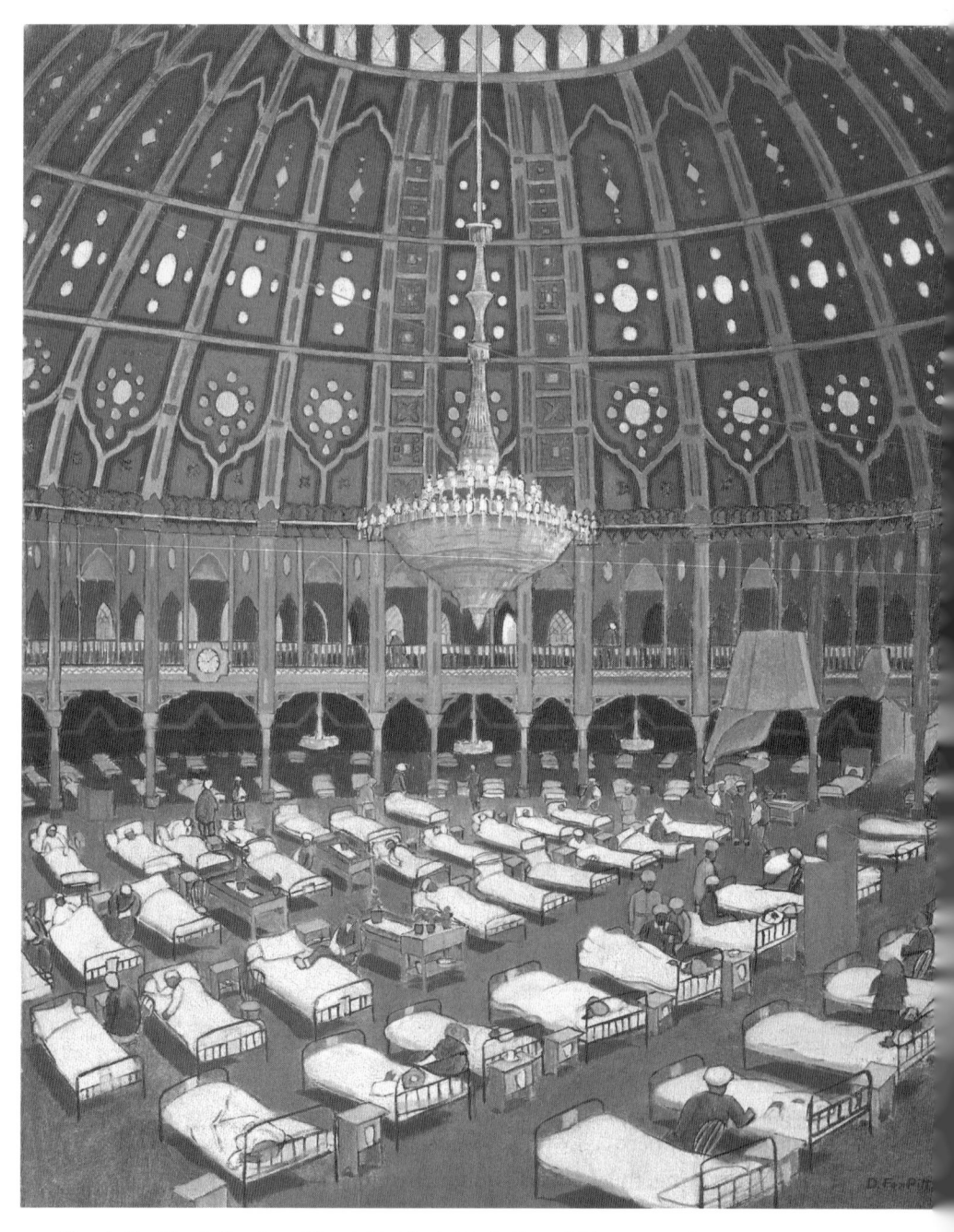

Douglas Fox-Pitt, *Indian Army Wounded in Hospital in the Dome*, Brighton, 1919, oil on canvas.

The former stables at Dunham Massey, Greater Manchester, built in the 18th century.

built in 2018 near the Chilean capital Santiago, blends in seamlessly with the local vernacular agricultural buildings; the simple, timber-framed and gabled structure featuring a striking skylight that runs along the ridge of the roofline, allowing enough natural light into the building for grooms to work indoors throughout the year.[35] This feature also recognizes the value of horses' well-being, since light and airy stables have long been held as indicative of happier and healthier captive animals.

In other contexts, horses sharing human space results in a much more disquieting sense of unease. Jannis Kounellis's controversial artwork *Untitled (Cavalli)*, first exhibited for a few days in Rome in 1969 and only five times since then, featured twelve live horses tethered in stalls in a former underground garage (refurbished as L'Attico Gallery). A prominent work in the Italian Arte Povera ('poor art') movement of the late 1960s and early 1970s, *Untitled* disturbs because seeing horses in an unlikely urban setting dissolves the boundary between what is considered human and animal space. In its original setting, the work also obliquely referenced the effects of the rapid economic growth of Italy's post-war years, which saw millions of people migrate from rural areas to industrial cities such as Turin. Here, otherwise rural animals appear in the heart of the city as a rebuke to the grand claims of industrial modernization.[36]

Horses, however, can enter our spaces without creating such a sense of unease. In December 2014, as a brutal storm hit northern Germany, a local doctor, Stephanie Arndt, invited a horse named Nasar into her farmhouse to shelter; after a few days the animal became so accustomed to indoor life that the doctor allowed Nasar to remain. Photographer Carsten Rehder's images of this interspecies cohabitation show the outsized animal completely filling a living room, looking out of a window and even playing a keyboard with his nose.[37] Reminiscent of the popular u.s. television series *Mister Ed* (1962–6), which featured a talking horse that undertook human occupations and was stabled in a garage, Rehder's photographs suggest that domestic space created for human needs might be appropriated by even the most unlikely of animals. In the 2021 film *Concrete Cowboy*, mentioned earlier, a horse permanently resides in a man's dilapidated apartment in a Black-majority inner-city area of Philadelphia, eventually developing a healing relationship with the man's troubled teenage son. In both of these examples, the incongruity of a horse living in a house (and the undoubted disruption this would cause) is offset by an optimistic sense of interspecies connection.

A far more discomforting take on horses and houses was provided by David Lynch in his 1992 film *Twin Peaks: Fire Walk With Me*, a prequel to the television series *Twin Peaks* (1990–91), created by Lynch and Mark Frost. In two memorable scenes, the mother of the doomed teenager Laura Palmer sees a white horse momentarily appear in her bedroom. The horse is a harbinger of death that draws on the symbolic power of the pale horse that personifies Death in the biblical Book of Revelation.[38] Lynch's melding of bedroom and horse unsettles because of the symbolic power of its animal subject. From the mythical white-winged Pegasus of ancient Greece onwards, white horses have been strongly suggestive to humans of certain symbolic attributes: in the case of Pegasus, supernatural gifts (the horse's ability to move between the heavenly and earthly realms); in Celtic mythology, fertility (the horse goddess Epona); in the Bible, both death and divine justice.[39] In *Fire Walk With Me*, the appearance of a white horse in the most private of domestic settings has the effect of shattering our sense of safe distance from the animal. While horses have long been brought under human control, they remain indelibly wild in some primal sense of their horse-being. As the eponymous horse protagonist of Anna

Sewell's 1877 novel *Black Beauty* muses, a captive animal may be well fed, its stables airy and light, its master kind and thoughtful; but a horse will always want but never attain its liberty – that is, freedom from standing up 'in a stable night and day except when I am wanted'.[40]

Cow

For Hindus, cows are the most sacred of all animals: the ur-cow was a mother goddess who emerged from a primeval ocean of milk. At the same time, bulls are revered for their fertility, the great Hindu god Shiva often taking the form of a bull in his earthly incarnations. The consequence of this bovine reverence, and a prohibition against killing cattle that it has inspired and continues to inspire, is the widespread presence of cows in Indian cities: there are an estimated 40,000 free-roaming animals living in New Delhi alone.[41] Researcher Rebecca Hui followed some of these urban cows, strapping a time-lapse camera beneath her headscarf and recording human interactions with individual animals. In the old districts of Mumbai and Ahmedabad, the cows she tracked took advantage of animal feeding stations built outside many of the houses, whereas in the new districts cows generally fed on rubbish or handouts. Such is the high status of cows in India that, when crossing roads, pedestrians will form human walls to protect the animals from oncoming vehicles.[42] A few favoured bulls even have their own temples: the Nandi (bulls) kept at the Shiva temples in Thanjavur, Rameshwaram and Mahalbalipuram in Tamil Nadu are held to be divine. The Vishwanath temple, built in 1002 CE, in Jhansi, Uttar Pradesh, is still home to a large bull.[43] Every November the countrywide Gopastami festival, dedicated to Lord Krishna and cows, sees bulls roaming the streets of Indian towns and cities, while cows are washed in temples and decorated with textiles and jewellery in the hope that their human handlers might receive a divine blessing.[44]

Although cattle are occasionally allowed into Western cities, for example for the annual Running of the Bulls event in Pamplona, Spain, a centuries-old practice that sees people trying to get as close as possible to a rampaging bull, cows generally have a very different status here to those present in Indian cities. In the West, cattle are domesticated animals that serve human needs: cows (females who have calved) are kept for their milk; steers (castrated

Free-roaming cow in Udalpur, India, 2019.

males) for their flesh; bulls (intact males) for their sperm; occasionally oxen (again, castrated males) are used as a source of power. In addition, beef hides become leather, while fatty acids derived from the carcasses of cows are vital ingredients in a whole panoply of products, including shoe creams, crayons, floor wax, margarine, deodorants, detergents, soaps, perfumes, insulation materials, refrigerants and confectionary.[45] The large range of structures that have been developed for the beef and dairy industries are designed to facilitate this utilitarian relationship between bovines and humans. Architecture for cows includes sheds and covered yards, dairies and cheese-making facilities, tanneries, feed-lots, storage areas (stockyards), cattle markets and slaughterhouses.[46]

At the top of the scale in terms of architectural importance, at least until the twentieth century, were structures associated with the dairy industry. Today, even utilitarian buildings used for milking cows, which now house milking machines rather than milkmaids, are still generally referred to in the UK and USA as 'parlours', reflecting the fact that dairy farmers would often spend a good proportion of their working lives inside these buildings. In previous centuries dairy buildings were often the most extravagant types of farm architecture. In the UK, these range from the Chinese dairy at Woburn, Bedfordshire, built from 1787 to 1802 by Henry Holland for the 5th Duke of Bedford, to the lavishly ornamental dairy built under the direction of Prince Albert in the grounds of Windsor Castle in 1848. Their unabashed exoticism reflected not only the high social status of their clients but that of the dairy products themselves which, until the advent of refrigeration, were generally regarded as luxuries. The design of both buildings, however, was also grounded in utility: the covered walkways and octagonal lantern of the Chinese dairy facilitated ventilation (essential in cooling warm milk); while the extraordinary faience decoration at Windsor was easy to keep clean. In the case of the latter, the luxuriant materials and exotic symbolism also fused product and patron. In the words of American diplomat Elihu Burritt, the decorative flourishes in the Royal Dairy seemed to link the imperial monarch with 'all the farmers' wives in the British Empire', the numerous marble-white basins taking 'up both [the] softness of look and sweetness of savor' of the regally infused cows' milk itself.[47]

Sectional drawing of the Royal Dairy, Windsor, 1848.

The widespread adoption of refrigeration in the twentieth century, together with changes in hygiene regulations, the centralization of production and an increasing reliance on imported milk and cheese, meant that the majority of these fanciful dairy buildings became redundant. From then on, milking parlours and cheese-making facilities shed symbolic decoration in favour of strict utility, a trend that, in line with stabling for horses, has only recently begun to shift.[48] In 2015 Abby Rockefeller, taking up her distinguished forebears' long tradition of philanthropic practice, opened Churchtown Dairy in Claverack, New York. Its most striking feature is a vast rotunda designed by architect Rick Anderson to house the cows during the winter months. When the cows are put out to pasture in spring, the building reverts back to human use: interlocking concrete slabs creating a platform over the hooded turf floor. Since 2015, it has variously functioned as a community space, temporary theatre and concert hall. With an emphasis on bovine well-being, the dairy practises 'biodynamic' farming: the dung of the resident cows collected and composted for recycling as an agricultural fertilizer. Every Christmas humans and cows are brought

Interior of Churchtown Dairy, Claverack, New York, 2015.

together when locals gather in the loft space of the rotunda to sing carols to the cows below.[49]

With an emphasis on animal well-being and community engagement, projects like Churchtown Dairy mark a welcome shift towards a more animal-centred approach to farm architecture. Yet it might also be argued that philanthropic projects only serve to deflect attention away from the much less palatable aspects of both the dairy and beef industries, which globally see 1.5 billion steers slaughtered every year for human consumption. It is also easily forgotten that cows produce milk only after calving, and that their lives thereafter are completely subjugated to human dictates, no matter how well they are cared for. Today, most dairy cows are producing far more milk than they did in the past and the majority are exhausted of their supplies within just a few years, as revealed in Andrea Arnold's film *Cow* (2021). Beef production, especially for the global fast-food industry, is even more hidden from public view. This is understandable if exposés such as Jennifer Abbott's *A Cow at My Table* (1998), Richard Linklater's *Fast Food Nation* (2006), based on Eric Schlosser's book of that title, and Kip Andersen and Keegan Kuhn's *Cowspiracy: The Sustainability Secret* (2014) are to be taken as benchmarks for current practices in the beef industry. Over a century ago, in his novel *The Jungle* (1906), Upton Sinclair described the notorious cattle stockyards in Chicago, where he had worked for seven weeks in 1904. Housing tens of thousands of imported cattle in countless stalls, the stockyards were antechambers of death. Driven up 4.5-metre-wide walkways into narrow chutes, the cattle were goaded with electric shocks, crammed into tiny pens and then killed by 'knockers' armed with sledgehammers.[50] The practices of killing cattle may have become more 'humane' since then but the architecture of death remains the same. Slaughterhouses exist for one purpose and one purpose alone. They are unpalatable reminders to most meat-eaters of the merciless mass-murder of animals.

Hard-hitting exposés of the meat industry might discourage humans from eating animals, but encouraging reconnection with cows is another matter. Chicago-based designers Allison Newmeyer and Stewart Hicks attempted the latter with their speculative Farmland World project. One of the runners-up in the 2011 Animal Architecture Awards, the project proposed the creation of a series of agro-tourist resorts in the American Midwest, not in the mould of an 'open' or 'petting' farm, but rather as a way of drawing attention to the 'hybrid human-animal-machine relationship' that characterizes contemporary farming.[51] These 'livestock Disneylands' would see human visitors engaging not just with real animals but a whole panoply of robotic, replicant or inflatable machines that would perform agricultural work. One of these is a giant structure in the shape of a cow (the cow combine), which would harvest crops through its mouth and into its body. The crops would then be processed by a series of machines that resemble internal organs. If required, the cow combine's human operator would sit within the chest area of the outsized animal. As architectural critic Geoff Manaugh has noted, the apparent outlandish fantasy of this project is actually rooted in the strange reality of contemporary farming: Manaugh cites his own childhood experience of visiting a farm in rural Wisconsin and seeing a cow that had a window surgically implanted into its side, allowing visitors to the farm to watch the cow digesting its food in its many stomachs.[52]

Confrontation with the mechanistic nature of human engagement with cattle certainly serves to raise awareness about the ways in which cows, humans and machines are inextricably enmeshed, but it does not move us beyond a utilitarian understanding of livestock. *Trufa* (the Truffle), a project by Spanish architect Antón García-Abril, cleverly subverts the idea of the cow as a passive servant of and product for humans.[53] The strikingly organic appearance of this house, completed in 2010, was the result of a cow named Paulina literally eating out its interior spaces. The project began with a hole being dug in the ground, the excavated earth formed into retaining walls. Hay bales were then stacked in the hole and unreinforced concrete poured in to create a solid structure. The whole was then extracted from the ground and an opening was cut into the concrete, allowing Paulina to feed on the hay contained within. A year later, after all the hay had been consumed, the cave-like concrete walls were all that remained of the interior space. Cleaned up and fitted out with minimalist furniture, together with a glass window fixed over Paulina's former entrance hole, the house quite literally retained the history of the cow's engagement with the building in its finished form.

In creating an ambiguous space somewhere between the natural and the artificial, *Trufa* asks us to think about cows in a much more creative way than is usually the case, particularly in terms of their agency as animals. While it is true that Paulina was building to serve human ends, the work that she

Perspective view of Allison Newmeyer and Stewart Hicks's proposed Farmland World theme park, 2011.

did was, for her, much more nourishing than being confined to a milking parlour. And in excavating rather than constructing an architectural space, Paulina also challenged the conventional notion of building as an agglomeration of materials; rather, in *Trufa*, the building was formed by a process of subtraction. This is architecture at its most primal, a return to the techniques used by our ancient ancestors, who dug holes in the ground or found shelter in crevices already provided by nature.

Pig

Pigs reared under human supervision are almost always destined for one place only: the slaughterhouse. Perhaps nowhere is this brought home more powerfully than in the closing moments of the 2021 film *Gunda*, directed by Victor Kossakovsky. For just over 90 minutes, the lives of a domesticated sow and her ten-strong litter of piglets (as well as interludes with groups of chickens and cows) are followed by a camera that adopts, with its close-up focus, an intimate relationship with the animals, showing them in their pigsty and foraging outside as the tiny piglets grow and develop. The only human presence in the film is when a tractor arrives and takes

Anton García-Abril's *Trufa* (Truffle), photographed when completed in 2010.

the young pigs away in a metal crate. After they have disappeared, the mother pig, clearly distressed, searches in vain for her missing family, her plaintive calls finally ceasing only when she returns to the now empty pigsty. These almost unbearable final 15 minutes of the film are a devastating indictment of the human view of pigs as simply 'units' of meat for our consumption.

It is also telling that the young pigs in *Gunda* simply disappear, even though their fate is obvious to (human) viewers, if not to their mother. Just as with other livestock ultimately destined for human consumption, the architecture of slaughterhouses for pigs has become increasingly invisible, revealed only when the intention is to shock us into awareness. In the nineteenth century attitudes towards slaughterhouses were quite different: for example, the famous pork 'disassembly line' developed in Cincinnati from the 1850s onwards became a tourist attraction, visitors finding wonder in its technologies of slaughter that were a mark of America's pre-eminence in pioneering rationalized forms of production. Frederick Law Olmsted, designer of New York's Central Park, visited one of Cincinnati's dozens of pork-producing plants in 1857, describing an 'immense low-ceiled room' filled with dead pigs lying on their backs, waiting to be moved to the 'human chopping-machine where [they] were converted into commercial pork'.[54]

By the time Upton Sinclair described the pork-processing stockyards of Chicago in *The Jungle* (1906), attitudes had changed. As one of a group of visitors, Sinclair described the long, narrow room where pigs were brought to be slaughtered. This room housed a 'great iron wheel', on both sides of which were narrow spaces into 'which came the hogs at the end of their journey'. Chained and borne aloft by the wheel, the pigs were then killed by men who slit their throats. Each carcass was then disassembled into various cuts of meat, with 'everything but the squeal' put to use. In unforgettable prose, Sinclair honed in on the incessant and 'terrifying shrieks' of the pigs that accompanied these scenes of mass slaughter. Sinclair ended his account with a lament to the lack of compassion shown by humans in this place of 'pork-making by machinery, pork-making by applied mathematics'.[55]

Gunda may end on a heartbreaking note, but for much of its running time it is the domestic life of the family of pigs that takes centre stage, much of which is focused on the pigsty, their timber-built, straw-filled home. In Britain and Ireland fields given over to pigs are generally identifiable by the half-cylinder pigsties that provide shelters as utilitarian as one might expect for farm animals. Occasionally, though, more elaborate pigsties have been constructed, often in conjunction with other agricultural buildings, such as poultry houses, cowsheds and dairies. On the Larchill estate in County Kildare, Ireland, for example, a complete *ferme ornée* which included castellated structures for goats, ducks and pigs was built by the Prentices, a Quaker family, between 1740 and 1780.[56] In the case of the miniature Grecian temple built for pigs on a hill near Robin Hood's Bay in northeast England, it seems that the landowner, John Warren Barry of Fyling Hall, had a particular fondness for the two Large White 'Yorkshire' pigs that he housed there. Today the building is owned by the Landmark Trust and can be rented as a bijou holiday apartment (for humans, that is).[57] Meanwhile, in 2015 an enterprising farmer in Wales converted a much more utilitarian pigsty into a holiday home, a novel take on humans getting back to nature.[58]

Scene from *Gunda* (2021), showing the sow alone in her pigsty after her piglets have been taken away.

Former pigsty built by John Warren Barry at Fyling Hall, Robin Hood's Bay, in the late 19th century.

But what if humans decided to live alongside the animals they also choose to eat? This is precisely the intention of Carsten Höller and Rosemarie Trockel's installation *Ein Haus für Schweine und Menschen* ('A House for Pigs and People'), exhibited at Documenta x in Kassel in 1997. The artists built a working pigpen behind a sheet of glass that allowed visitors to watch the animals without disturbing them. Yet because the glass was reflective on the pig's side, it was only the humans who were able to observe their 'subjects'. This aspect of the work reminds us that, even though we are surrounded by animals, they remain strangers to us because we generally perceive them in a wholly anthropocentric way.[59] But, like *Gunda*, the installation also draws attention to the animal qualities within ourselves, emotions and values that we actually share with pigs, but which we so often treat as passive objects for our consumption (whether looking at or eating them).

In both works, we are drawn into the lives of pigs through structures that humans have built for them, a sign that we perhaps also share an understanding of domestic space with these animals, however human-centred that understanding may be. This probably derives from the long history of small-scale pig husbandry that has all but disappeared in the Global North but which is still part of everyday life in rural China, Vietnam and other 'developing' countries. Back in the nineteenth century pigs were a common sight in industrializing cities such as London and New York, before they were targeted by sanitary reformers as inescapably 'dirty' animals that were anathema to their modernizing agendas. Henry Mayhew's mid-century *London Labour and the London Poor* captured the moment when urban pigs in London moved from everyday life into the realm of the monstrous. Incorporated into his observations about sewer workers and the ferocious rats that menaced them, Mayhew referred to a 'strange tale in existence . . . of a race of wild hogs inhabiting the sewers in the neighbourhood of Hampstead'. This group of feral pigs apparently originated from a pregnant sow who accidentally entered the sewers and then reared her young there, the pigs finding ample sustenance in the sewage itself.[60] This apocryphal story resonated with Victorian fears of monsters lurking beneath the city, especially in the context of rapid urban change that created ambivalence in the minds of middle-class observers such as Mayhew. On the one hand, feral pigs roaming the sewers pointed back to an atavistic past, a time when nature exerted real agency in cities; on the other, they pointed forward to a modernized urban future, where the monstrosity of the pig lay more in its negative associations with dirt and disease.[61]

Today, pigs are generally absent in cities in the Global North, even as urban farming is growing in significance, especially in post-industrial cities where brownfield sites offer new opportunities for future development. In 2000 an early project by Dutch architecture firm MVRDV proposed a radical vision of urban pig-farming in the year 2021. Titled *Pig City*, this project envisioned the development of organic pig husbandry without the vast amount of land generally needed for it, namely through the creation of a series of supertall (622-metre) skyscrapers dedicated to the rearing and slaughtering of pigs. Although a seemingly fantastical solution to the problems associated with contemporary pig farming, *Pig City* was grounded in detailed statistical analysis that was focused on achieving a closed-loop system of pork production, where everything (food, waste and water) is recycled back into the process. With the towers distributed in Dutch cities and clustered around the country's ports, *Pig City* would not only make pig farming a much more visible part of the Dutch landscape, but significantly intensify the notion of pigs as solely utilitarian units for human consumption. The 76 towers proposed by MVRDV would supply the Netherlands' entire demand for pork, as well as its significant export market; in the 1990s this was around 15.2 million pigs spread over 29 per cent of the surface of the country.[62]

American science-fiction author John Scalzi has provided an implicit literary take on MVRDV's project in his 2009 short story 'Utere nihil non extra quiritationem suis', which formed part of the *METAtropolis* collection he assembled and edited. In a dystopian future, 'new' St Louis is one of dozens of fortified city-states aross the world; its pig towers part of the enclave's 'virtuous' vision of achieving a zero-carbon footprint. But this comes at a high price: the closed-loop agriculture is a mirror of the gated city-state, 'sealed like a medieval fortress, with only a few entrances, all guarded'. Eventually the pig towers are breached by desperate inhabitants of old St Louis, who steal skin samples from the pigs in order to sequence their genomes and so democratize the technologies of vertical farming.[63] In giving the skyscraper pig farm a distinctly social meaning, Scalzi's story challenges the overt technological emphasis of MVRDV's project, showing that questions of utility in agriculture are always grounded in wider social contexts.

There is also a central problem with purely technological solutions to pig farming that only intensifies as science advances. Alongside the

Still from MVRDV's short film *Pig City*, released in 2000.

undoubted freedoms gained by farmers (and consumers) in imposing efficiency-based systems on pigs, there are always increasing levels of domination and control of the animals. Breaking this cycle requires, first and foremost, a change in human attitudes towards pigs. Stripping away the technological high jinks of *Pig City*, *Gunda* returns us to the basics of pig husbandry, namely a makeshift pigsty and a muddy field beyond. The power of the film lies in the way in which it uses up-to-date technology (in this case a high-spec digital camera) to dissolve the distance between humans and pigs. The very rudeness of the pigsty is what allows us to identify with it, the pigs humanized as we ourselves are in some sense 'piggified'. Such an interspecies identification challenges how humans perceive pigs, the sow's home a mirror of our own, her family as cherished as ours.

Chicken

It is perhaps fitting that the final animal considered in this book should also be the one that humans have arguably exploited the most. Globally, around 60 billion chickens (known as broilers) are reared for meat every year, and this number is continuing to grow at a rapid rate, especially in industrializing countries such as China and India. By the time you have read to the end of this paragraph, 60,000 chickens will have been slaughtered across the world (around 2,000 every second). Factory-farmed chickens live an average of 42 days in completely artificial environments, gigantic sheds crowded with tens of thousands of birds who never venture outside and are specially bred to gain weight as quickly as possible. On average, each individual chicken lives in a space smaller than an A4 sheet of paper: barely enough for them to move, let alone turn around, scratch or dust bathe (all 'natural' chicken behaviours).[64] In these factory systems, chicken farmers have very little contact with the animals, the rearing process now being almost fully mechanized. Egg-producing hens suffer no less than their male counterparts, the young females transferred to battery farms when they are four months old, spending the rest of their lives in cramped cages, with thousands of these lined up and stacked in vertical tiers. While some countries have outlawed battery cages for laying hens, the vast majority of both chicken meat and eggs are still produced by factory-farming methods, their architectures of incarceration all but invisible to consumers.[65]

In 1994 American artist Doug Argue completed an enormous untitled painting showing innumerable layer hens in battery cages, a barely exaggerated depiction of life inside a chicken farm. In the foreground of the painting, each individual hen is rendered in painstaking detail, even as their features dissolve as our eyes follow the perspective lines towards the vanishing point in the far distance. An animal equivalent of the images of human incarceration in Hariton Pushwagner's graphic novel *Soft City*, Argue's painting was inspired by Franz Kafka's short story 'Investigations of a Dog' (1922), in which a canine narrator enquires into the practices of his own culture, more particularly how dogs acquire their food.[66] The sheer size of Argue's painting (3.35 × 5.5 metres) not only magnifies the horror of the incarnation of chickens in the modern factory system, but forces an identification with factory-farming and standardization and monotonous repetition in mass housing of the post-war period. Modern housing may not be quite the horrifying animal dystopia that is the modern factory farm; but Argue's painting nevertheless questions where the tendency in high-rise design will eventually take us, a question that is arguably even more pertinent now than it was in the mid-1990s, given the proliferation of supertall buildings in recent years.

The global dominance of the factory system, and the still growing rate of demand for chicken meat, means that proponents of 'alternative' methods of chicken husbandry must always be sanguine about enacting systemic change. Perhaps some hope resides in regions, particularly sub-Saharan Africa, where small-scale chicken farming is still the norm, even in urban contexts such as Gaborone, Botswana, subject of in-depth research by Alice Hovorka.[67] In European and North American cities, the past two decades have seen the growth of movements that attempt to reinstate local food networks as well as others that promote the 'backyard' farming of livestock for household and community use. Indeed, chicken farming even featured in the first episode of the satirical comedy-sketch series *Portlandia* (2011), when two ultra-hipster diners in Portland learn about the food they are considering ordering, namely Colin the Chicken, whose 'local' credentials are vetted assiduously by the couple to the point where they leave the restaurant in order to visit the farm where Colin was raised.[68]

For any would-be chicken farmer, the biggest single expense will be the housing needed for the birds themselves: the chicken coop. In 2003, responding to the renewed interest in small-scale farming in London, four students at the Royal College of Art designed and built the Eglu, a relatively inexpensive structure incorporating a plastic-moulded chicken coop and an attached wire-mesh run (by 2021 their company, Omlet, was selling a variety of Eglu-based coops as well as structures and accessories for other domestic animals).[69] Today, prefabricated chicken coops are aggressively marketed in the media outlets that serve chicken-keeping organizations, and regular tours of coops bring prospective chicken-keepers into contact with a whole array of designs, from the utilitarian to the luxurious. It is not surprising that chicken coops featured alongside dog homes and cat shelters in *Pet-tecture*: architect-designed coops are now just as much a status symbol for small-scale chicken-farmers as bespoke dogs homes are for some dog owners. These high-end chicken houses include Nogg, a visually striking egg-shaped timber coop; The Moop, a 'modern and stylish chicken coop made for the urban garden'; and Germaine, a metal trapezoid designed for an indoor coop that aims to promote 'the inclusion of chickens in humans' daily life'.[70]

Doug Argue, *Untitled*, 1994.

Omlet-designed
chicken coop.

Larger-scale interventions by architects seek to provide alternative housing for industrial-scale farming. In 2019 Istanbul-based practice SO? completed a modular coop for eight hundred chickens on an artist's farm in rural eastern Turkey. Although far smaller than any factory-farm coop, this design nevertheless suggests a middle ground in terms of scale between backyard and industrial chicken farming. Built from simple, inexpensive materials – oak plywood, oxidized metal panels and a corrugated metal roof – the design reappropriates the standardized components used in factory farms to create chicken housing that is as utilitarian for the birds as it is for the humans farming them. The interior spaces are comprised of identical roosting bays that lead to stacked wooden nesting boxes, the internal spaces cross-ventilated and suffused with natural light.[71] In a similar vein, Kengo Kuma's coop, designed to provide eggs for the Casa Wabi Foundation in Mexico, comprises a network of gridded walls made from

so?'s chicken farm located in rural Turkey, 2019.

interlocking wooden boards. Photographs of the interior show a structure that resembles a smaller-scale and far more humane version of Doug Argue's painting. Kuma has stated that the design was inspired by collective housing projects for humans: the individual cells for nesting chickens are the animal equivalent of standardized human housing that is rooted in a socialist politics of autonomy and equality, rather than oppressive uniformity.[72]

This cross-species approach becomes even more prominent in chicken farms built with an expressly educational purpose. The complex known as Chickenville in Rakov Potok, a small town in Croatia, is a poultry farm that is attempting to produce eggs with zero carbon footprint and raise awareness about eco-friendly methods of poultry farming to the local population. Chickenville's designers, Skroz Architecture, have opened up every stage of egg production to public scrutiny, building a complex of coops alongside a 'public' street that is also used by farmers for the feeding, maintenance and cleaning of the coops. Creating distinct 'neighbourhoods' for the four different chicken breeds housed on the site, the architects have brought together chicken and human spaces to make a direct connection between human and avian social life.[73] This is intended to challenge consumers to meaningfully reconnect with the usually hidden processes that produce their food, and which also has the potential to generate more empathy on the part of humans for the otherwise unheeded plight of factory-farmed chickens.

Empathy for animals can also be fostered by thinking beyond their utilitarian value. In countless myths and legends, the main product of chickens – their eggs – have been regarded as powerful symbols of creative agency, the shape of an egg an afterimage of our mothers' wombs. The bodies of adult chickens have also fascinated humans for centuries, not least their remarkable feet, which are quite literally the vestigial remains of the dinosaur species Tyrannosaurus rex, from whom they ultimately evolved. Perhaps it is this pre-human association with chicken feet that has led them to occupy a central place in the centuries-old Slavic folk tale of Baba Yaga. In this story an old woman with witch-like powers lives deep in the endless Russian taiga in a strange house that is supported on four outsized chicken legs and which spins around when Baba Yaga becomes angry. This animated dwelling seems to embody contradictory meanings: in some stories Baba Yaga eats the children who stumble across her hut; in others she offers counsel and comfort to those in distress. It has been argued that the hut's

Skroz Architecture's Chickenville in Rakov Potok, Croatia, 2018.

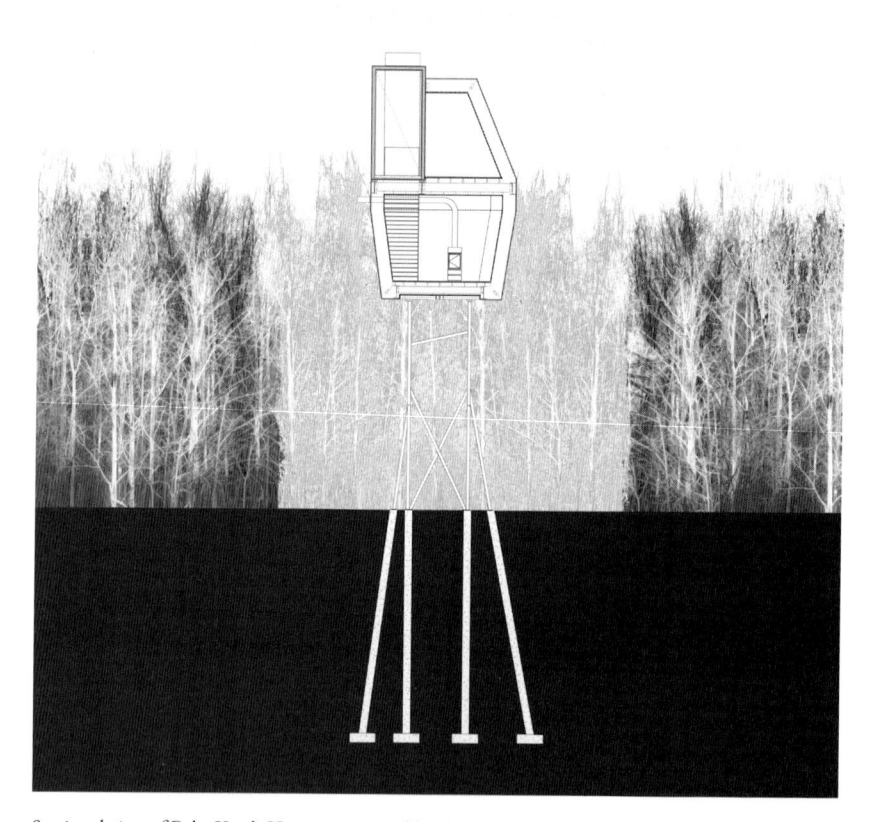

Sectional view of Baba Yaga's House, conceived by Kate and Andrew Bernheimer, 2011.

chicken-feet supports stem from Slavic healing rituals that involve hens and chickens, still commonplace animals in the Russian countryside. For example, babies who constantly cry might be taken to the household chicken coop, which is asked to restore sleep to the infant by giving him or her a 'human life' instead of a 'chicken life'.[74]

In 2011 writer Kate Bernheimer and her architect sibling Andrew Bernheimer curated a series of works in which designers were invited to explore the relationship between fairy tales and architecture. The Bernheimers' own contribution was a contemporary reinterpretation of the chicken house at the centre of the Baba Yaga folk tale. In their speculative design,

Baba Yaga's house is located on the main flight path to Vladivostok airport in a forest clearing in Russia's far east. The metal-framed house is wrapped in tree bark 'like a chicken's belly perched on a steel structure'.[75] In this re-conception of the folk tale, giant jet aircraft passing overhead are the contemporary equivalents of the broomstick-flying witch. Responding to these movements in the air, the upper part of the house would spin on a built-in turntable. The architects leave the question open as to how this structure would fit into a modern retelling of the Baba Yaga story.

In an even stranger twist, in 2018 a photograph of the supposed real-life home of Baba Yaga was posted on Reddit. Here, in an unspecified location in the Russian countryside, a makeshift log cabin was built and raised up off the ground on four tree trunks that look uncannily like chicken legs. The form of this structure was likely an ad hoc solution to the problem of keeping out hungry animals from a store of human foodstuffs, yet its reso-nance with the fairy tale lends that utility a powerful sense of enchantment. In effect, this chicken-like building reverses the conventional meanings of utility in animal architecture, holding out the hope that other buildings for livestock might serve to enrich rather than impoverish our understanding of the lives of their inhabitants.

Coda

A startling confirmation of what is increasingly being called the Anthropocene, a new epoch in which humans are the dominant planetary force, came in 2020 in the form of a study published in *Nature*. This revealed that, for the first time in history, the mass of everything made by humans exceeded that of all living biomass (the latter being approximately 1.1 teratonnes).[1] We have, quite literally, created an artificial environment that increasingly threatens the very existence of what we commonly refer to as nature. On the one hand, it might be argued that such a revelation merely reinforces the boundary between what we make and the natural 'environment' outside of which the human-built world supposedly stands. On the other, it is proof, if proof were needed, of the inescapable *entanglement* of these two worlds. Framed in a negative way, the world we build is at the expense of nature, which we only come to value when it has already been destroyed. Such are the contradictions inherent in the very notion of the Anthropocene, especially for those determined to counter its destructive character.

This book has offered a modest contribution to what are now many and varied attempts to shift humans from the centre of things, while also acknowledging that the very idea of so doing almost certainly comes from an awareness of our increasing dominance over all other life forms. We can never escape this contradiction but, as I have shown in this book, it can, through the tension it produces, generate rich forms of creativity. By leaning into contradiction, many pathways open up. The argument made throughout this book is that humans are capable – perhaps uniquely so among all animals – of imagining the lives of other beings, what might be called creative empathy. The imaginative faculty need not be dismissed as a 'decorative' embellishment of the rational mind, but rather cherished and nurtured as the very foundation of what it means to be human in a world of others.

One way to bring together the vast range of works explored in this book is through the concept of home. Taking his cue from the work of Martin Heidegger, philosopher David Wood has explored how the word 'dwelling' means much more than simply 'snuggling up in a lair, venturing out for food, and returning to relative safety'. Rather, dwelling 'has always incorporated distance'.[2] Taking his cue from Vitruvius, Wood reimagines the primeval time when humans first learnt to build. Here, he sees a contradiction at the heart of home-making, a tension between removing ourselves from that which threatens (what we would now call nature) and a sense of loss at that displacement – our inevitable disconnection from the teeming world of others. One of the most effective ways of enlarging our imaginative identification with these others is to recognize that all animals are in the business of home-making. There is no organism that does not need to disconnect itself from the environment in which it emerges but in which it must also remain. Indeed, the environment itself is the product of this tension: it is created by countless acts of retreat from others and countless other unavoidable entanglements.

So, returning to Chapter One, think of spiders entering our homes in order to make their own. If we come to the realization that spiders have the same desire as us for safe shelter, then perhaps we would be more inclined to tolerate them as fellow guests. Moving to Chapter Two, we might discover a starling taking advantage of a 'defect' in our home and finding a safe place to nest under a broken roof tile or inside a gap in the eaves. Viewed in this way, the things we would conventionally regard as problems are actually creative opportunities for homemaking by other animals. This is, of course, not without a cost to our own sense of well-being; but is this not precisely the kind of encounter where we are actually able to test how much we care about the well-being of other creatures? Pushing a bit further (as Chapter Three does), are we going to continue to assert that some animals are 'pests' while others are not? What about a rat finding its home under a shed or compost heap? We might argue that it is justifiable to exterminate such 'vermin', but surely being open to a questioning of that very definition might be an opportunity to hold fire. Why indeed are rats not entitled to a home, just as other animals are?

When animals make their homes in or near water (the subject of Chapter Four), it is perhaps easier to accept them, distant as we and our buildings generally are from this element. But here there is a tendency for humans to want to relate to these animals solely on their terms: think of dolphins performing in an aquarium or oysters and beavers becoming unwitting agents in the human fight against climate change. As scientists such as John C. Lilly have shown, living alongside aquatic animals is not merely about respecting their intelligence, but rather about developing an awareness of their radical *difference* to us, even as we cannot but help assimilate them through anthropomorphic identification. Perhaps the onus to assimilate should be more on us than aquatic animals: what might it mean for humans, for instance, to live alongside dolphins rather than the other way around?

We are perhaps on more comfortable ground with our pets, the subject of the final chapter. We willingly share our homes with all manner of other life forms; and even for those who do not, it seems obvious that the commonest pets – dogs and cats – are able to cohabit relatively happily with humans. Some design with these animals in mind, although the results are sometimes glaringly human-centred. Yet, even the owners of animals we would not conventionally regard as anything like us, such as reptiles, spiders and other 'exotic' pets, often become convinced that their pets communicate with them. To live with another animal is perforce to discover hitherto unknown qualities of that animal and, perhaps, that process is mutual. It is easy to dismiss the culture of pets as rooted in a human desire for control, namely for a relationship with another being that is entirely on our own terms. But animals are not merely commodities; they bite back in ways that we cannot usually foresee.

What unites all animals, and what connects us to them and vice versa, is a shared vulnerability. All animals are, at root, both at home in, and displaced from, the world. Of course, some are more displaced than others. Human domination is both an inevitable consequence of our own arrogance and a heavy responsibility that far outweighs that of any other animal; for, unlike beetles or elephants, we surely know what we do. No other animal is as seemingly exempt as humans are from what is being termed the Sixth

Mass Extinction; today, the vulnerability of the vast majority of animals is a consequence of our actions and not those of other beings. And yet we can listen to, notice, care about and respond to other animals, which is undoubtedly a very modest gain in the face of apocalyptic losses, but a gain nonetheless.

Can we sense the pain of other animals even when we know we are responsible for that pain? Yes, if we can bear it, and that is undoubtedly a matter of personal choice. But there is more, I think. When we share vulnerability with other animals, we come to understand that it is not only vulnerability that connects us with them, but our very existence as animals. For example, we are told by biologists that our bodies contain more microbes than human cells; that the flourishing of what we might call 'human' bodies depends utterly on the flourishing of other lives; and that all of those other lives depend on many others for their own flourishing. It is worth thinking again about the word 'environment', which is so often used to describe everything outside of the human-built world. It bears repeating: that environment is nothing less than the sum total of all living beings making their homes in the world; and that there is no dividing line between our environment and theirs.

Let us return, then, to that insignificant moss plant growing on the rubber gasket of one of the metal rivets that hold together the steel-and-glass superstructure of Ian Simpson's Urbis building in Manchester. That little tufted patch of green is in all probability home to a tremendous number of tiny invertebrates – tardigrades, springtails, nematodes, mites and rotifers being the most common. It is quite literally a life world of its own, but one that seems completely at odds with the inert surfaces of rubber and metal on which it has grown. It is commonly said that 'life finds a way'; but this insignificant patch of moss forcefully brings that truth to hand. And if we stay long enough and try to imagine that microcosmos, we also feel the extraordinary sense of threat that this truth brings in its wake. If life does indeed always find a way, then our attempts to build outside of that life will be doomed to destruction. It is high time that we stopped to consider what healthier – quite literally, more sustainable – alternatives might be.

References

Introduction: Going to Ground

1 Vitruvius, *Ten Books of Architecture*, trans. Morris Hicky Morgan (Cambridge, MA, 1914), p. 38.
2 See Joseph Rykwert, *On Adam's House in Paradise: The Idea of the Primitive Hut in Architectural History* (Cambridge, MA, 1981).
3 Ibid., p. 192.
4 See Marsh McLennan, 'The Future of Construction: A Global Forecast for Construction to 2030 Issued in Partnership with Oxford Economics and Guy Carpenter', 2021, www.marsh.com.
5 Stephen Graham, *Vertical: The City from Satellites to Bunkers* (London, 2016), pp. 372–87.
6 Tim Ingold, *Correspondences* (Cambridge, 2021), p. 9.
7 Ibid., p. 107.
8 See www.insulatebritain.com, accessed 10 May 2022.
9 See Stephen Cairns and Jane M. Jacobs, *Buildings Must Die: A Perverse View of Architecture* (Cambridge, MA, 2014).
10 See Rosi Braidotti, *The Posthuman* (Cambridge, 2013) for a comprehensive theoretical overview of post-humanism, but which does not consider the more recent emergence of Object-Oriented Ontology.
11 See Joseph Bedford, ed., *Is There an Object-Oriented Architecture? Engaging Graham Harman* (London, 2020). For an accessible introduction to Object-Oriented Ontology, see Graham Harman, *Object-Oriented Ontology: A New Theory of Everything* (London, 2018).
12 Harman, *Object-Oriented Ontology*, pp. 61–102; and Timothy Morton, *Being Ecological* (London, 2018), pp. 33–5.
13 Timothy Morton, *Humankind: Solidarity with Nonhuman People* (London, 2019), p. 143.
14 Ibid., p. 144.
15 See Mike Hansell, *Built by Animals: The Natural History of Animal Architecture* (Oxford, 2009).
16 Ibid., p. 60.
17 George Orwell, *Animal Farm* [1945] (London, 1971), p. 114.

18 Thomas Nagel, 'What Is It Like to Be a Bat?', *Philosophical Review*, LXXXIII/4 (1974), pp. 435–50.

19 Ian Bogost, *Alien Phenomenology; or, What It's Like to Be a Thing* (Minneapolis, MN, 2012), pp. 62–5.

20 Jane Bennett, *Vibrant Matter: A Political Ecology of Things* (Durham, NC, 2000), p. 120.

21 J. M. Coetzee, *The Lives of Animals* (Princeton, NJ, 1999), pp. 33–5.

22 See Alex Thornton, 'This Is How Many Animals We Eat Each Year', World Economic Forum, www.weforum.org, 8 February 2019.

23 See, for example, Michael Pawlyn, *Biomimicry in Architecture* (London, 2016); and William Myers and Paola Antonelli, *Bio Design: Nature + Science + Creativity* (London, 2018).

24 On the two silk pavilions at MIT, see 'Neri Oxman', MIT Media Lab, www. media.mit.edu.

25 Paul Dobraszczyk, *Future Cities: Architecture and the Imagination* (London, 2019), pp. 129–39.

26 Timothy Morton, *The Ecological Thought* (Cambridge, MA, 2010), p. 29.

27 Ingold, *Correspondences*, p. 200.

28 See www.expandedenvironment.org.

29 See Fritz Haeg, 'Animal Estates', www.fritzhaeg.com, accessed 9 May 2022.

30 Jennifer Wolch, 'Zoöpolis', in *Animal Geographies: Place, Politics, and Identity in the Nature-Culture Borderlands*, ed. Jennifer Wolch and Jody Emel (London, 1998), pp. 122–3.

31 Bennett, *Vibrant Matter*, p. 116.

1 Miniature

1 Karl Marx, *Capital* [1867] (London, 1930), pp. 169–70.

2 Tim Ingold, 'The Architect and the Bee: Reflections on the Work of Animals and Men', *Man*, n.s., XVIII/1 (1983), p. 4.

3 A useful summary of this research can be found in Tim Ireland and Simon Garnier, 'Architecture, Space and Information in Constructions Built by Humans and Social Insects: A Conceptual Review', *Philosophical Transactions of the Royal Society B*, CCCLXXIII/1753 (2018).

4 Richard Jones, *House Guests, House Pests: A Natural History of Animals in the Home* (London, 2015), pp. 216–75.

5 See Jussi Parikka, *Insect Media: An Archaeology of Animals and Technology* (Minneapolis, MN, 2010).

6 Timothy Morton, *The Ecological Thought* (Cambridge, MA, 2010), p. 14.

7 Francisco Sánchez-Bayo and Kris A. G. Wyckhuys, 'Worldwide Decline of the Entomofauna: A Review of Its Drivers', *Biological Conservation*, CCXXXII (2019), pp. 8–27.

8 See Jones, *House Guests*.

9 China Miéville, *Perdido Street Station* (London, 2000), pp. 255–6.

10 Franz Kafka, 'Metamorphosis' [1915], in *Metamorphosis and Other Stories*, trans. Michael Hofmann (London, 2007), p. 73.

11 Adam Dodd, *Beetle* (London, 2016), pp. 15–16.

12 Lidija Grozdanic, 'Vaulout & Dyèvre's Insectopia Installations Look Like Densely-Populated Bug Hotels', https://inhabitat.com, 8 August 2015.

13 See Fritz Haeg, 'Animal Estates', www.fritzhaeg.com, accessed 9 May 2022.

14 Ibid.

15 Henrietta Rose-Innes, *Nineveh* (London, 2011), pp. 104–5.

16 See University of Stuttgart Institute for Computational Design and Construction, 'ICD/ITKE Research Pavilion 2013–14', 2014, www.icd.uni-stuttgart.de.

17 See, for example, Michael Pawlyn, *Biomimicry in Architecture* (London, 2016), pp. 62–5.

18 See Blaine Brownell, 'Arachnid Architecture as Human Shelter', *Architect*, www.architectmagazine.com, 27 July 2015.

19 Katarzyna Michalski and Sergiusz Michalski, *Spider* (London, 2010), p. 7.

20 On the construction of spiderwebs, see William Eberhard, *Spider Webs: Behavior, Function and Evolution* (Chicago, IL, 2020).

21 Ovid, *Metamorphoses*, Book 6.

22 Michalski and Michalski, *Spider*, p. 81; and pp. 93–4 on spiders and the *femme fatale*.

23 Sir Tim Berners-Lee, British Computer Society's Lovelace Lecture, London, 13 March 2007, available at www.openobjects.org.uk, accessed 10 May 2022.

24 See Berthold Burkhardt, 'Natural Structures: The Research of Frei Otto in Natural Sciences', *International Journal of Space Structures*, XXXI/1 (2016), pp. 9–15.

25 See Geoff Manaugh, 'Architecture-by-Bee and Other Animal Printheads', www.bldgblog.com, 16 July 2014.

26 See Studio Tomás Saraceno, 'Hybrid Webs', https://studiotomassaraceno.org.

27 See Kimberly Bradley, 'With Spiders and Space Dust, Tomas Saraceno Takes Off', *New York Times*, 19 October 2018; and David Rothenberg, 'Spider Music', *PAJ: A Journal of Performance and Art*, XL/1 (2018), pp. 31–6.

28 Wilson Tarbox, 'Tomás Saraceno: How Spiders Build Their Webs', *Frieze*, www.frieze.com, 21 January 2019.

29 See Simon Sadler, *Archigram: Architecture Without Architecture* (Cambridge, MA, 2005), p. 88.

30 Italo Calvino, *Invisible Cities* [1972], trans. William Weaver (London, 1997), p. 67.

31 Ordinary Ltd, 'Arachnia', available at http://cargocollective.com, accessed 10 May 2022.

32 Michalski and Michalski, *Spider*, pp. 44–53.

33 Karl Abrahams, 'The Spider as a Dream Symbol', *International Journal of Psycho-Analysis*, 4 (1923), pp. 313–18.

34 John Wyndham, *Web* (London, 1979).

35 *Tape*, Museum of Science and Industry, Manchester, 2017; see Joe Roberts, 'Behind the Scenes: Building Tape', 24 October 2017, https://blog. scienceandindustrymuseum.org.uk, accessed 10 May 2022.

36 For descriptions and images of the various incarnations of *Tape*, see www.numen.eu, accessed 10 May 2022.

37 Hannah Moore, 'Are All the Ants as Heavy as All the Humans?', *BBC News*, www.bbc.co.uk, 22 September 2014.

38 Italo Calvino, 'The Argentine Ant', *Esquire*, 1 October 1960, p. 154.

39 Ibid.

40 See Walter R. Tschinkel, 'The Nest Architecture of the Florida Harvester Ant, *Pogonomyrmex badius*', *Journal of Insect Science*, IV/21 (2004), pp. 1–19.

41 The process of excavating the nest was documented in the film *Ants! Nature's Secret Power* (2004; dir. Wolfgang Thaler).

42 Julian Gavaghan, 'The Bug Society: Scientists Excavate Underground Ant City that "Rivals the Great Wall of China" with a Labyrinth of Highways', *Mail Online*, www.dailymail.co.uk, 2 February 2012.

43 See Charlotte Sleigh, *Ant* (London, 2003), p. 34.

44 Israel Fernández, 'What Have Ants Taught Architecture?', *Ferrovial*, https://ferrovial.com, 18 November 2016, accessed 10 May 2022.

45 Ed Yong, 'Ants Write Architectural Plans into the Walls of Their Buildings', *National Geographic*, www.nationalgeographic.com, 18 January 2018.

46 'Learning from Ants', LYCS Architecture, http://lycs-arc.com.

47 'Urban Ant Farm: Colony Encouraged to Hack City of Glass and Sand', https://weburbanist.com.

48 Sleigh, *Ant*, p. 30.

49 Ibid., p. 111.

50 See Rafael Gómezbarros, *Casada Tomada* (*House Taken Over*), 2013.

51 On the variety of wasp nest construction, see Robert L. Jeanne, 'The Adaptiveness of Social Wasp Nest Architecture', *Quarterly Review of Biology*, 30 (1975), pp. 267–87.

52 The experiment received wide coverage in the design and other press; see 'Outreach: Wasp Is Art', www.mattiamenchetti.com.

53 See Eric Bonabeau, Marco Dorigo and Guy Theraulaz, *Swarm Intelligence: From Natural to Artificial Systems* (New York, 1999).

54 Philip Ball, 'Bright Lights, Bug City', *New Scientist*, 27 February 2010.

55 For a short film of the prototype house being constructed, see WASP Team, 'Gaia: 3D Printed Earth House with Crane WASP: Presentation Video', www.youtube.com.

56 See '3D Printing Architecture: TECLA', www.3dwasp.com; and Mario Cucinella Architects, 'TECLA', www.mcarchitects.it.

57 Calvino, *Invisible Cities*, p. 115.

58 E. Lily Yu, 'The Cartographer Wasps and the Anarchist Bees', *Clarkesworld*, 55 (April 2011).

59 Graham Harman, *Object-Oriented Ontology: A New Theory of Everything* (London, 2018), p. 88.

60 See Count Bubs, 'An Abandoned Hornet's Nest My Dad Found in His Shed That He Hadn't Been in for a Couple Years', www.reddit.com, 23 April 2014, accessed 10 May 2022.

61 See Mike Hansell, *Built by Animals: The Natural History of Animal Architecture* (Oxford, 2007), p. 29.

62 Claire Preston, *Bee* (London, 2006), p. 7. On the history of apiculture, see Eva Crane's comprehensive *The World History of Beekeeping and Honey Hunting* (Abingdon, 1999).

63 Langstroth patented his invention in 1852 and described it in his influential book *Langstroth on the Hive and the Honey-Bee: A Bee Keeper's Manual* (Northampton, 1853).

64 See Juan Antonio Ramírez, *The Beehive Metaphor: From Gaudí to Le Corbusier* (London, 2000), p. 31.

65 Ibid., p. 25. On vernacular granaries, see Bernard Rudofsky, *Architecture Without Architects: A Short Introduction to Non-Pedigreed Architecture* (New York, 1964), pp. 94–8.

66 See 'Bee Shelter History', *Hartpury Heritage Trust*, www.hartpuryheritage. org.uk.

67 Ned Doddington, 'Hive City', www.expandedenvironment.com, 9 April 2012.

68 Raffaello Rosselli and Luigi Rosselli, 'The Beehive', *Architizer*, https://architizer.com.

69 Elisabeth Schneyder, 'A Beehive as a Model for Living', *UBM Magazine*, www.ubm-development.com.

70 'Honeycomb Refugee Skyscraper', *eVolo*, www.evolo.us, 28 July 2017.

71 Maurice Maeterlinck, *The Life of the Bee*, trans. Alfred Sutro (New York, 1903), p. 48. A contemporary equivalent is Laline Paull's *The Bees* (London, 2015).

72 See Stephanie Strasnick, 'Step Inside a Massive Beehive in London's Kew Gardens', *Architectural Digest*, www.architecturaldigest.com, 29 June 2016.

73 See Ramírez, *The Beehive Metaphor*, pp. 87–9.

74 Manaugh, 'Architecture-by-Bee and Other Animal Printheads'.

75 Recounted in Charles Butler, *The Feminine Monarchie; or, The Historie of Bees* (London, 1609), pp. B2V–B3R.

76 Quoted in Colin Fernandez, 'Termite Mound with Cathedral's Dreaming Spires', *Daily Mail*, 24 November 2017.

77 See Richard Dawkins, *The Extended Phenotype* (Oxford, 1982).

78 For the full story, see Fernandez, 'Termite Mound with Cathedral's Dreaming Spires'.

79 See Lisa Margonelli, *Underbug: An Obsessive Tale of Termites and Technology* (London, 2019), p. 31.

80 See Scott Turner, *The Extended Organism: The Physiology of Animal-Built Structures* (Cambridge, MA, 2000), pp. 195–200.

81 Amia Srinivasan, 'What Termites Can Teach Us', *New Yorker*, 17 September 2018.

82 See Lee Billings, 'The Termite and the Architect', *Nautilus*, https://nautil.us, 8 December 2013.

83 Philip Ball, 'For Sustainable Architecture, Think Bug', *New Scientist*, www.newscientist.com, 17 February 2010.

84 Quoted in Margonelli, *Underbug*, p. 251.

85 See Guy Theraulaz and Eric Bonabeau, 'A Brief History of Stigmergy', *Artificial Life*, V/2 (1999), pp. 97–116.

86 See the video by the Self-Organizing Systems Research Group, 'TERMES: Autonomous Robot Construction Crew', Wyss Institute, available at https://wyss.harvard.edu.

87 William Morton Wheeler, 'The Ant-Colony as an Organism', *Journal of Morphology*, XXII/2 (1911), pp. 307–25.

88 Eugène Marais, *The Soul of the White Ant* [1936], trans. Winifred de Kok (Cape Town, 2006), p. 18.

89 Quoted in Margonelli, *Underbug*, p. 250.

90 Marais, *The Soul of the White Ant*, p. 42.

91 Quoted in Billings, 'The Termite and the Architect'.

2 Aerial

1 Dillon Marsh, 'Assimilation', www.dillonmarsh.com.

2 Gaston Bachelard, *The Poetics of Space* [1957], trans. Maria Jolas (Boston, MA, 1994), pp. 91–104.

3 A comprehensive overview of birds' nest design and construction is in Peter Goodfellow and Mike Hansell, *Avian Architecture: How Birds Design, Engineer and Build* (Lewes, 2013).

4 Mark Cocker, *Crow Country* (London, 2008), p. 12.

5 On the conflicting association of pigeons, see Barbara Allen, *Pigeon* (London, 2009).

6 On the development of dovecotes in the Middle East, south Asia and Europe, see Peter Hansell and Jean Hansell, *A Dovecote Heritage* (Bath, 1992).

7 A comprehensive history of British dovecotes is found in Peter Hansell and Jean Hansell, *Doves and Dovecotes* (Bath, 1988).

8 Ibid., p. 39.

9 Ibid., p. 225.

10 Allen, *Pigeon*, pp. 50–55.

11 Colin Jerolmack, *The Global Pigeon* (Chicago, IL, 2013).

12 Ned Dodington, 'Interview: Carla Novak', www.expandedenvironment.org, 7 February 2012.

13 See 'Racing Pigeons: Garbage City Hosts World's Oddest Pastime', https://weburbanist.com, 4 September 2014.

14 Gordan Savičić and Selena Savić, *Unpleasant Design* (London, 2016).

15 See Cara Giaimo, 'What Pigeon Spikes Can Teach Us About People', *Atlas Obscura*, www.atlasobscura.com, 22 September 2017.

16 Jerolmack, *The Global Pigeon*, pp. 44–77.

17 Allen, *Pigeon*, pp. 59–60, 74–9.

18 Aranda\Lasch, 'The Brooklyn Pigeon Project', http://arandalasch.com; see also David Gissen, *Subnature: Architecture's Other Environments* (Princeton, NJ, 2009), pp. 186–7.

19 S. A. Rogers, 'Pigeons on Patrol: Birds with Backpacks Monitor London Air Pollution, https://weburbanist.com, 9 May 2016.

20 Stella Burney and Natsko Seki, *Architecture According to Pigeons* (London, 2013).

21 See Derek Ratcliffe, *The Peregrine Falcon* (London, 1980), pp. 64–6.

22 See Helen Macdonald, *Falcon* (London, 2006), pp. 136–44.

23 Ibid., pp. 31–2.

24 Robert Macfarlane, introduction to J. A. Baker, *The Peregrine* [1967] (New York, 2005), p. xiii.

25 Ibid., p. 35.

26 See Adam Kuby, 'Cliff Dwelling', www.adamkuby.com.

27 Steve Hinchliffe and Sarah Whatmore, 'Living Cities: Towards a Politics of Conviviality', *Science as Culture*, xv/2 (2006), p. 127.

28 The most comprehensive survey of falconry practices around the world is Karl-Heinz German and Oliver Grimm, eds, *Raptor and Human: Falconry and Bird Symbolism Throughout the Millennia on a Global Scale* (Hamburg, 2014).

29 Macdonald, *Falcon*, p. 83, p. 97; Phillip Glasier, *Falconry and Hawking* (London, 1978), is still a key work on the subject.

30 Macdonald, *Falcon*, p. 180.

31 On the symbolic meanings of swallows and other hirundines, see Angela Turner, *Swallow* (London, 2015).

32 See Stephen Moss, *The Swallow: A Biography* (London, 2020).

33 Vitruvius, *Ten Books of Architecture*, trans. Morris Hicky Morgan (Cambridge, MA, 1914), p. 38. See also Jason Rhys Parry, 'Primal Weaving: Structure and Meaning in Language and Architecture', *SubStance*, xlvi/3 (2017), pp. 125–49.

34 Turner, *Swallow*, pp. 33–4.

35 See Deniz Onur Erman, 'Bird Houses in Turkish Culture and Contemporary Applications', *Procedia: Social and Behavioral Sciences*, 122 (2014), pp. 306–11.

36 Helen Macdonald, 'Nestboxes', in *Vesper Flights* (London, 2020), pp. 118–19.

37 See 'Birdhouse by J. Warren Jacobs', *Pennsylvania Heritage*, http://paheritage. wpengine.com (Summer 2004).

38 See 'Purple Martin Capital of the Nation – Griggsville, IL', www.waymarking. com, 7 April 2017.

39 James Rennie, *The Architecture of Birds* (New York, 1844), p. 333.

40 Mary Douglas, *Purity and Danger: An Analysis of Concepts of Pollution and Taboo* [1966] (London, 2002).

41 Vincent Callebaut Architectures, 'Swallow's Nest', https://vincent.callebaut. org.

42 Turner, *Swallow*, p. 146.

43 Paul D. Kyle and Georgean Z. Kyle, *Chimney Swifts: America's Mysterious Birds above the Fireplace* (College Station, TX, 2005).

44 Paul D. Kyle and Georgean Z. Kyle, *Chimney Swift Towers: New Habitats for America's Mysterious Birds* (College Station, TX, 2005).

45 David Lack and Andrew Lack, *Swifts in a Tower* [1956] (London, 2018).

46 Ibid., pp, 237–8. See also the 2015 report published by the RSPB, Mark Eaton et al., 'Birds of Conservation Concern 4: The Population Status of Birds in the UK, Channel Islands and Isle of Man', *British Birds*, 108 (2015), pp. 708–46.

47 See Something & Son, 's.w.i.f.t code', www.somethingandson.com.

48 Will Nash, 'Swift Tower', 2020, www.willnash.co.uk.

49 See Menthol Architects, 'Swift Tower', www.menthol.pl, 1 August 2015.

50 Personal correspondence with Andy Merritt, 8 March 2021.

51 Lack, *Swifts in a Tower*, p. 96.

52 See Giacomo Balla, *Swifts: Paths of Movement + Dynamic Sequences*, 1913, Museum of Modern Art, New York.

53 Helen Macdonald, 'Vesper Flights', in *Vesper Flights* (London, 2020), pp. 136–44.

54 Mengying Xie, 'Porous City', MSc thesis, Royal Institute of Technology, Stockholm, 2020.

55 Mark Cocker, *Crow Country* (London, 2008), pp. 115, 122, 132.

56 Ibid., pp. 65–6.

57 Dickens visited St Giles in 1851 in the midst of writing *Bleak House*. See Charles Dickens, 'On Duty with Inspector Field', *Household Words*, 14 June 1851.

58 On the history of the St Giles rookery and others in the city, see Thomas Beames, *The Rookeries of London: Past, Present and Prospective* (London, 1850).

59 See Pascal Tréguer, 'History of "Crow's Nest" (Lookout Platform on a Ship's Mast)', https://worldhistories.net, 16 August 2018. The biblical story is recounted in Genesis 8:6–7.

60 See 'Survey of the Metropolis', *Illustrated London News*, 22 April 1848, p. 259; and 'Ordnance Survey of London And Its Environs', 24 June 1848, p. 414.

61 See Paul Dobraszczyk, *Into the Belly of the Beast: Exploring London's Victorian Sewers* (Reading, 2009), pp. 24–5.

62 Boria Sax, *Crow* (London, 2017), p. 6.

63 See Llowarch Llowarch Architects, 'Ravens Night Enclosures', www.llarchitects.co.uk.

64 See Paul Wilson, 'Architecture at zsl London Zoo, Regent's Park', www.zsl.org.

65 Russell Hoban, 'The Raven', in *The Moment Under the Moment* [London, 1992]; repr. in *A Russell Hoban Omnibus* (Bloomington, IN, 1999), pp. 743–9.

66 On the origin of this nursery rhyme and its adaptation for the film, see Christopher Laws, 'The Birds (1963): "Risseldy Rosseldy"', *Culturedarm*, https://culturedarm.com.

67 See 'Biography', https://katemccgwire.com.

68 Recounted in Lyanda Lynn Haupt, *Mozart's Starling* (London, 2017), pp. 54–6.

69 See C. J. Feare, *The Starling* (Princes Risborough, 1985).

70 The story of Mozart's starling was first explored in detail in Meredith West and Andrew P. Kind, 'Mozart's Starling', *American Scientist*, LXXVIII/2 (1990), pp. 106–14.

71 Haupt, *Mozart's Starling*, pp. 82–94, 98.

72 Timothy Q. Gentner, Kimberly M. Fenn, Daniel Margoliash and Howard C. Nusbaum, 'Recursive Syntactic Pattern Learning by Songbirds', *Nature*, CDXL/7088 (2006), pp. 1204–7.

73 See Andrea Procaccini et al., 'Propagating Waves in Starling, *Sturnus Vulgaris*, Flocks under Predation', *Animal Behaviour*, LXXXIV/4 (2011), pp. 759–65.

74 Seamus Perry, ed., *Samuel Taylor Coleridge: Collected Notebooks, a Selection* (Oxford, 2002), p. 39.

75 Andy Morris, 'Educational Landscapes and the Environmental Entanglement of Humans and Non-Humans through the Starling Murmuration', *Geographical Journal*, CLXXXV/3 (2019), pp. 303–12.

76 Perry, ed., *Coleridge: Collected Notebooks*, p. 39; on Crombie's image see Rosita Bolland, 'Murmuration of Starlings: How Our Stunning Front-Page Photograph Was Taken', *Irish Times*, 4 March 2021.

77 A useful summary of this research can be found in Andrew J. King and David J. T. Sumpter, 'Murmurations', *Current Biology*, XXII/4 (2012), pp. 12–14.

78 Haupt, *Mozart's Starling*, pp. 232–5.

79 SO-IL, 'Murmuration, Atlanta, Georgia, USA, 2021', http://so-il.org.

80 'Museum Musings: A Chat with Squidsoup', Scottsdale Center for the Performing Arts, https://smoca.org, 6 May 2020.

3 Wild

1 See, for example, 'The Urban Wild: Animals Take to the Streets Amid Lockdown – in Pictures', *The Guardian*, 22 April 2020.

2 See Frances Stonor Saunders, 'Feral: Searching for Enchantment on the Frontiers of Rewilding by George Monbiot – Review', *The Guardian*, 24 May 2013.

3 Ivan Illich, *Tools for Conviviality* (London, 1973).

4 See Jon Adams and Edmund Ramsden, 'Rat Cities and Beehive Worlds: Density and Design in the Modern City', *Comparative Studies in Society and History*, LIII/4 (2011), pp. 722–56.

5 Jonathan Burt, *Rat* (London, 2004).

6 See Jon Adams and Edmund Ramsden, 'Escaping the Laboratory: The Rodent Experiments of John B. Calhoun and Their Cultural Influence', *Journal of Social History*, XLII/3 (2009), pp. 762–92; see also John B. Calhoun, 'Population Density and Social Pathology', *Scientific American*, CCVI/2 (1962), pp. 139–49.

7 Adams and Ramsden, 'Rat Cities', pp. 736–7, 750.

8 Thomas Beames, *The Rookeries of London: Past, Present and Prospective* (London, 1850), pp. 26–7; Charles Dickens, *Bleak House* [1852–3] (London, 2003), pp. 235–6.

9 The classic book on this subject is Hans Zinsser, *Rats, Lice and History* (London, 1935).

10 Burt, *Rat*, p. 13.

11 Henry Mayhew, *London Labour and the London Poor*, vol. III (London, 1851), p. 3.

12 Ibid., pp. 7–10.

13 Robert Sullivan, *Rats: Observations on the History & Habitat of the City's Most Unwanted Inhabitants* (New York, 2004), p. 12.

14 Ibid., p. 103.

15 Neil Gaiman, *Neverwhere* (London, 1996), p. 69.

16 On the Rat King, see Adrian Daub, 'All Hail the Rat King', https://longreads.com, 11 December 2019.

17 China Miéville, *King Rat* (London, 1998), p. 338.

18 Roy Wagner, *Anthropology of the Subject: Holographic Worldview in New Guinea and Its Meaning and Significance for the World of Anthropology* (Berkeley, CA, 2001), pp. 136–7.

19 Tessa Laird, *Bat* (London, 2018), p. 74.

20 See Will Brooker, *Batman Unmasked: Analysing a Cultural Icon* (London, 2000). Laird brings the batman story more up-to-date in *Bat*, pp. 103–5.

21 An informative compilation of batcave references in television, film, anime and video games can be found at 'Secret Entrances to the Batcave: Evolution (TV Shows, Movies and Games)', www.youtube.com.

22 See Jeremy Deller, 'Bats', www.jeremydeller.org.

23 Charles A. Campbell, *Bats, Mosquitoes and Dollars* (Boston, MA, 1925).

24 Ibid., p. 91. See also Elisabeth D. Mering and Carol L. Chambers, 'Thinking Outside the Box: A Review of Artificial Roosts for Bats', *Wildlife Society Bulletin*, XXXVIII/4 (2014), p. 742.

25 See Asher Elbein, 'Where to See the Most Historic Bat Roost in Texas', https://texashighways.com, 15 April 2019.

26 See Jeremy Deller, 'Bat House', www.jeremydeller.org.

27 Rebecca Boyle, 'Inside the World's First Manmade Batcave Built for Wild Bats', *Popular Science*, www.popsci.com, 14 September 2012.

28 See 'South Congress Bridge Bats', www.batsinaustin.com.

29 See 'Bat Observatory', Texas Architecture, https://soa.utexas.edu, March 2014.

30 '12. Bat Cloud', www.antsoftheprairie.com.

31 '10. Bat Tower', ibid.

32 Thomas Nagel, 'What Is It Like to Be a Bat?', *Philosophical Review*, LXXXIV/4 (1974), pp. 435–50.

33 J. M. Coetzee, *The Lives of Animals* (Princeton, NJ, 1999), pp. 35, 33.

34 Richard Morecroft, *Raising Archie: The Story of Richard Morecroft and His Flying Bat* (East Roseville, NSW, 1991), pp. 58–61.

35 Laird, *Bat*, p. 146.

36 See Dorothy Yamamoto, *The Boundaries of the Human in Medieval English Literature* (Oxford, 2000), pp. 29, 60–74.

37 Martin Wallen, *Fox* (London, 2006), p. 50.

38 Ronald Nowak, *Walker's Carnivores of the World* (Baltimore, MD, 2005), p. 74.

39 'The Architecture of Burrows', Terrierman's Daily Dose, https://terriermandotcom.blogspot.com, 22 April 2005.

40 Quoted in Wallen, *Fox*, p. 17.

41   See 'The Architecture of Burrows'; and Anthony J. Martin, *The Evolution Underground: Burrows, Bunkers, and the Marvelous Subterranean World Beneath Our Feet* (New York, 2017).

42   Franz Kafka, 'The Burrow' [1924], in *Metamorphosis and Other Stories* (London, 1999), pp. 129–66.

43   See Eric Paul Meljac, 'The Poetics of Dwelling: A Consideration of Heidegger, Kafka, and Michael K', *Journal of Modern Literature*, XXXII/1 (2008), pp. 69–76.

44   J. M. Coetzee, *The Life and Times of Michael K* [1983] (London, 1998), pp. 114–15.

45   Ibid., pp. 101, 124.

46   Stephen Harris, Phil Baker and Guy Troughton, *Urban Foxes* (London, 2001).

47   See Angela Cassidy and Brett Mills, '"Fox Tots Attack Shock": Urban Foxes, Mass Media and Boundary-Breaching', *Environmental Communication*, VI/4 (2012), pp. 494–511.

48   Tim Dowling, 'Is the Dog's Friendship with the Fox Sweet or a Bad Omen?', *The Guardian*, 10 April 2021.

49   Wallen, *Fox*, p. 56.

50   Angus M. Woodbury, 'Study of Reptile Dens', *Herpetologica*, X/1 (1954), pp. 49–53.

51   Ned Dodington, 'Interview: Prosthetic Lizard Homes', www. expandedenvironment.org, 29 February 2012.

52   Results of a search for 'reptile house' carried out by the author at www. amazon.co.uk, 3 May 2021.

53   See, for example, Paul Demas, 'Designing and Building a Vivarium', *Reptiles Magazine*, www.reptilesmagazine.com, 9 January 2013.

54   'History of the Reptile House', www.zsl.org, accessed 18 July 2022; 'Conserving Architectural Heritage', https://nationalzoo.si.edu, accessed 18 July 2022; Gregorio Astengo, 'White Whale: The Aquarium and Reptile House At the Turin Zoo and the Architecture of Enzo Venturelli (1955–65)', *Architectural Histories*, VI/1 (2019), pp. 1–16; Jared Ranahan, 'This Is the Largest Reptile Zoo in the World', *USA Today 10Best*, www10best.com, 2 September 2019.

55   J. G. Ballard, *The Drowned World* (London, 1962), p. 18.

56   See Joe Cain, 'Why Benjamin Waterhouse Hawkins Created Crystal Palace Dinosaurs', https://profjoecain.net; and Alexandra Ault, 'A Dinosaur Dinner and Relics from "One of the Greatest Humbugs, Frauds and Absurdities Ever Known"', https://blogs.bl.uk, 16 June 216.

57   Quoted in Nathaniel Robert Walker, 'Paleostructure: Biological, Spiritual, and Architectural Evolution at the Oxford Museum', in *Function and Fantasy: Iron Architecture in the Long Nineteenth Century*, ed. Paul Dobraszczyk and Peter Sealy (London, 2016), p. 61.

58   Ibid., p. 67.

59   Frank Lloyd Wright, *An Autobiography* (New York, 1943), p. 146.

60   See Philip Wilkinson, *Phantom Architecture* (London, 2017), pp. 50–55.

61 See Hubert Naudeix, Mathilde Bejanin and Matthieu Beauhaire, *L'Eléphant de Napoléon* (Paris, 2014).

62 Victor Hugo, *Les Misérables* [1862] (London, 1988), pp. 822–3, 826.

63 'Le Grand Eléphant', *Les Machines de l'île Nantes*, www.lesmachines-nantes.fr.

64 On the history of Lucy the Elephant, see https://lucytheelephant.org.

65 Matt Hickman, 'New Jersey's Most Famous Work of Novelty Architecture Is Now on Airbnb', *The Architect's Newspaper*, www.archpaper.com, 2 March 2020.

66 See https://lucytheelephant.org.

67 See Mark Haywood, 'A Brief History of European Elephant Houses: From London's Imperial Stables to Copenhagen's Post-modern Glasshouse', available at www.academia.edu, accessed 12 May 2022.

68 See Ned Dodington, 'Elephant House', www.expandedenvironment.org, 4 June 2009.

69 See Emily Hooper, 'Kaeng Krachan Elephant Park Shell', *Architect Magazine*, www.architectmagazine.com, 27 October 2015.

70 For a poetic description of the project by the design team, see 'Elephant Study Centre', http://bangkokprojectstudio.co.

71 These numbers are quoted in Dan Wylie, *Elephant* (London, 2008), pp. 139–40, 168.

72 Quoted in 'Elephant Study Centre'.

73 Gottfried Semper, *The Four Elements of Architecture and Other Writings* [1851], trans. Harry Francis Mallgrave and Wolfgang Herrmann (Cambridge, 1989), pp. 226–7.

74 Fiona Anne Stewart, 'The Evolution of Shelter: Ecology and Ethology of Chimpanzee Nest Building', PhD thesis, University of Cambridge, 2011, p. 1.

75 Ibid., pp. 1, 6–9.

76 Ibid., pp. xix, 2, 7.

77 Tim Ingold, 'Of Blocks and Knots: Architecture as Weaving', *Architectural Review*, www.architectural-review.com, 25 October 2013. See also Ingold's book *Making: Anthropology, Archaeology, Art and Architecture* (London, 2013).

78 See John Sorenson, *Ape* (London, 2009), pp. 105–26, for an outline of various kinds of ape fictions.

79 For a detailed account of the production design of *Planet of the Apes*, see 'Ape City (East Coast), https://planetoftheapes.fandom.com, accessed 12 May 2022. Huebner's original sketches for Ape City are reproduced in J. W. Rinzler, *The Making of Planet of the Apes* (2018).

80 On the history of King Kong, up until Peter Jackson's 2005 remake, see Cynthia Marie Erb, *Tracking King Kong: A Hollywood Icon in World Culture* (Detroit, MI, 2009).

81 Discussed at *Things Magazine*, www.thingsmagazine.net, 19 December 2005, accessed 12 May 2022.

4 Aquatic

1 See Julia Watson, *Lo-TEK: Design by Radical Indigenism* (Cologne, 2019), pp. 272–377.
2 Quoted in Rachel Poliquin, *Beaver* (London, 2015), p. 11.
3 Vitruvius, *Ten Books of Architecture*, p. 39.
4 Ibid., pp. 311–15.
5 Louise M. Pryke, *Turtle* (London, 2021), pp. 7–8, 15.
6 Ibid., pp. 11, 23–5.
7 See Yaniv Shelef and Benny Bar-On, 'Surface Protection in Bio-Shields via a Functional Soft Skin Layer: Lessons from the Turtle Shell', *Journal of the Mechanical Behavior of Biomedical Materials*, 73 (2017), pp. 68–75.
8 See Marc Dessauce, ed., *The Inflatable Moment: Pneumatics and Protest in '68* (New York, 1999). Utopie demonstrated the potential of air-filled buildings in their 'Structures Gonflables (Inflatable Structures)' exhibition in Paris in March 1968, which featured designs for not only inflatable houses but all manner of objects, from machines and tools to furniture and vehicles.
9 See William Firebrace, 'Learning from the Tortoise', https://drawingmatter. org, 9 August 2019.
10 Ibid.
11 Andy Knaggs, 'Vietnamese Folklore Inspires Aquarium by Legacy Entertainment', *CLADnews*, www.cladglobal.com, 15 October 2019.
12 Pryke, *Turtle*, pp. 49–51, 68.
13 See Kenneth D. Rose, *One Nation Underground: The Fallout Shelter in American Culture* (New York, 2001), p. 128.
14 Ibid., pp. 152–3.
15 See 'Ancient Chinese "Turtle Town" Is a Tortoise-Shaped Fortress', http://petslady.com, 4 June 2019.
16 On the franchise, see Richard Rosenbaum, *Raise Some Shell: Teenage Mutant Ninja Turtles* (Toronto, 2014); and Andrew Farago, *Teenage Mutant Ninja Turtles: The Ultimate Visual History* (San Rafael, CA, 2014).
17 See David L. Pike, 'Urban Nightmares and Future Visions: Life Beneath New York', *Wide Angle*, XX/4 (1998), pp. 9–50.
18 Q. V. Hough, 'What to Expect from the Teenage Mutant Ninja Turtles Movie Reboot', https://screenrant.com, 1 September 2020.
19 See Rebecca Stott, *Oyster* (London, 2004). On Turner's project, see 'City Audio Services: Arts Projects', http://cityaudioservices.com.
20 See Karen Hardy et al., 'Shellfishing and Shell Midden Construction in the Saloum Delta, Senegal', *Journal of Anthropological Archaeology*, 41 (2016), pp. 19–32.
21 Stott, *Oyster*, pp. 14–16.
22 For details on the 2010 exhibition, see 'Inside/Out' blog posts, 3 November 2009–1 November 2010, www.moma.org; for the original Oyster-tecture project, see 'Oyster-tecture', www.scapestudio.com.
23 On oysters and New York, see Mark Kurlansky, *The Big Oyster: A Molluscular History of New York* (London, 2007).

24 For details of the Living Breakwaters project, see 'Living Breakwaters: Design and Implementation', www.scapestudio.com. See also Kate Orff, 'Shellfish as Living Infrastructure', *Ecological Restoration*, XXXI/3 (2013), pp. 317–22.

25 The story of the project was documented in episode 282 of Roman Mars's *99% Invisible* podcast, available at https://99percentinvisible.org.

26 The course of the project was described to the backers of the Billion Oyster Pavilion during 2015 at www.kickstarter.com; Dameron Architecture, 'Billion Oyster Project Headquarters', https://dameronarch.com.

27 Stephanie Wakefield and Bruce Braun, 'Oystertecture: Infrastructure, Profanation, and the Sacred Figure of the Human', in *Infrastructure, Environment and Life in the Anthropocene*, ed. Kregg Hetherington (Durham, NC, 2018), pp. 193–215.

28 Gaston Bachelard, *The Poetics of Space* [1957], trans. Maria Jolas (Boston, MA, 1994), p. 123.

29 Edward Forbes, 'Shell-fish: Their Ways and Works', *Westminster Review*, LVII (January 1852), pp. 44–5.

30 Francis Ponge, *Le Parti pris des choses* [Paris, 1942], trans. C. K. Williams and Wake Forest University Press (Winston-Salem, NC, 1994).

31 Quoted in Francis Ponge, *Selected Poems* (London, 1998), p. 26.

32 Quoted in Bachelard, *The Poetics of Space*, pp. 130–31.

33 Ibid., p. 132.

34 See Stott, *Oyster*, p. 27.

35 W. M., 'On Some Remarkable Examples of Irregular Growth in the Oyster', *Illustrated London News*, 11 August 1855, p. 190.

36 Stott, *Oyster*, pp. 148–50.

37 On the evolution of cephalopods and their intelligence, see Peter Godfrey-Smith, *Other Minds: The Octopus and the Evolution of Intelligent Life* (London, 2017); and Sy Montgomery, *The Soul of an Octopus: A Surprising Exploration into the Wonder of Consciousness* (London, 2015).

38 Godfrey-Smith, *Other Minds*, p. 48.

39 Quoted in Richard Schweid, *Octopus* (London, 2014), pp. 28–30.

40 Godfrey-Smith, *Other Minds*, p. 64.

41 Illustrated at Francesca Myman, Poulpe Pulps, https://francesca.net.

42 On cephalopods in cinema, see William Brown and David H. Fleming, *Squid Cinema from Hell: Kinoteuthis Infernalis and the Emergence of Chthulumedia* (Edinburgh, 2020).

43 On the Kraken myth, see Rodrigo B. Salvador and Barbara M. Tomotani, 'The Kraken: When Myth Encounters Science', www.scielo.br, 2014.

44 For octopus-related political imagery, see Dave Gilson, 'Octopi Wall Street!', *Mother Jones*, www.motherjones.com, 6 October 2011; and 'Victor Hugo's Devil-Fish', https://vulgararmy.tumblr.com.

45 H. P. Lovecraft, 'The Call of Cthulhu', *Weird Tales*, 11/2 [February 1928], pp. 159–78; repr. in *Collected Stories, vol. 1* (Ware, 2007), pp. 34–60. On Lovecraft and architecture, see Will Wiles, 'The Corner of Lovecraft and Ballard', *Places*, https://placesjournal.org, June 2017.

46 The *Kodiak Queen* art reef is described at https://1beyondthereef.com. This page also contains a link to *The Kodiak Queen* (2018), a documentary by Rob Sorrenti on the construction and sinking of the project.

47 For a short description and photographs of the project, see Bethany Ao, 'An Inflatable Sea Monster Takes Over the Navy Yard', *Philadelphia Enquirer*, 8 October 2018.

48 Alan Bauch, *Dolphin* (London, 2014), pp. 7–40.

49 See Diana Reiss, *The Dolphin in the Mirror: Exploring Dolphin Minds and Saving Dolphin Lives* (Boston, MA, 2011).

50 Jeff VanderMeer, *Annihilation* (London, 2014), p. 97.

51 Bauch, *Dolphin*, pp. 79–82, 127–9.

52 Lilly's books include *Man and Dolphin* (Garden City, NY, 1961) and *The Mind of the Dolphin: A Nonhuman Intelligence* (Garden City, NY, 1967).

53 See Christopher Riley, 'The Dolphin Who Loved Me: The Nasa-Funded Project That Went Wrong', *The Guardian*, 8 June 2014. Lovatt's experiences were documented in the film *The Girl Who Talked to Dolphins* (dir. Christopher Riley, 2014).

54 The most comprehensive source on Ant Farm remains Constance M. Lewallen and Steve Seid, eds, *Ant Farm, 1968–1978* (Los Angeles, CA, 2004), published to accompany the first retrospective of the group's work held in 2004 at the Berkeley Art Museum and Pacific Film Archive, University of California.

55 See Tyler Survant, 'Biological Borderlands: Ant Farm's Zoopolitics', *Horizonte*, 8 (2013), pp. 49–64, available at https://tylersurvant.com, accessed 10 May 2022.

56 Ibid.

57 See Paul Dobraszczyk, *Future Cities: Architecture and the Imagination* (London, 2019), pp. 51–65.

58 Lewallen and Seid, eds, *Ant Farm*, pp. 82–3.

59 On the spiritual meanings of dolphins, see Mette Bryld and Nina Lykke, *Cosmodolphins: Feminist Cultural Studies of Technology, Animals and the Sacred* (New York, 2000).

60 See Stefan Linquist, 'Today's Awe-Inspiring Design, Tomorrow's Plexiglass Dinosaur: How Public Aquariums Contradict Their Conservation Mandate in Pursuit of Immersive Underwater Displays', in *The Art and Beyond: The Evolution of Zoo and Aquarium Conservation*, ed. Ben A. Minteer, Jane Maienschein and James P. Collins (Chicago, IL, 2018), pp. 329–43.

61 Ibid., pp. 342–3.

62 Tom Anstey, 'U.S. National Aquarium Considers Retiring Dolphins to One-of-a-Kind Sanctuary', *Attractions Management*, 12 June 2014, www.attractionsmanagement.com.

63 See Peter Coates, *Salmon* (London, 2006), pp. 59–65.

64 'Purpose', https://salmonnation.net.

65 See Yongwook Seong, 'Becoming Salmon', *Architect Magazine*, www.architectmagazine.com, 10 August 2019.

66 Christopher Dunagan, 'New Seattle Seawall Improves Migratory Pathway for Young Salmon', www.eopugetsound.org, 9 June 2020.

67 'James Smith (1789–1850)', www.gracesguide.co.uk.
68 See Amy Kraft, 'Upstream Battle: Fishes Shun Modern Dam Passages, Contributing to Population Declines', *Scientific American*, www.scientificamerican.com, 20 February 2013.
69 Coates, *Salmon*, pp. 95–6.
70 Anders Furuset, 'Norway Unveils New Aquaculture Strategy, Seeks to Overhaul Wide Range of Regulations', www.intrafish.com, 8 July 2021.
71 Coates, *Salmon*, pp. 96–105.
72 See 'Business Intelligence Report: Land-Based Salmon Farming: A Guide for Investors and Industry', www.intrafish.com, 17 October 2019.
73 Andy Knaggs, 'Interactive Aquacentre Venue with "Fish-Eye" Design Planned for Norway', *CLADnews*, www.cladglobal.com, 7 May 2019.
74 On ancient and modern uses of salmon skin as clothing, see Hermann Ehrlich, *Biological Materials of Marine Origin: Vertebrates* (London, 2015), pp. 264–71.
75 Richard Dawkins, *The Extended Phenotype* [1982] (Oxford, 1999), pp. 304–6.
76 See Poliquin, *Beaver*, pp. 53–98, 126–34.
77 Lewis Henry Morgan, *The American Beaver and His Works* (Philadelphia, PA, 1868).
78 Ibid., p. 256.
79 See Irene Cheng, 'The Beavers and the Bees: Intelligent Design and the Marvelous Architecture of Animals', *Cabinet*, 23 (2006), www.cabinetmagazine.org.
80 Bernard Rudofsky, *The Prodigious Builders* (New York, 1977), pp. 13, 57, 59.
81 Poliquin, *Beaver*, pp. 159–62.
82 'Grey Owl's Strange Quest' [1934], available to view at www.youtube.com.
83 See Stacy Passmore, 'Landscape with Beavers', *Places*, https://placesjournal.org, July 2019.
84 See 'Brutalist Beaver Constructs Paul Rudolph-Inspired Dam', *The Onion*, www.theonion.com, 29 March 2019.
85 Poliquin, *Beaver*, p. 184.
86 See Thomas Hynes, 'The Boogie Down Beavers of NYC's Bronx River', *Untapped New York*, https://untappedcities.com, 10 May 2021.
87 'No Design on Stolen Land', https://nodesignonstolen.land.
88 Passmore, 'Landscape with Beavers'.
89 See Poliquin, *Beaver*, pp. 123–5.

5 Domestic

1 Jessica Glenza, 'Shakira Says Two Wild Boars Attacked Her in Barcelona Park', *The Guardian*, 30 September 2021.
2 Bernhard Warner, 'Boar Wars: How Wild Hogs Are Trashing European Cities', *The Guardian*, 30 July 2019.
3 Angela Giuffrida, 'Rome Residents Impose Curfew After Spate of Wild Boar Attacks', *The Guardian*, 3 May 2022.
4 See John Bradshaw, *In Defence of Dogs* (London, 2012), pp. 31–46.
5 Donna J. Haraway, *When Species Meet* (Minneapolis, MN, 2007).

6 Bradshaw, *In Defence of Dogs*, p. 35.

7 See Tom Wainwright, *Pet-tecture* (London, 2018). 'Architecture for Dogs',
   a travelling exhibition curated by Kenya Hara at various venues from 2012,
   was last held at Japan House, London, 19 September 2020–10 January 2021;
   for a virtual tour of the exhibition, see 'Architecture for Dogs', *Japan House*,
   www.japanhouselondon.uk, accessed 13 May 2022. See also 'Dogchitecture
   Expo in Mexico City', *Bunker Arquitectura*, www.bunkerarquitectura.com.

8 Wainwright, *Pet-tecture*, pp. 43–4.

9 Ibid., pp. 92–3.

10 Ibid., p. 7. According to Wainwright, in 2016, in the USA alone, the pet
   industry was estimated at $66.75 billion, with a similar proportionate amount
   in the UK.

11 Rahm's video work was shown at the 'Bêtes Off' exhibition; see *Bêtes Off*,
   exh. cat., ed. Claude d'Anthenaise, Conciergerie, Paris, January–March 2012.

12 See, for example, John Plaw, *Ferme Ornée; or, Rural Improvements*
   (London, 1823), Plate IX.

13 Examples of surviving dog kennels from the eighteenth and nineteenth
   centuries in the UK are illustrated in Lucinda Lambton's *Palaces for Pigs:
   Animal Architecture and Other Beastly Buildings* (Swindon, 2011), pp.
   64–73.

14 Ibid., pp. 68–9.

15 Sandra Kaji-O'Grady, 'Architecture and the Interspecies Collective: Dog and
   Human Associates at Mars', *Architecture and Culture*, IX/4 (2020), pp. 569–86.

16 See Maria Laken, 'UK's Stray Dog Numbers Decrease but More Needs Doing',
   Dogs Today, https://dogstodaymagazine.co.uk, 26 November 2018.

17 For a useful summary, see Rebecca F. Wisch, 'Detailed Discussion of State
   Cat Laws', Animal Legal and Historical Center, Michigan State University
   College of Law, www.animallaw.info, 2005.

18 See John Bradshaw, *Cat Sense* (London, 2013), p. 243. See also 'U.S. Pet
   Ownership Statistics', *American Veterinary Medical Association*,
   www.avma.org, based on statistics for 2017–18.

19 Wainwright, *Pet-tecture*, p. 81.

20 Ibid., pp. 46, 96–7.

21 Eleanor Gibson, 'Six Houses Designed as Playgrounds for Cats', *Dezeen*,
   www.dezeen.com, 22 November 2016.

22 Rose Etherington, 'Inside Out by Takeshi Hosaka Architects', *Dezeen*,
   www.dezeen.com, 31 March 2011.

23 See 'Secret Life of the Cat: The Science of Tracking Our Pets',
   www.bbc.co.uk, 12 June 2013.

24 See Brigitte Schuster, *Architektur für die Katz/Arcatecture: Schweizer
   Katzenleitern/Swiss Cat Ladders* (Basel and Bern, 2019).

25 Ibid. See also Kurt Kohlstedt, 'Swiss Cat Ladders: Documenting and
   Deconstructing Feline-Friendly Infrastucture', https://99percentinvisible.org,
   25 September 2020.

26 See 'The Fragmented Courtyard: Architecture for Cats',
   https://concentrico.es, 2016.

27 See Edward William Lane and Edward Stanley Poole, *An Account of the Manners and Customs of the Modern Egyptians* (London, 1871), vol. I, p. 362.

28 See T. C. Barker and Michael Robbins, *A History of London Transport: Passenger Travel and the Development of the Metropolis* (London, 1963). On horse-drawn cabs, see Trevor May, *Gondolas and Growlers: The History of the London Horse Cab* (Stroud, 1995). On the London omnibuses, see 'From Omnibus to Ecobus: A Social History of London's Public Transport, 1829–2000', formerly available at www.ltmuseum.co.uk, and now at https://web.archive.org, accessed 13 May 2022.

29 Victor Deupi, Introduction to Oscar Riera Ojeda and Victor Deupi, *Stables: High Design for Horse and Home* (New York, 2020), p. 11.

30 Ibid., p. 10.

31 See Elaine Walker, *Horse* (London, 2008), pp. 94–100.

32 See Geoffrey Tyack, 'A Pantheon for Horses: The Prince Regent's Dome and Stables at Brighton', *Architectural History*, LVIII (2015), pp. 141–58.

33 Jonathan Foyle, 'Equine Architecture and the Era of Stables as Grand Monuments', *Financial Times*, 25 July 2014.

34 Ojeda and Deupi, *Stables*, pp. 50–62. A more utilitarian approach is provided in Keith Warth, *Design Handbook for Stables and Equestrian Buildings* (London, 2014).

35 Ojeda and Deupi, *Stables*, pp. 154–62.

36 See Penelope Smart, 'Twelve Live Horses', https://medium.com, 24 November 2019.

37 'Horse Lives in House Like a Normal Person', HuffPost, www.huffpost.com, 10 February 2014.

38 Revelation 6:8, New King James Version.

39 See Walker, *Horse*, pp. 21–63.

40 Anna Sewell, *Black Beauty* [1877] (Ware, 1993), p. 39.

41 Govindasamy Agoramoorthy and Minna J. Hsu, 'The Significance of Cows in Indian Society Between Sacredness and Economy', *Anthropological Notebooks*, XVIII/3 (2012), pp. 5–12.

42 Rebecca Hui, 'MOOving Along: Following Cows in Changing Indian Cities', *Tekton*, II/1 (2015), pp. 8–24.

43 Agoramoorthy and Hsu, 'The Significance of Cows', p. 7.

44 See Hannah Velten, *Cow* (London, 2007), pp. 74–5.

45 Ibid., p. 158.

46 On building types in the UK, see Jeremy Lake and Paul Adams, 'National Farm Building Types', 2 October 2014, available at https://historicengland. org.uk, accessed 13 May 2022.

47 Quoted in Lambton, *Palaces for Pigs*, p. 124.

48 See, for example, Daniel P. Gregory, *The New Farm: Contemporary Rural Architecture* (Princeton, NJ, 2020).

49 See Abby Luby, 'Churchdown Dairy, a Castle for Cows', *Edible Hudson Valley*, https://ediblehudsonvalley.ediblecommunities.com, 15 June 2016.

50 Upton Sinclair, *The Jungle* (New York, 1906), pp. 44–6.

51 See Design With Company, 'Farmland World', www.designwith.co.

52 Geoff Manaugh, 'Farmland World', www.bldgblog.com, 22 August 2011.

53 For information on the project, including a short film, see Ensamble Studio, 'The Truffle: Costa da Morte, 2010', www.ensamble.info.

54 Quoted in Brett Mizelle, *Pig* (London, 2011), p. 48.

55 Sinclair, *The Jungle*, pp. 39–41.

56 Lambton, *Palaces for Pigs*, pp. 100–102.

57 See 'The Pigsty, Robin Hood's Bay', *The Landmark Trust*, www.landmarktrust.org.uk, accessed 13 May 2022.

58 See Ian Belcher, 'Your Room's a Pigsty', *Sunday Times*, 21 June 2015.

59 Quoted in Daniel Birnbaum, 'Mice and Man: The Art of Carsten Höller and Rosemarie Trockel', *Artforum*, XXXIX/6 (2001), pp. 114–19.

60 Henry Mayhew, *London Labour and the London Poor*, vol. II (London, 1851), pp. 154–5. The legend is also discussed in relation to Victorian sensationalist culture in Thomas Boyle, *Black Swine in the Sewers of Hampstead: Beneath the Surface of Victorian Sensationalism* (London, 1990).

61 See Peter Stallybrass and Allon White, *The Politics and Poetics of Transgression* (Ithaca, NY, 1986), pp. 48–50.

62 See MVRDV, 'Pig-City', www.mvrdv.nl. A short film of the project made by MVRDV can be viewed at Sara Marzullo, 'Pig City: The Economy of Meat', www.architectureplayer.com, accessed 13 May 2022.

63 John Scalzi, 'Utere nihil non extra quiritationem suis', in *METAtropolis*, ed. John Scalzi (New York, 2009), pp. 174–230.

64 See '10 Things You Should Know About Factory-Farmed Meat Chickens', www.worldanimalprotection.org.uk, 11 January 2019.

65 See Annie Potts, *Chicken* (London, 2012), pp. 158–63.

66 See Mary Abbe, 'Doug Argue: Big Picture', *ARTnews*, XCIV/1 (1995), p. 95.

67 Alice Hovorka, 'Transspecies Urban Theory: Chickens in an African City', *Cultural Geographies*, XV/1 (2008), pp. 95–117.

68 A more academic study is Jennifer Blecha and Helga Leitner, 'Reimagining the Food System, the Economy, and Urban Life: New Urban Chicken-Keepers in U.S. Cities', *Urban Geography*, XXXV/1 (2014), pp. 86–108.

69 For the origins of Omlet Ltd, see www.omlet.co.uk.

70 See, respectively, Wainwright, *Pet-tecture*, pp. 104, 157, 159.

71 India Block, 'so? Builds Modular House of Chickens on a Farm in Turkey', *Dezeen*, www.dezeen.com, 26 February 2019.

72 Bridget Cogley, 'Kengo Kuma Builds Blackened-Wood Chicken Coop at Casa Wabi Artist Retreat', *Dezeen*, www.dezeen.com, 20 June 2020.

73 See 'Chickenville, a Chicken's Ambition: Interview with Skroz Architecture', https://archis.org, 5 December 2018.

74 See Potts, *Chicken*, p. 87.

75 See Kate Bernheimer and Andrew Bernheimer, 'Fairy Tale Architecture: The House on Chicken Feet', *Places*, https://placesjournal.org, December 2011.

Coda

1 Emily Elhacham et al., 'Global Human-Made Mass Exceeds All Living Biomass', *Nature*, 588 (2020), pp. 442–4.
2 David Wood, *Thinking Plant Animal Human: Encounters with Communities of Difference* (Minneapolis, MN, 2020), p. 6.

Further Reading

Adams, Jon, and Edmund Ramsden, 'Rat Cities and Beehive Worlds: Density and Design in the Modern City', *Comparative Studies in Society and History*, LIII/4 (2011), pp. 722–56

Ball, Philip, 'Bright Lights, Bug City', *New Scientist*, 27 February 2010

Baratay, Eric, and Elisabeth Hardouin-Fugier, *Zoo: A History of Zoological Gardens in the West* (London, 2004)

Bogost, Ian, *Alien Phenomenology; or, What It's Like to Be a Thing* (Minneapolis, MN, 2012)

Cheng, Irene, 'The Beavers and the Bees: Intelligent Design and the Marvelous Architecture of Animals', *Cabinet*, 23 (2006), www.cabinetmagazine.org

The Expanded Environment, www.expandedenvironment.org

Firebrace, William, 'Learning from the Tortoise', https://drawingmatter.org, 9 August 2019

Gissen, David, *Subnature: Architecture's Other Environments* (Princeton, NJ, 2009)

Gunnell, Kelly, Brian Murphy and Carol Williams, *Designing for Biodiversity: A Technical Guide for New and Existing Buildings* (London, 2013)

Haeg, Fritz, 'Animal Estates', www.fritzhaeg.com

Hansell, Mike, *Built by Animals: The Natural History of Animal Architecture* (Oxford, 2007)

Haraway, Donna, *The Companion Species Manifesto: Dogs, People, and Significant Otherness* (Chicago, IL, 2003)

Hwang, Joyce, www.antsoftheprairie.com

—, 'Toward an Architecture for Urban Wildlife Advocacy', *Biophilic Cities*, 1/2 (2017), pp. 24–31

Ingold, Tim, 'Of Blocks and Knots: Architecture as Weaving', *Architectural Review* 25 October 2013, pp. 26–7

—, *Correspondences* (Cambridge, 2020)

Lambton, Lucinda, *Palaces for Pigs: Animal Architecture and Other Beastly Buildings* (Swindon, 2011)

'LA+Creature: Winning Designs', LA+ [*Landscape Architecture Plus*], https://laplusjournal.com, 2020

Manaugh, Geoff, and John Becker, 'Architecture-by-Bee and Other Animal Printheads', www.bldgblog.com, 16 July 2014

Morton, Timothy, *The Ecological Thought* (Cambridge, MA, 2010)

Passmore, Stacy, 'Landscape with Beavers', *Places*, https://placesjournal.org, July 2019

Philo, Chris, and Chris Wilbert, *Animal Spaces, Beastly Places* (Abingdon, 2000)

Rhys Parry, Jason, 'Primal Weaving: Structure and Meaning in Language and Architecture', *SubStance*, XLVI/3 (2017), pp. 125–49

Rykwert, Joseph, *On Adam's House in Paradise* (Cambridge, MA, 1997)

Smith, Nancy, Shaowen Bardzell and Jeffrey Bardzell, 'Designing for Cohabitation; Naturecultures, Hybrids, and Decentering the Human in Design', *Proceedings of the CHI Conference on Human Factors in Computing Systems: Denver, CO, 6–11 May 2017*, pp. 1714–26

Survant, Tyler, 'Biological Borderlands: Ant Farm's Zoopolitics', *Horizonte*, 8 (2013), pp. 49–64

Wainwright, Tom, *Pet-tecture: Design for Pets* (London, 2018)

Wakefield, Stephanie, and Bruce Braun, 'Oystertecture: Infrastructure, Profanation and the Sacred Figure of the Human', in *Infrastructure, Environment and Life in the Anthropocene*, ed. Kregg Hetherington (Durham, NC, 2018), pp. 193–215

Wolch, Jennifer, and Jody Emel, *Animal Geographies: Place, Politics and Identity in the Nature-Culture Borderlands* (London, 1998), especially Wolch's chapter 'Zoöpolis', pp. 119–38

—, and Marcus Owens, 'Animals in Contemporary Architecture and Design', *Humanimalia*, VIII/2 (2017), pp. 1–18, available at https://humanimalia.org, accessed 10 May 2022

Wood, David, *Thinking Plant Animal Human: Encounters with Communities of Difference* (Minneapolis, MN, 2020)

Acknowledgements

This book was mostly written during the second year of the COVID-19 pandemic. Like many others, the enforced social isolation during the winter and spring of 2021 provided me with ample opportunity to pay more attention to the natural world. I vividly remember the research I was doing on certain animals coinciding with their appearance in my immediate environment: a starling nesting in a neighbour's roof; a brown rat scouring my garden for scraps of food; our newly acquired puppy Charlie teaching me about the peculiar domestic habits of dogs. So, first and foremost, I must thank animals, near and far, for what they themselves have brought to the writing of this book.

I'm also grateful to a large number of people who've already devoted themselves to researching and writing about animals – it's a hugely exciting field in itself and such a pleasure to engage with. I am particularly grateful to Jonathan Burt at Reaktion for editing the marvellous Animal series of books, which have been an invaluable resource for me and many others (and which is still ongoing). Several authors of books in this series have been extremely generous in their engagement with earlier versions of chapters in this book: Claire Preston, Boria Sax, Charlotte Sleigh, Rebecca Stott, Martin Wallen and Dan Wylie. Thanks also to Lisa Margonelli, Nathaniel R. Walker, Andy Merritt and Joyce Hwang for their generous comments. Vivian Constantinopoulos at Reaktion has, once again, proved to be a generous, patient and supportive editor – and I'm grateful to her and Martha Jay for making the publication process so smooth. In addition, David Rose's copy-editing went far beyond the call of duty in honing the text and correcting errors that I really shouldn't have made.

I've also been heartened by the generosity of artists and designers who have kindly provided images for the book, including Tim Knowles, Fritz Haeg, Mattia Menchetti, Geoff Manaugh and John Becker, Joyce Hwang, Scott Turner, Dillon Marsh, Carla Novak, Adam Kuby, Kate MccGwire, Renee Davies, Bangkok Studio, Kate Orff, Studio Gang, OPSYS, Allison Newmeyer and Stewart Hicks, Roland Halbe, and Andy and Kate Bernheimer. Grateful thanks also to the Bartlett School of Architecture, who funded image permissions and reproduction fees through their Architecture Research Fund.

Family have been equally important in making this book possible. I'm grateful to my mother, Anne, who instilled in me at an early age a love for animals in her care for sundry species. At various times she took in a rook with a broken wing, a particularly recalcitrant feral cat, a clutch of abandoned swallow chicks, and many unwanted cats, kittens and guinea pigs, as well as a much-loved dog. Finally, I'm grateful, as always, to my wife Lisa and daughter Isla, who have been patient once again with my obsessions and absences, even as one of the payoffs was an adorable puppy.

Photo Acknowledgements

The author and publishers wish to express their thanks to the below sources of illustrative material and/or permission to reproduce it. Every effort has been made to contact copyright holders; should there be any we have been unable to reach or to whom inaccurate acknowledgements have been made, please contact the publishers, and full adjustments will be made to any subsequent printings.

07BEACH: p. 192; Alamy: pp. 36 (Eden Breitz), 158 (Imaginechina Limited), 205 (Heritage Image Partnership Ltd); Jean Aubert: p. 155; Avery Library, Columbia University: p. 139; Bangkok Studio Architects: p. 144; John Becker and Geoff Manaugh: p. 61; Berkeley Art Museum & Pacific Film Archive, 2005.14.66: p. 174; Andrew and Kate Bernheimer: p. 230; Bosnic+Dorotic: p. 229; Fredrik Brauer: p. 110; British Museum: p. 101; University of Calgary Digital Collections: p. 184; Vincent Callebaut Architectures: p. 90; D3architecture: p. 199; Paul Dobraszczyk: pp. 11, 17, 41, 59, 74, 80, 94, 108, 142, 209; Flickr: pp. 77 (Surfing The Nations/CC BY-NC-ND 2.0); 83 (Washington State Department of Transportation), 95 (Vasyl Vaskivskyi/CC BY 2.0), 103 (Charlie Dave/CC BY 2.0), 123 (Jim Linwood/CC BY 2.0), 134, 143 (malouette/CC BY 2.0), 202 (A. Davey/CC BY-NC-ND 2.0/Used with permission); Fritz Haeg: p. 33; Roland Halbe: p. 218; Joyce Hwang: pp. 125, 126 (Photo by Albert Chao); *Illustrated London News*: pp. 100, 136; Tim Knowles: p. 13; Adam Kuby: p. 82; Library of Congress: p. 168 (API01.P7 1898 (Case X) [P&P]); Logroño School of Design: p. 203; LYCS Architecture: p. 47; Kate MccGwire: p. 105; Dillon Marsh: p. 70; Mattia Menchetti: p. 50; Allison Newmeyer and Stewart Hicks: p. 217; Carla Novak: p. 75; Ordinary Ltd: p. 40; © 2018 OPSYS: p. 186 (collage adapted from original base infrared photograph by Paolo Pettigiani, 2018); Pixabay: pp. 56 (Dave Noonan) 57 (Dave Noonan), 119 (Thankful Photography), 128 (Thomas Wilken), 131 (wal_172619); Reddit: p. 53 (CountBubs); Royal Collection Trust: p. 213; SCAPE: p. 161; Yongwook Seong: p. 178; Shutterstock:p. 87 (Celalettin Gunes); The Soane Museum: p. 194; Squidsoup: p. 111; Fiona Stewart: p. 62; © Studio Gang: p. 175; Takeshi Hosaka Architects: p. 200; Ali Taptık, Onagöre, 2018.10.25, Palanga Kümes, SO?Architects: p. 228; Scott Turner: p. 64; Stephen Turner: p. 160; WASP: p. 51; Wikimedia Commons: pp. 6 (Hyperion924 at English Wikipedia/CC-BY-SA 3.0 Unported), 34 (Andreas

ANIMAL ARCHITECTURE